Health Inequality
Second Edition

Health Inequality

An Introduction to Concepts, Theories and Methods

Second Edition

Mel Bartley

polity

First edition published in 2004 by Polity Press
This second edition first published in 2017 by Polity Press

Polity Press
65 Bridge Street
Cambridge CB2 1UR, UK

Polity Press
350 Main Street
Malden, MA 02148, USA

ISBN-13: 978-0-7456-9109-1
ISBN-13: 978-0-7456-9110-7(pb)

A catalogue record for this book is available from the British Library.

Library of Congress Cataloging-in-Publication Data

Names: Bartley, Mel, author.
Title: Health inequality : an introduction to concepts, theories and methods / Mel Bartley.
Description: 2nd edition. | Cambridge, UK ; Malden, MA : Polity, 2016. | Includes bibliographical references and index.
Identifiers: LCCN 2016014155 (print) | LCCN 2016018268 (ebook) | ISBN 9780745691091 (hardcover : alk. paper) | ISBN 0745691099 (hardcover : alk. paper) | ISBN 9780745691107 (pbk. : alk. paper) | ISBN 0745691102 (pbk. : alk. paper) | ISBN 9780745691121 (mobi) | ISBN 9780745691138 (epub)
Subjects: | MESH: Health Status Disparities | Models, Theoretical | Socioeconomic Factors
Classification: LCC RA418 (print) | LCC RA418 (ebook) | NLM WA 300.1 | DDC 362.1--dc23
LC record available at https://lccn.loc.gov/2016014155

Typeset in 10.5 on 12 pt Plantin by Servis Filmsetting Ltd, Stockport, Cheshire
Printed and bound in the UK by Clays Ltd, St Ives PLC

For further information on Polity, visit our website: www.politybooks.com

Contents

Figures and Tables

Figures

Tables

Acknowledgements

Mel Bartley thanks the Centre for Longitudinal Studies, Institute of Education, for the use of the 1958 birth cohort data and the United Kingdom Data Archive and Economic and Social Data Service for making those data available. None of the organizations that provided access to data had responsibility for the analysis or interpretation of these data.

This book owes a great deal to past and present colleagues, in particular Amanda Sacker, Meena Kumari, Pekka Martikainen, Archana Sing-Manoux, Paul Clarke, Mai Stafford and Eric Brunner, Updating the British official data on health inequality would not have been possible without the help of Peter Goldblatt.

Introduction to the Second Edition

Many of those who studied health inequality in the 1970s and 1980s saw it as a chance to improve our understanding of disease and our ability to prevent ill health in the whole population, regardless of social background. Social differences in premature mortality from almost all causes were so large; it seemed that if we could understand the ways in which socio-economic adversity 'gets under the skin' to produce disease, this might lead to major improvements in population health and ways of making medical care more effective. What is the point, we asked, of treating someone's bronchitis in hospital and then sending them back to a damp, cold house to become ill again? The existence of health inequalities was seen as proof that diseases were indeed preventable by changes to the environment. Since 1948 the British National Health Service offered medical care free at the time of use to all citizens, but by the 1970s it was clear that free health care was not reducing the size of health inequalities; in fact, they increased (see chapter 2). This was all the more encouragement to regard prevention as better than cure. After all, even free operations are not a pleasant experience; most people would prefer not to become ill in the first place. But more surprising was that health inequalities continued to increase even after 40 years of a welfare state that in theory prevented the worst extremes of poverty and that had actually succeeded in reducing income inequality.

The Black Report of 1980 was the first attempt to drill down into the statistics and identify what it was about social class (the measure of social inequality used in British official statistics) that produced these large differences in risk. The Black Report put forward four possible models of explanation: selection, artefact, material and behavioural-cultural. In the early 2000s, the artefact explanation had been completely discredited and the selection explanation was little considered outside of economics. Accordingly, the first edition of this book concentrated on the material and behavioural-cultural models and tried to assess how well each of them fitted the existing evidence. It also described and assessed three additional factors that had been increasingly investigated in research between 1980 and 2000: psycho-social stress at work, social isolation and life-course effects. In this second edition, this evidence will be updated, but consideration will also be given to some of the more recent thinking that has arisen, particularly what the evidence has to say about the importance of individual characteristics for health inequality.

Between 1997 and 2001, when the ideas behind this book were being gestated and written down, the United Kingdom had a 'New Labour' (moderate social democratic) government that was in many ways determined to reduce health inequality and was prepared to do so by addressing at least some of the social and economic factors (the so-called 'upstream factors') believed to be involved, such as the absence of a minimum wage, low pensions, widespread educational failure and child poverty. The successor to the Black Report, the Acheson Report, set out a large number of rather precise recommendations (Acheson 1998), and a government plan published in 2002 described the ways in which many of these would be met (Department of Health 2002). As pointed out by Mackenbach (Mackenbach 2010a, 2010b), the British programme was 'by far the best resourced of all the Western European strategies to reduce health inequalities which started during the decade'. It should have been a golden age during which the research paid off in terms of real-world reductions in health disparities between social groups, and overall improvements in population health.

So it has been surprising and dismaying to see the verdict on the past 10 years of policy initiatives: that they have not succeeded in reducing health inequality in the United Kingdom (Department of Health 2009; Mackenbach 2010a; Law, Parkin and Lewis 2012). At least, not as far as we can tell. It is not easy to trace the changes in health inequality since 1997 because the availability of data that can be used to evaluate the success or failure of new policies has changed. This has made it quite hard to compare the situation now with that in 1997 and 2014 (let alone any further back). When I decided it was time to update *Health Inequality*, the first thing to do was to revise the tables and figures. This seemed like it would be a simple task. But it did not turn out that way. For a start, the evaluations proposed in the 2002 report 'Tackling Health Inequalities' only required a comparison of mortality by geographical areas, not by social class as had been done every 10 years since 1921 in England and Wales. Social class gaps were only assessed in infant mortality. It appears that the degree of class inequality in infant mortality did begin to fall quite a lot (Bambra 2012), though it may have risen again after 2010. The gaps in adult life expectancy between the most and least deprived areas, at least in England, have remained stubbornly unchanged, or even slightly increased (Law et al. 2012; Vizard and Obolenskaya 2013). But that is not the same as being able to extend the 70-year old analysis of social class differences in premature death that gave rise to the whole issue of health inequality in the first place.

Should we be surprised that policy measures left the health gap between more and less advantaged citizens untouched? Many people do not think so (Howden-Chapman 2010; Mackenbach 2010a, 2010c). When, after its election in 1997, the New Labour government, so as to design policies, asked the experts what were the causes of health inequality, the answers were all too vague.

Part of the motivation for the first edition of *Health Inequality* was to set out the different explanations that were being offered, and how they were being tested, in such a way as to encourage a wider group of people to participate in the search for explanations and hence for solutions. But this is not what has happened. Health inequality research seems to have become rather an arcane topic beset with mysterious numbers. The influential think tank the Kings Fund published blogs pointing out the retreat from serious consideration (Buck 2014). There seems to have been a reduction in the gathering and use of evidence of changes in the differences in health between more and less socially advantaged groups. Kat Smith's study, which is one of the recommended readings to accompany this chapter, goes 'Beyond evidence-based policy' (Smith 2013) to give an instructive account of the politics of research in this area. Once it was shown that policy initiatives did not seem to be effective, what took over was an increase in philosophical arguments about the injustice of health inequality, rather than detailed attention as to why policy changes had had such little effect. No one, for example, went out and asked citizens in the most deprived areas of Britain (termed 'spearhead' areas for policy purposes) why the energetic attempts to discourage smoking in these areas had had so little influence.

Another view of the political paralysis, however, is that we can now return to the more serious science involved in understanding health inequality. There have been major advances in related areas of research that will, I am sure, have considerable effects on our understanding. There are now several large international data sets, designed to make the experiences of people in different countries comparable. One of these, the Survey of Health, Ageing and Retirement in Europe (SHARE), is an international study of ageing which focuses on health. Although SHARE does not contain data on all phases of the life course, participants complete a life-grid in which they report on major life changes after young adulthood. Another is EU-SILC, the European Study of Income and Living Conditions, which collects far fewer data on health but is beginning to be used in interesting ways. Outside of SHARE, there now exists a collection of comparable ageing studies in the United Kingdom (the English Longitudinal Study of Ageing: ELSA), the United States (the Health and Retirement Study: HRS), the Korean longitudinal ageing study (KLOSE) and the Japanese longitudinal study of older people (J-STAR), with other nations joining as time passes. The first hugely influential comparative studies using these data to compare health in older people in the United Kingdom, the United States and Europe showed large health disadvantages in the United States compared to English citizens, and similar US health deficits in older people compared to European nations (Banks et al. 2006; Avendano et al. 2009). However, these studies have not as yet been used to throw light on inequalities in health between social groups within nations.

How should a second edition of this book respond to these changes? One possibility would be to stick to the initial basic structure of the first edition in term of the models that attempt to explain health inequality. Is the classification of approaches into material, behavioural, psycho-social and life-course models still useful when we try to understand more recent trends? It is interesting that, while the amount of commentary on national trends in health equality has declined, there are still fairly lively debates about the relative importance of risky health behaviour (Dunn 2010; Stringhini et al. 2010, 2011; Nandi, Glymour and Subramanian 2014) and psycho-social factors such as work stress, effort−reward imbalance and work−life balance (Kivimäki et al. 2012; Landsbergis, Dobson and Schnall 2013; Theorell 2014). There has also been a strong revival in the 'indirect selection' model in the shape of a series of papers showing strong associations between childhood cognitive abilities and adult health (Batty et al. 2007a, 2007b). Not surprisingly, genetic research has gone from strength to strength as the ability to analyse the human genome has improved due to technical advances, although as yet there is little evidence of any association of genetic variants with a measure of social position such as social class or income.

The most important advance in social epidemiology since 2004, however, has been the rapid increase in understanding the life course (Power and Hertzman 1997; Wadsworth 1997; Hertzman et al. 2001; Case, Fertig and Paxson 2005). This is now possible because of the maturing of the British birth cohorts, representative samples of citizens born in 1946, 1958, 1970 and 2000 (see chapter 10). Detailed health measures are now also available for all participants in the British Household Panel Study and its far larger (40,000 households) successor, *Understanding Society*. So the content of the different aetiological models needs to be revised in the light of what has happened in life-course research. No one thinks any more that cross-sectional (relating health at one time point to social circumstances at the same time point) research on work stress, poor housing or even smoking can enlighten us any further or help in the design of more effective policies. This is partly because there are now so many new and extended data sets available that trace what happens to people either from birth or over many years of adulthood and into old age. When we observe the health of people in a certain social class, we now know that we are observing the accumulated consequences of their material, emotional and cultural histories. 'Selection' arguments always were life-course explanations. But we are now in a far better position to investigate what went on before; for example, poor school performance led to a risky job in adulthood, or low self-efficacy resulted in addiction to tobacco (Sweeting et al. 2016). This new capability in health research has been enriched by an important innovation, a focus on life-course justice. Researchers in France and the United Kingdom are beginning to ask: Can we regard differences in health behaviours as a matter of personal choice? Or, if such behaviours are seen in life-course studies to be strongly linked to disadvantage in early life, should inequalities in smoking, exercise and diet also be regarded as unjust (Jusot, Tubeuf and Trannoy 2013)?

In the first edition, a whole chapter was devoted to the work of Wilkinson and others on the relationship of health to income inequality at the macro-level of whole nations or other geopolitical units. But at this level, income inequality is no longer the only variable of interest to health inequality researchers. In the years since 2002, a lot of research has been carried out into health and health inequality in different welfare regimes. It took more than a decade for the path-breaking work of Esping-Andersen (1990) to penetrate social epidemiology. But once it had been realized that it was highly plausible to link the commodification of labour power with poor health and the de-commodification with better health, this became a welcome task. The revised chapter on the macro-level determinants of health (chapter 7) will therefore need to put this work alongside that of Wilkinson and Pickett's powerful analysis of overall income inequality (Wilkinson and Pickett 2009). To somewhat anticipate the contents of this chapter, the weight of evidence shows that more generous welfare regimes do not have lower levels of health inequality. This has been one reason for the revival of interest in the importance of selection by personal characteristics (Mackenbach 2012).

Despite, or perhaps because of, the failure to show that what looked like promising policies, or policy changes, are linked to lower health inequality, there is now a rising concern with the more philosophical issues involved. A leading researcher, author and proponent of policy change is Michael Marmot, whose Whitehall II study has figured prominently in the research literature for more than 30 years. Whitehall II findings figured prominently in the first edition of *Health Inequality*. The recent monitoring exercises of the successes and failures of British policies have mostly been carried out by Marmot's group. At the same time, some of the Whitehall II research, particularly into the importance of psycho-social work conditions and the relative importance of behavioural versus material and psycho-social factors, has come under attack. In fact, these have been some of the most controversial contributions to the research base since 2004. However, increasingly Marmot has been on record as emphasizing the philosophical and ethical over the scientific importance of health inequality. Health inequality, he and his colleagues argue, is fundamentally a matter of social justice (Marmot, Allen and Goldblatt 2010). In his view, we will know when we have socially just policies because at this point social inequalities in health will start to decline. This is, for some people, a long way from an initial interest in the phenomenon because of what it might be able to tell us about the ways in which disease arises and thereby how to prevent disease. It is as if we have more or less given up on understanding health inequality well enough to design appropriate policies. Rather, policies must be changed for the sake of fairness, and a decline in health disparities will act as evidence that new policies are really fair. To take an example, 40 years of anti-smoking advice has failed to reduce inequalities in premature death from smoking-related disease. This has to be one of the most reliable bits of evidence ever derived from a public health intervention. The response − that when we start to see a reduction in the differences in smoking between social classes we will know that policies (economic and social) have become more just – is actually rather appealing, certainly more so than the prospect of endlessly repeated anti-smoking advice.

Some of the most exciting advances in research are now combining philosophical concepts of freedom and fairness with a life-course approach to take a more fruitful perspective (Jusot et al. 2013) and to revive the area as a 'progressive research programme'. I am going to take the view that this interdisciplinary programme is in the process of revolutionizing our work. However, problems do remain, as will become evident in the 'applied' chapters of the book on ethnicity and gender. It may be that applying a social justice approach over the whole of the life course will do more to counter health disparities in the longer term. But we also know that population health can respond very quickly to policy changes that occur during adulthood. A life-course approach must not become a reason to ignore adult social conditions at work and at home (Edwards, Gillies and Horsley 2014).

It is not the purpose of this book to set out a general theory of health inequality. Rather, it aims to provide readers with the wherewithal to understand and evaluate arguments and explanations put forward by other researchers (and possibly to think up their own explanations). However, the researcher should admit her own biases and prejudices, and of course I do have my own hunches about why health inequality exists and is so persistent in the face of rising living standards and improving general levels of health. These hunches centre around the problems involved in the negotiation of personal identity (Bunton and Burrows 1995; Langman 1998; Howard 2000). The prospect of young people deserting apparently safe homes in western nations to risk their lives fighting to establish a caliphate in the Middle East is an extreme example of how the struggle for identity can tragically shorten life.

Identities are shifting and have highly variable sources, making generalization hazardous (Giddens 1991). But it is possible that the 'psycho-social' and the 'behavioural' processes thought to be involved in health inequality, and even the importance of money, have their roots to some extent in problems of identity (Elstad 2010). Where an individual's sense of identity is assured by the stable occupation of 'central life roles' (Siegrist 2000a), such as worker, partner or parent, and/or by acceptance in a reasonably stable community, the cost of identity management is lower. But these sources of stability may be accompanied by extensive constraints on factors such as occupational choice or sexual behaviour or orientation. Where there is no stable community of acceptance, identity may depend more on outward symbolic display, which needs to be constantly repeated and updated. Individuals gain little sense of inherent worth just by 'being themselves'. Large cities are places where the shackles of traditional role performance may be gladly shaken off but where making and retaining alternative sets of social ties may present other problems. Such circumstances may increase the importance of high numbers of material goods, and goods of the culturally symbolic kind. Living in a fragmented society tends to be expensive. The advent of social media may well have exacerbated these problems. In fact, one could surmise that one reason for the relentless rise of health inequality at a time of rising overall living standards and falling income inequality (Bartley 2012) is to be found in the increase in communication media. The years following the widespread introduction of television in homes in the 1950s were at the origin of the puzzle of rising health inequality.

Identity may be supported or threatened by any of the major forms of inequality. High prestige protects against adverse events of shorter duration. For example, living in a run-down student flat for a few years does not threaten someone from a secure middle-class family who knows they are sacrificing income at the present time in order to secure a satisfying, high-status long-term career. Security and autonomy at the workplace support a stable sense of self, even for people without high income or status. And income? As indicated above, this may act as a means to an end in terms of the prestige and security it can buy. In other cases, the purchase of consumer goods may act as a substitute for other sources of stable identity. The implication of this is that money for conspicuous consumption may be more important when autonomy, security or other sources of support for identity are not present.

As societies modernize, institutional constraints exerted by religion, family, caste or clan loosen, and freedom for many (in particular, for everyone who is not an adult male of the 'majority' or dominant cultural or ethnic group) increases. But under these conditions the maintenance of stable identity may become more problematic. In order to maintain social acceptance, the individual may need to devote more resources to identity-sustaining relationships. Identity maintenance for those in dominant positions has traditionally depended on being able to exert superior power and has been provided by women for everyone else. If traditional forms of dominance are breaking down and women's time is more occupied with paid employment and the 'public sphere', this changes. Along with greater individual freedom comes the necessity for every individual, male and female, and, increasingly, older children as well as adults to do their own work in creating and maintaining the relationships that contribute to a sense of creditable identity. There is an ever-greater premium on the capacity for internal self-regulation and the management of one's own identity and the creation of one's own community.

Here again, a life-course approach offers useful sources of understanding. Those individuals whose experiences in their family of origin have given them an inner sense of security and the ability to form and maintain relationships may revel in the freedom of a less constrained community, even if social ties are looser. In Beck's words:

> The ability to choose and maintain one's own social relations is not an ability everyone has by nature. It is . . . a learned ability which depends on special social and family backgrounds. The reflexive conduct of life, the planning of one's own biography and social relations, gives rise to a new inequality: the inequality of dealing with insecurity and reflexivity. (Beck 1992: 98)

Those with fewer inner resources may adopt images from the mass media as a substitute source of identity. For these individuals, periods with relatively little money can be catastrophic for the sense of self. If self-esteem depends on possession of symbolic goods, these will be given priority over, for example, nutrition and warmth. And the cost of imitating cultural, mass-media images is what will determine in part how much health will suffer during financially insecure periods.

One way of understanding the dynamic that produces health inequality may be the vital importance of social participation to identity and the effect of social inequality on the costs of social participation. But wider social inequality has another effect. This is the influence of the experience of inequality on the consumption of mood-altering substances. This means not only drugs such as heroin and cocaine, or even alcohol. In the early 1980s, Cameron and Jones termed alcohol and tobacco 'drugs of solace' (Cameron and Jones 1985). They argued that, while doctors and health educators see alcohol and tobacco as a 'problem', for those who use them they are in fact a solution. To these, I would add a wide range of 'comfort foods', all of which are consumed to dull the experiences of uncertainty and isolation. The importance of the struggle for a stable identity in the causation of health inequality is shown by the age-patterned nature of many of these influences. Very large numbers of adolescents become obsessed with expensive consumer items, and take up smoking and the use of recreational drugs. It is a period when the struggle for identity is at its most acute and the outcome is uncertain. As they grow older, adolescents from the more socially (and perhaps emotionally) favoured backgrounds tend to moderate their attachment to these (Giesinger et al. 2014) – they find other sources of identity in work and in stable adult relationships. Difficulty in establishing adult identity can have a number of different sources: disturbed parental relationships and an inability to find work which is sufficiently well paid to make independent life possible are two of the most common. For those with very disturbed emotional backgrounds, even great riches may not be sufficient to feed an unsuccessful quest for identity, as is frequently seen in media 'stars' and in members of rich and aristocratic families who engage in self-destructive forms of behaviour.

In what follows, we shall see whether existing research on health inequality can be understood with the help of a model of accumulated biological, psychological and social advantages and disadvantages within the contexts of different national and local economies and cultures. There are numerous potential combinations of circumstances that individuals may pass through in their life course, all of which may contribute to healthy life expectancy many years into the future. The challenge for research is to arrive at adequate measures of these, and adequate methods for putting them together in causal models that are useful for policy discussion.

Further reading

On the relationship of research to policy in health inequality:
Smith, K. (2013), *Beyond Evidence-Based Policy in Public Health: The Interplay of Ideas*. London: Palgrave Macmillan.

The full selection of reports carried out by Michael Marmot and colleagues is available on the website of the Institute of Health Equity, http://www.instituteofhealthequity.org/
Elstad, J.-I. (2010), Indirect health-related selection or social causation? Interpreting the educational differences in adolescent health behaviours. *Social Theory and Health* 8(2): 134–50.

1

What is Social Inequality?

Before being able to go any further into the description of health inequality, we need to think carefully about what is meant by *social* inequality. From 1931 to 2001, official statisticians in England and Wales used a consistent measure of social class, the Registrar General's Social Classes (RGSC) schema to compile a series of reports on health inequality, the contents of which will be described in the next chapter. This pioneering work has stimulated a large literature using many different measures of social inequality. The measure used in British official statistics itself changed in 2001. So although we now have many studies from different nations and at different times, it is actually very difficult to make comparisons between nations or to look at trends over time.

It has become a lot clearer in the past 10 years that the conflict and confusion around how we should understand social inequality has major implications for the study of health inequality. If you read the research that has been published over this period, it is striking how awkward many papers are when describing their measures of social position. The terms 'high' and 'low' are used in a vague manner, attached to income, status or social class without further explanation. What is the difference between class and status in any case? Do they always have the same relationship to each other, or to income? There seems to be little consideration of the possibility that different people might have very different ideas about what might count as 'high' and 'low' status or income. In fact, the measure of social position presently used in British official statistics does not have a simple ranking of high to low at all. There is a hidden theme throughout most research on health inequality which explains a lot of this confusion. This chapter aims to clarify the confusion and describe the danger it poses to understanding health inequality.

A seminal paper by Krieger and colleagues in 1997 (Krieger, Williams and Moss 1997) used a general term, 'social position' to encompass class and status and 'socio-economic position (SEP)', to include income or wealth differences. These terms are proposed only as a tool for taking things forward and are by no means a perfect expression of the underlying ideas. For example, income and assets are not really types of 'position' in society, although one's place on the income ladder (your income relative to that of other people) might be regarded in this way. Two people with the same amount of monthly income, whether or not they own their home and have a car, central heating, a computer and so on, may be in different socio-economic positions in terms of their social class, status or income relative to that of their friends, neighbours or workmates.

Importantly, Krieger and colleagues also suggested that in actual research these dimensions of inequality need to be kept separate. The most suitable measure, they argue, will depend on the ways in which the researcher thinks social inequality is producing inequalities in a specific health outcome. For example, there are social inequalities in accidental death and in death from heart disease, but obviously different processes must be at work. Chapters 4, 5 and 6 of this book set out three different 'aetiological pathways', and chapters 9 and 10 give some examples of how different pathways may be at work in different cases. But first it is necessary to spell out the differences between the dimensions of class, status and income/wealth, and how these have been measured. In order to try and incorporate the newer research, it is also now necessary to discuss how education might fit into the measurement of social inequality.

Measures of social position

There are two ways in which social position (leaving out income and wealth) is usually represented: social class and social status or prestige. Although in many studies these two concepts have been used interchangeably, these dimensions of inequality may not have the same relationships to different types of disease outcomes. When we understand what social class and status are supposed to measure, we can see more clearly what kinds of effects they might be expected to have on health and how these effects may come about.

Social class

Measures of social class are based on theories of social structure: people choose their measure according to the theory they prefer. The two most prominent theories of social structure used in studies that work with a concept of class are based on the thinking of Marx and Weber. They divide occupations into groups according to typical employment conditions and employment relationships. These groups are the social classes (and there is no concept of some being 'higher' or 'lower' than others). Both schools of thought agree on the importance of two things. The first is the ownership of assets, such as property, factories or firms. That is what determines whether a person needs to work at all or whether she or he is the owner of a business, land or other assets sufficient to make working for a wage or salary unnecessary. The second feature of social class which is of generally agreed significance is the relationship of all those who do have to work for a living with those who own and manage the establishments in which they work, with those who supervise their work and also with any others whose work they in turn manage or supervise.

The definition of social class most widely used in British sociological and political research is based on the work of Weber, developed by John Goldthorpe and his co-workers. The earliest of these measures was first used in work on social mobility in the United Kingdom (Goldthorpe, Llewellyn and Payne 1980). Social classes are described as combining occupations whose members would tend to have similar sources and levels of income job security and chances of economic advancement, and who would have a similar location within systems of authority and control within businesses, and hence similar degrees of autonomy (Marshall et al. 1988). Erikson, Goldthorpe and Portocarrero further developed the original Goldthorpe schema in order to conduct a large international comparative study of social mobility (Erikson and Goldthorpe 1992). The most basic classificatory division in this schema is between those who are owners, either of a company or of property such as real estate or farmland, and those who are not. Within the group of 'owners', there are those who employ large numbers of others, those with a few employees and those with none. Those who own no property or company may either be employees or self-employed workers. The much larger group of people who are employees has more sub-divisions. They are divided according to the skill needed for their work, whether it is manual or non-manual, and the nature of their employment contract.

Erikson and Goldthorpe distinguish two basic forms of employment contract: the 'service contract' and the 'labour contract'. The service contract is what you find in managerial and professional work. Employees with this kind of contract of employment have to be trusted: their work cannot be supervised in any simple way by monitoring their time-keeping or counting how many nuts or bolts they have produced by the end of the day. In order to motivate performance, employees with this kind of job are offered more job security, salary increments and a progressive career as incentives to good and loyal service. In addition, this type of work entails a degree of command, either over the work of other people or at least autonomy over one's own work. Workers with a service contract are usually paid monthly, may have share options or a similar stake in the profitability of the company and seldom have to do things like clocking in and out. In contrast, employees with a labour contract perform work that is more easily monitored. They have little autonomy and tend to be more closely supervised and restricted in their patterns of work. Payment is more closely tied to hours of work and, in some cases, to how much is produced in that time ('piece rates'). There is less likelihood of career progression and no annual salary increment, and job security is lower. The Erikson–Goldthorpe–Portocarrero (EGP) classification acknowledges that many occupations have a mix of these conditions, so that allocating them into classes is a matter of deciding which occupations more closely resemble each other in these respects (Evans 1992).

The principles behind the EGP schema, of employment relations and conditions as the basis for defining social classes have been further developed into the new class schema, the National Statistics Socio-economic Classification (NS-SEC). The NS-SEC is now used in all official government reports in the United Kingdom, such as the 2001 and 2011 censuses of England and Wales and of Scotland and the annual Health Surveys. The most important difference between the EGP schema and the NS-SEC is that both the notion of 'skill' and the manual/non-manual divide have disappeared from the classificatory principles. The criteria for allocating occupations to the different classes have been made totally explicit. They are: the timing of payment for work (monthly versus weekly, daily or hourly); the presence of regular increments; job security (over or under one month); how much autonomy the worker has in deciding when to start and leave work; promotion opportunities; degree of influence over planning of work; and level of influence over designing their own work tasks (Coxon and Fisher 2002). Because it will be used for a wide

---

Box 1.1   National Statistics Socio-Economic Classification (NS-SEC)

1. Higher managerial and professional occupations, including employers in large firms, higher managers and professionals, whether they are employees or self-employed.
2. Lower managerial and professional occupations and higher technical occupations.
3. Intermediate occupations (clerical, administrative, sales workers with no involvement in general planning or supervision but high levels of job security, some career prospects and some autonomy over their own work schedule).
4. Small employers and self-employed workers.
5. Lower technical occupations (with little responsibility for planning own work), lower supervisory occupations (with supervisory responsibility but no overall planning role and less autonomy over own work schedule).
6. Semi-routine occupations (moderate levels of job security; little career prospects; no pay increments; some degree of autonomy over their own work).
7. Routine occupations (low job security; no career prospects; closely supervised routine work).

---

range of official statistics as well as for research, the NS-SEC in its 'full' form has a large number of categories which can be combined in different ways according to the purpose at hand. A seven-category version is likely to be that most frequently used in reports and studies (see Box 1.1).

Extensive empirical work went into deciding which occupations to put in each social class. Questions covering each of the seven criteria were asked of some 60,000 citizens in the United Kingdom Labour Force Survey of 1997. Occupations could then be allocated to social classes according to the typical answers of members of each occupation to these questions. For example, among biological scientists, 78.6 per cent had incremental pay and 76 per cent planned their own work; among kitchen porters, the comparable percentages were 27 per cent and 3.8 per cent. As may be imagined, the amount of work involved in the construction of this measure was enormous, and it will be necessary to carry out regular updating of the classification as job conditions change over time, and new occupations appear.

Social status

The sociological definitions of social class described above are very different to what is often meant by 'class' in lay terms. In everyday talk, people often use 'social class' to refer to what a sociologist would call 'status'. Unlike social class, the concept of status centrally involves the idea of a hierarchy or ranking 'from top to bottom' of society. The term 'status' is used often in everyday talk, and everyone thinks they know the meaning of the word. Sociologists and anthropologists use the synonymous term 'prestige' to refer to the differential ranking of respect and 'social honour' accorded to persons in a society.

Social classes are essentially groups of occupations. Social status is often an attribute of an individual, derived from their family, religious, tribal or ethnic background and independent of their occupation. In Hindu cultures, fine gradations of prestige are represented by the caste system, based on the traditional occupations of extended kin groups (Beteille 1992). Figure 1.1 is a very simplified version of the Hindu caste system found in India. As you can see, the caste groups are associated with different types of occupation (priest, warrior, merchant) but this does not mean every member

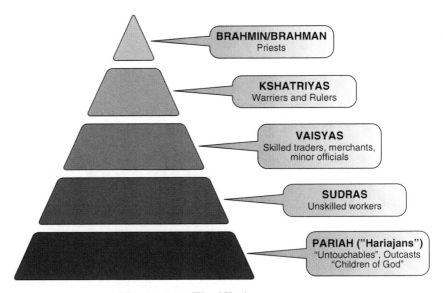

BRAHMIN/BRAHMAN
Priests

KSHATRIYAS
Warriers and Rulers

VAISYAS
Skilled traders, merchants,
minor officials

SUDRAS
Unskilled workers

PARIAH ("Hariajans")
"Untouchables", Outcasts
"Children of God"

Figure 1.1   The Hindu caste system
Source: © Julesunlimited/Dreamstime

exercises that occupation. Rather, a member of a caste is regarded as descended from ancestors who exercised a certain occupation.

Whereas ownership of a large amount of property or large business gives the most advantageous employment conditions in the social class schema, the organizing idea of this caste hierarchy is that of closer proximity to the Divine. The highest status is accorded to those descended from priestly ancestors, who devote their lives to prayer and study rather than earthly power or wealth.

Anthropologists regard the mark of caste membership to be the willingness of people to live close together, worship in the same church, eat together and marry each other. Members of higher castes maintain 'social distance' from members of lower castes (those with less prestige) by avoiding these forms of contact. Having close contact with lower castes risks rendering the individual 'impure' so that, for example, the marriage prospects of everyone in a family are damaged if one member marries a member of a lower caste.

Although caste is most strongly associated with the Hindu people of India, a very similar prestige ranking system existed in Regency England, which formed the central theme of Jane Austen's *Pride and Prejudice*. The book tells the story of the romance between Mr Darcy, a man of self-consciously very high status and Elizabeth Bennet, an intelligent and dignified woman. Despite his strong attraction to Elizabeth, Darcy and his relatives clearly regard her as of too low a status to be a suitable marriage partner. In contrast, Darcy's friend Bingley, who is also wealthy, seems to have no such issue about marrying Elizabeth's sister Jane. It was a puzzle to me where Darcy got his pretensions from, as in my simple understanding of British prestige ranks, the highest-status people usually had titles (Sir, Lord, etc.). As both Darcy and Bingley were wealthy and neither had titles, why were their attitudes to the two sisters so different?

A blog, *Juanita's Journal*, explains it in a way that is helpful for our present purposes. It demonstrates the links between class and status group in England at this historical period. In fact, both Mr Darcy and Elizabeth's father, Mr Bennet, would have been considered 'gentlemen' because neither of them needed to work since they could both live off the proceeds of land that they owned, despite the fact that Darcy owned a lot more land and had a far higher income. This would also put both of them today in the most advantaged of the NS-SEC classes. Their unequal *status* came from the fact that Mr Bennet's father-in-law *had* needed to work for a living; he was 'in trade'. By the same logic, Jane Bennet's husband Bingley, though also a very rich landowner, did not consider himself to have 'married down' because his father had also had to work, and he had bought his land with money from his father's business, rather than inheriting it from his ancestors. The difference between the status of the two men, Darcy and Bingley, had nothing to do with income or with the simple ownership of land, but whether the land had been recently bought with the proceeds of work or had been inherited. As Bingley's land had been bought with money that came from business ('trade') while Jane's father's far smaller estate was inherited from his landowning ancestors, Jane was a good catch for Bingley (this brilliant account of status in Regency England is given by 'Juanita' in *Felice's Log* [2014]).

This story will seem quite alien to many readers outside England (even perhaps people in Scotland) because, unlike class, the sources of status are specific to historical time and place (Chan and Goldthorpe 2007). Social groups may display caste-like social distancing behaviour for many different reasons. A famous modern example was the insistence in many American states that African-American people go to different schools, sit in a different section of buses and eat in different restaurants to white Americans. This segregation was regardless of the occupations or income of the discriminated group.

It might seem bizarre that the study of health inequality in modern industrialized nations would use measures of status, whose uses seem outdated to us. However, you do not have to look far to see that status differences are still a powerful influence on social life. Box 1.2 gives a description from a widely read London newspaper of the ways in which a British audience might decide on the status of Catherine Middleton, the first woman with neither royalty nor landowning nobility in her background to marry the future heir to the British throne.

In the United Kingdom, there are two measures of social position which explicitly depend on patterns of interactions between members of different occupations. The first of these, the Cambridge Scale, was developed by Stewart and colleagues in the early 1970s (Stewart, Prandy and Blackburn 1973) and has been used in the study of health inequality (Chandola 1998; Bartley et al. 1999; Prandy 1999). More recently, Goldthorpe and Chan turned their attention to developing a measure of social status, also based on the degree of friendship between members of different occupational groups (Chan and Goldthorpe 2004, 2007). In this measure, prestige is more explicitly based on the 'degree of manuality' of occupations (Chan and Goldthorpe 2004: 387) – that is, people tend to have friends from among occupational groups with a similar degree of manual or non-manual work to their own. Non-manual work (as in the Hindu caste system) is associated with higher prestige.

Box 1.2   A modern example of caste-like status distinctions

Nothing in the past four years has so exposed Britons' obsessions with policing class [*sic*] boundaries as the coverage of Catherine Middleton's family, wealth, upbringing and ancestors. The undertone of much of it has . . . been . . . incredulous and indignant. Newspapers have dwelt endlessly on the fact that her family tree includes *coal miners, domestic servants, road sweepers and butchers.* Her origins are described as humble . . . There is far less criticism of her father, or his family. He comes from a background described as 'solid'; lines of *provincial solicitors and landed gentry.* The worst that is said of him is that he is *self-made.* ('As a society, we still distrust the upwardly mobile': Jenni Russell, *London Evening Standard*, 18 April 2011: my italics)

So in the terms of the caste diagram above, Mr Middleton's 'caste' lies partly in the fact that his ancestors included gentlemen of leisure and scholarship ('Brahmin') although he himself has had to make his own money ('Vaishya'). But, horrors! Mrs Middleton's ancestors include servants ('Shudra') and even people with 'untouchable' occupations such as butchers and road sweepers.

Socio-economic status in American sociology

The concept of status in American social epidemiology has somewhat different origins. The United States does not have an established hereditary aristocracy, and the idea that those people who do not need to work are of high status is less prevalent. It is a powerful (though incorrect) belief that the United States is a far less 'class-bound' society than the United Kingdom, and who your ancestors were does not matter. An influential school of sociology in the United States has long understood inequality in terms of a theory called 'structural-functionalism'. This school of thought was led by Talcott Parsons, who put forward a clear logic for social inequality. According to Parsons, people naturally have unequal abilities. Society needs its most able members to be attracted to the jobs that are (according to this theory) most important for its basic functions, such as law, medicine, science and senior management in industry (Marshall et al. 1988). These occupations therefore offer advantageous employment conditions (as described in the NS-SEC), plus high income and prestige. Members of certain occupations, therefore, have 'high socio-economic status' because of their qualities, as illustrated for example by their success in education. Any society will offer high rewards to attract such people into 'functionally essential' jobs. So people who enjoy a high income and good employment conditions are doing so as the result of their talents. Their status is not due to their family's ownership of assets, or to their own conditions of work, but to the positive personal characteristics they must have in order to gain access to a functionally essential occupation with privileged employment conditions.

The first attempts to measure status in the United States took the form of studies of small towns where everyone knew everyone else, rather like the Indian villages where some of the most detailed studies of caste have been undertaken (Beteille 1992). In these small communities, it was possible to ask about the reputation of different individuals and families, so the method became known as a 'reputational' method (Oakes and Rossi 2003). However, when large-scale surveys started to be carried out, it was obviously no longer possible to do this. So instead a sample of the population, sometimes called 'a panel of judges', were given a list of occupations and asked to rank these in order of prestige (Duncan 1961). There are, however, enormous problems in developing measures of prestige for very large numbers of occupations. How many 'judges' should be used? How many of the myriad occupations in a society is it fair or sensible to ask them to rank or to score? The original study of this kind was carried out by the National Opinion Research Center in the United States in 1947, and it asked respondents to rank ninety occupations. But there are many hundreds of occupations in any society. One way around this, used in American research, was to find out the average income and education level of the jobs which had been given a score, and to use this to transfer a score to all other occupations (Duncan 1961; Hollingshead 1971; Nam and Terrie 1982). Suppose, in other words, in the last big national study of prestige (using a panel of judges), a doctor had a prestige ranking of 2, and a bricklayer had a ranking of 9. Suppose also that doctors on average earned £50,000 a year and had 20 years of education while bricklayers earned £5,000 a year and had 10 years of education. Then a new occupation arises, that of web page designer. On average, they earn £25,000 a year and have 15 years of education, so their prestige score could be estimated at around 6.5 (because in terms of education and income they are about halfway between the doctor and the bricklayer).

It is clear from these accounts of the development of the measures in the United States that neither income nor education was what the researchers were really interested in. They were just using these as a more feasible way to get at the 'social judgements' of characteristics of individuals which gave them high or low prestige. However, this process led increasingly to the practice of using combined income and education as the sole measure of social position, and calling this 'socio-economic status' (Featherman and Hauser 1976).

The extent to which status measures are really an attempt to measure the qualities of individuals has been further clarified in the recent Great British Class Survey (Savage et al. 2013). This study used a large number of criteria to arrive at something which they labelled 'social class'. As well as the value of their homes and their salaries, people were asked the occupations of their best friends (which were classified according to how 'manual' their work was), and things like their taste in music and their favourite entertainment. The Dutch sociologists Kraaykamp et al. give a succinct rationale for this: 'school can be regarded as a selection device that separates the cognitively talented . . . from the less talented . . . [so] if it is true that highbrow cultural activities are to a large extent more difficult . . . it is likely that students with higher levels of education will participate . . . in highbrow activities' (Kraaykamp, van Eijck and Ultee 2010: 176).

So a measure of social position (even if this is erroneously termed 'social class') that includes whether a person partakes in 'highbrow' or 'lowbrow' leisure pursuits is able to get closer to the real merits of that person in terms of their intellectual capacities. In functionalist terms, this would indeed make it a better measure than income or ownership of assets such as land or a business.

In fact, it would be unfair to state that the Great British Class Survey consciously aimed at improving a functionalist model of social inequality. It has the virtue of pointing out the existence of a small 'elite' with large amounts of wealth in money and housing values, and of a growing 'precariat' of workers in very insecure situations (Savage et al. 2015). But it is not clear what is added to the quality of the measure by all the information on cultural pursuits, until one remembers the functionalist roots of American research on social inequality. A lot of what goes on in epidemiological research on inequality happens in a kind of fog of assumptions about the relationship between the individual and society, assumptions that can be traced back to American functionalism.

Registrar General's Social Classes (RGSC)

Although we have spent some time carefully thinking through concepts of class and status, we have not considered the most commonly used measure of social position in British research up to 2001, the

Table 1.1 Classification of the Registrar General's social classes (RGSC)

Class number	Description
I	Professional
II	Managerial
III non-manual (NM)	Clerical, sales
III manual (M)	Skilled manual
IV	Semi-skilled manual
V	Unskilled manual

Source: Office of Population Censuses and Surveys 1980

Registrar General's social classification. This measure, or something regarded as very similar, was the most commonly used indicator of social inequality in British studies of health inequality and many studies that are still relevant use such a measure.

The Registrar General's classes are said to be based on either 'general standing in the community' or 'occupational skill'. The classification consists of six categories (see Table 1.1). To those familiar with British research on health inequality, it may seem strange to reiterate yet again the names of the RGSCs. But now that we have discussed the concepts and measures of class and status that are widely used in social and political research, it is helpful to think a little more carefully about how these relate to the 'classes' distinguished by the Registrar General's schema. The schema is in fact not a measure of class at all, in the sense used by Erikson and Goldthorpe or the NS-SEC. It is usually regarded as a hierarchy, that is, I is 'higher' than II, which is 'higher' than IIINM, and so on. There is an assumption that any form of non-manual work is 'higher' on this continuum than any form of manual work. There is the further assumption that any professional is 'higher' than any manager. This would mean that a junior doctor or a minister of religion, for example, would have a superior social position to that of a manager in a company, regardless of their relative incomes or the amount of authority they exercise (as in the Hindu caste system). Implicitly, it is clear that prestige is the underlying ordering principle which takes precedence over all other characteristics of occupations. Although this is never said in so many words, the assumption seems to be that occupations requiring more skill are held to be of higher 'standing in the community'. The equation, vague as it is, of 'general standing in the community' with 'occupational skill' reveals that, at least implicitly, the RGSC is a functionalist measure in which skill results in prestige. Marshall et al. accuse the RG classification of being a Parsonian functionalist measure as described above: 'embod[ying] the now obsolete and discredited conceptual model . . . of society as a hierarchy of inherited natural abilities, these being reflected in the skill level of different occupations' (Marshall et al. 1988: 19).

There is no evidence that the Registrar General's different classes are actually widely regarded by the British population as having different levels of general standing in the community, and no 'reputational' studies have been carried out equivalent to those in the United States to investigate perceptions of status among the general public. Nor have there been any studies to see whether the Registrar General's classes are an accurate grouping of occupations with different levels of education or skill.

The Registrar General's classification is a bit like aspirin: everyone knows that it works (i.e. there are large differences in health between the different groups), but nobody knows why. So knowing that it works is of little help in further explanation, just as knowing about the effectiveness of aspirin has not helped to explain the causes of osteoarthritis. However, such is the power of the phenomenon of health inequality that even such a vague measure has produced large and consistent differences over a very long period of time, as we will see in chapter 2.

Education

Increasingly, research on health inequality over the past 10 years has used education as the measure of social inequality (Elo 2009). There have been some practical reasons for this. Much more international comparative research is now feasible, and many nations use measures of social class, if of widely varying types. As more longitudinal research is done, we begin to see how much movement there is between social classes, income, or status groups over time. In contrast, education is thought of as being fixed by the time of entry into work. Education is often found to be a powerful predictor of health outcomes. So what is the problem with using education as a measure of social inequality in studies of health?

There is no doubt that education has very strong associations with health (Mirowsky and Ross 2003). But in fact using it as a simple measure of social position does not do justice to the complexity of health inequality. What happens over the whole of childhood is increasingly understood to have a cumulative effect on both personal development and social destination. In general, the greater the number of favourable influences during this period, whether they be quality living standards, family culture or relationships, the better the child and young person will do in education. It will not diminish the health gap between more and less socio-economically advantaged groups of adults to reduce these powerful processes in early life to a one-dimensional measure.

The second problem with using education as a simple measure of social position is that, over time and between nations, the number of people who reach a given level varies enormously. In 1965, around 6 per cent of the 18–19 year old age cohort, and only 2 per cent of women, went to university in Great Britain (Egerton and Halsey 1993). In 2013, it was around 43 per cent (Department for Business Innovation and Skills 2014). However, is it possible, then, to regard 'degree-level education' as the same thing for people born in these two cohorts? Or, indeed, for men and women? In the United States, those with a high-school diploma in 1959 had much higher pay on average than those without one; but by 2012 this 'income premium' had reduced greatly, and merely having a degree was sufficient to ensure a high income (Chen et al. 2013). The differences between different nations, and how these have varied over time, are also significant.

The third closely related problem relates to the differences in access to education for girls and boys, and for people of different ethnic or status groups. In some nations, ethnicity, caste and gender either exclude people from university (or indeed from school at all) or raise significant barriers. For my own age cohort, there were quotas in the United Kingdom limiting how many girls could attend certain types of technical training, including medical school, and quotas limiting the numbers of Jewish people who could be admitted to some US universities.

The fourth problem with regard to education as a measure of social position is that it is far too easy to fall into 'functionalist' assumptions and let these influence the ways in which we reason about health inequality. It is clear from a lot of what gets written in the literature on health inequality that educational attainment, like taste in music, art or literature, is actually being used as a measure of individual 'virtues' which have resulted in the 'socio-economic status' of the person. It has been easy, for example, for some social epidemiologists to move from this kind of assumption to the investigation of intelligence as 'the fundamental cause of health inequality' (Gottfredson 2004).

The position that is taken in this book is that, if we want to measure status, we need to use the results of studies that do in fact show how the prestige of different occupations is ranked in people's minds, and which groups mix together socially and intermarry. If we want to measure social class, we need to use a measure such as the NS-SEC and the growing number of adaptations for nations other than the United Kingdom, based on employment relations and conditions. If we want to measure income or wealth, then we can use other pretty obvious methods (such as asking people what their income is and how much savings they have, although this is not as simple as it sounds). We may want to look at these in conjunction with asking whether, for example, income is more or less important than occupational class or status (Geyer et al. 2006). If so, then we should use the separate measures in the same analysis. As subsequent chapters will show, there are often good reasons for being interested in this kind of question. As for education, if it is the only measure available, then using it may be unavoidable. But this needs to be done cautiously, keeping in mind it is only a 'proxy' or a probabilistic indicator. Education does not measure class, status or income at all but gives some indication of what these may be, which will vary by time, place, gender and ethnicity among other things.

Why measurement matters

The importance of knowing about these different measures for understanding health inequality is twofold. First, it alerts us to the necessity of defining what we mean by whatever concept of 'inequality' we are using, and of making sure we use valid measures of the concept. Secondly, it reminds us that we need to specify what we think it is about socio-economic position (the general term that I am using to refer to class, income and status) that may relate to health. Is it money, status or the conditions in which people work? And if, as is likely, what matters is different combinations of these for different illnesses, which forms of inequality are the most important for which conditions? Both health and social policy makers need answers to these questions. Because if, for example, we try to reduce inequalities in a certain illness by giving people more income when it is actually work conditions which are significant for that illness, effort and resources are wasted.

In terms of understanding health inequality, we need to think carefully about what it might be about class position, income and prestige that might plausibly affect health. It is no longer sufficient to observe that a large variety of measures based on a large number of different concepts (or none at all) repeatedly appear to yield similar 'health gradients' (Bartley et al. 1999; Torssander and Erikson 2010). For one thing, this is not true for women nor for members of all ethnic groups. The theoretically based social class measures (E-G classes, NS-SEC) offer one kind of possibility. This is because some of the criteria used to classify occupations into E-G classes in their various forms, such as work autonomy and job security, have been found in other studies to be related to major diseases, such as heart disease (Karasek 1996; Kivimäki et al. 2012; Nyberg et al. 2014).

Prestige may be thought of as having a different kind of effect. Caste groups display their prestige by distancing themselves from forms of activity and people which are considered unclean or unworthy. They also mark their social status by bodily adornment, clothing and various other aspects of what sociologists of industrial societies might call 'lifestyle'. These include dietary practices and attitudes towards mood-altering substances such as alcohol. There are strong similarities between the display of prestige in both more and less traditional societies (Bourdieu 1984a). In both, individuals mark their actual prestige, and attempt to increase it, by confining themselves to what are considered worthy activities and attempting to associate only with others who are perceived as of appropriate rank (Chan and Goldthorpe 2007). An essential part of the claim to prestige includes the adoption of certain forms of lifestyle. A 'cultural' theory of the relationship between prestige and lifestyle makes more sense of the social distribution of smoking, diet and exercise, for example, than a theory based purely on income, as neither non-smoking nor vigorous exercise need cost any money. In contrast, being a non-smoker is more or less obligatory in certain high- and medium-status social circles in northern Europe and the United States, and being seen to go jogging certainly helps to establish one's status credentials.

It is this use of measures of social position to construct 'causal narratives' (Marshall 1997; Rose and O'Reilly 1998) that makes it possible to take our attempts to understand health inequality forward more quickly, not because any one of the measures is superior to the others, but because we can see that inequality can be of different kinds and may influence health in different ways. As the originators of the Cambridge score have observed, 'it may be that policemen and skilled workers . . . interact with each other as equals, yet their relations to the productive system are different and this can have important behavioural consequences under certain conditions' (Stewart, Prandy and Blackburn 1980: 28). So we can, for example, test whether lower prestige may affect diet or smoking even within the same set of employment relations. There are rich possibilities for developing more complex and sensitive causal models which, at the same time, are more likely to be useful for health policy (Sacker et al. 2001; Torssander and Erikson 2010).

Further reading

An excellent account of the social theories lying behind different social class measures, combined with an empirical study of class differences (not in health):

Marshall, G., Rose, D., Newby, H. and Vogler, C. (1988), *Social Class in Modern Britain*. London: Hutchinson.

The best summary of British work on social inequality: indispensable:

Crompton, R. (2008), *Class and Stratification*, 3rd edn. Cambridge: Polity.

Describes the development of the new British government class schema and includes very useful discussion of the surrounding issues:

Marshall, G. (1997), *Repositioning Class*. London: Sage.

2

What is Health Inequality?

Since the first edition of this book was written, the directions taken in much of the research have been quite different to those I expected. Measures have changed and concepts become more rather than less confused. It has become more difficult, for example, to show a consistent series of statistics on health inequality in different nations that allows us to compare them. So what is presented in this chapter cannot claim to show uncontroversial facts and figures, merely the best efforts of scholars and national statistical authorities over the past decade or so.

How unequal is health?

Health inequality in England and Wales

This chapter gives some examples of what health inequality research in the past 40 years or so has told us about the size of social differences in health, and the extent to which these are growing or shrinking. Although the research effort began in the United Kingdom (or, to be more precise, in England and Wales), there is now a large body of work covering many nations. Here, I will concentrate on the industrial economies of Europe and the United States.

Health inequality was put firmly on the map of both public policy and academic study with the publication in the United Kingdom of the Black Report in 1980 (Department of Health and Social Security 1980; Townsend, Davidson and Whitehead 1986). This compilation of data on the relationship between ill health and mortality in England and Wales between the 1950s and the 1970s showed that the prospect of death at most ages, and therefore of the length of life, were strongly related to a measure of social and economic position referred to as 'social class' (see chapter 1). In the British context, the term 'social class' created such a powerful popular image that then, and for many years afterwards, the relationship to health seemed to require little further explanation. Formally, social class was defined in the official British government reports, going back to 1931 and from which the Black Report took its facts and figures, as 'general standing in the community based on occupational skill'. The official statistical information system of England and Wales made it possible, every 10 years at the census, to match up the occupations given on death certificates for people dying around the times of the censuses (1931, 1951, etc.) with a sample of census records for how many people there were in each occupation. Occupations were grouped into 'social classes', and death rates could be calculated from the numbers of people in each social class who died divided by the total number in that class at the Census.

Many other European nations' official statistical organizations use rather similar measures. In the United States, Canada and Australia, the notion of social class is less familiar and less widely used in research. However, interest in, and concern about, health differences between people with more and less favourable situations in respect of income, prestige ('standing in the community') and education has continued to grow in most industrialized and many developing nations.

Table 2.1 is the one that drew attention to the phenomenon of health inequality in Britain. It showed that the introduction of a national health service paid for by taxation and free to use at the time of need in 1947 had apparently done nothing to reduce differences in death risk between the social classes. Even worse, these differences had in fact grown considerably larger. These figures were arrived at by taking advantage of the Census of Population that takes place every 10 years. The census gives the numbers of people in each social class (defined according to their occupation); this is the denominator. Official death registrations give the numbers of people in each social class who die in the three years around the Census; this is the numerator. In simple terms, this can be thought of as a percentage and can be calculated the same way.

The measure of mortality risk in Table 2.1 is not a percentage but an SMR or 'standardized mortality ratio'. The SMR was often used up until around 2000 as a way to describe the size of health differences between groups. It is no longer widely used but can be read

Table 2.1   Health inequality in England and Wales, 1931–1991:
Standardized Mortality Ratios by Registrar General's Social Classes
(RGSC) in men aged 15–64

RGSC	1931	1951	1961	1971	1981*	1991*
I: Professional	90	86	76	77	66	66
II: Managerial	94	92	81	81	76	72
IIIN: Routine non-manual (1991)						100
III: Routine non-manual & skilled manual (1931–1981)	97	101	100	104	103	
IIIM: Skilled manual						117
IV. Semi-skilled manual	102	104	103	114	116	116
V. Unskilled manual	111	118	143	137	166	189

*ages 20–64
Sources: Wilkinson 1986: 2, Table 1.1; Drever, Bunting and Harding 1997: 98,
Table 8.2

simply. If you take 100 as the death rate for the average person, a
number lower than 100 indicates a lower risk for that social group,
and one above 100 a higher risk. For a more detailed explanation of
how to work out an SMR, see the Appendix to chapter 3.

The reason why the figures from 1931 to 1971 in the Black Report
attracted so much attention was that the differences between the
social classes were clearly increasing. This was not what was supposed to happen after the introduction in 1947 of a free National
Health Service. The figures for 1981–1991 show that this increase in
inequality continued.

What happened after 1991? Since the first edition of this book
was written, more information on health inequality in England and
Wales has appeared, but in a rather different form. The numbers
that provide the closest we have to a comparison between the series
1931–1991 and 2001 were provided by the Office for National
Statistics for England and Wales and are shown in Table 2.2, which
needs to be read in conjunction with the account of the NS-SEC
given in chapter 1.

Table 2.2 is obviously very different from Table 2.1. It has been
simplified drastically by only including the most and least advantaged occupational classes at each time point. Like Table 2.1,
however, what makes it possible to calculate these figures is having a

Table 2.2 Trend in inequality in mortality between 1970s and 2001–2, using old and new social class measurements (England and Wales, men aged 25–64, directly age standardized rates per 100,000)

	1970–72	1979–83	1991–93	2001–03	2010
RGSC I	500	373	280		
RGSC V	897	910	806		
Rate Ratio	1.8	2.4	2.9		
NS-SEC 1.1				182	128
NS-SEC 7				513	458
Rate Ratio				2.8	2.8

Sources: White et al. 2007; Office for National Statistics 2012

numerator (numbers who die) taken from official death records, and a denominator taken from Censuses or other official statistics. These are proper rates (not SMRs) and can be thought of as exactly the same as a percentage:

$$\frac{\text{Number in social class who die}}{\text{Total number in social class}} \times 100,000$$

only you divide by 100,000 rather than 100 because death is a rare event in most age groups. The 'age standardization' just means that an adjustment has been made to take into account the possibility that different social classes may have different average ages (see chapter 3). For example, many manual jobs require considerable physical strength so that people doing this kind of work tend to be younger. If no attention was paid to this, then mortality among manual groups might appear lower, not because of any less exposure to risk but just due to their younger average age.

The numbers in Table 2.2 give deaths per 100,000 in the most and the least advantaged social classes. The 'rate ratio' summarizes this difference by dividing one by the other (e.g. 897/500 = 1.8). For 2001–2003 and 2010, the way the mortality rates and the rate ratio are arrived at is just the same, but the most and least advantaged classes are defined according to the new NS-SEC which was described in some detail in chapter 1. It is generally agreed that the change from the old Registrar General's class schema to the NS-SEC did not make it look as if social inequality in mortality is lower than it 'should' be. So the important number is really the ratio for each year. And we can see that, in agreement with the (differently calculated)

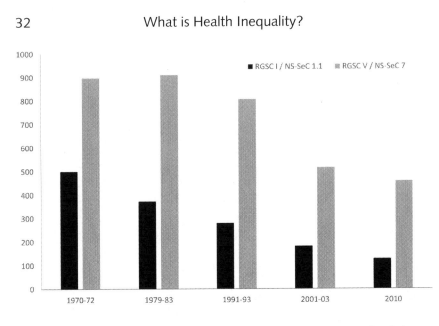

Figure 2.1 Trends in mortality rates (directly age standardized) in England and Wales 1970–2010 (men aged 20–64)
Source: Data from Table 2.2

inequality measures of Table 2.1, inequality rose quite a lot between 1970–2 and 1991–3, and then seems to have fallen very slightly in 2001–3 and remained the same in 2010.

Looking at these trends on a chart (Figure 2.1) shows more clearly what happened, at least between the 1970s and 2010. Because the directly standardized rates can be read just the same way as a percentage, we can see how mortality declined remarkably over this period in both the most (RGSC 1 or NS-SEC 1.1) and the least (RGSC V or NS-SEC 7) advantaged social classes. But the decline was steadier in men in the most advantaged occupations. In the least advantaged jobs, there was a bigger fall in mortality between 1991 and 2001 than in any other period.

Many readers will rightly ask why only men are considered in these statistics of health inequality. This is the downside of having such a long series stretching back to the 1920s and 1930s. During much of this period, women in the United Kingdom participated less in paid work, so that any placing of a woman within a 'social class' was problematic. Many women only worked for a small proportion of their lives. Women were excluded from many jobs by discriminatory practices. Many women did not receive an occupational title on their death certificates, which meant it was not possible to carry out matching between population numbers and numbers of deaths in each occupational class.

Health inequality in the United States

It is very difficult to create picture of health inequality in the United States that can be properly compared with the United Kingdom (England and Wales), and totally impossible to trace the trends back to the 1930s. The United States has excellent official statistical organizations which produce a huge amount of information, all made freely available without copyright restrictions. For example, it is quite easy to look at trends in what are called the 'health disparities' between ethnic and racial groups, which we will see in chapter 10. But there never has been a concept of 'social class' in the United States similar to that in European nations, and there is no way to replicate the 'class differences in mortality' in the same way even today, let alone before the Second World War.

In the latest research on health inequality in the United States, it has been possible to use education as a measure of social position. In chapter 1, we saw the problems involved in this kind of exercise. Education can have a very different meaning for different age cohorts, given that throughout the twentieth century an increasingly higher proportion of people undertook longer periods of education and gained more qualifications (Chen et al. 2013). This can mean that the people 'left behind' in the lowest educational groups are those with a more and more disadvantaged life course (or, some would say, less and less 'intelligence'). So the fact that people with the fewest years of education have increasingly worse health might be regarded as due to this kind of selection.

Since 1989, in 26 American states, anyone who dies has the number of years of their education written on their death certificate. Ma et al. used this information combined with estimates of the numbers of people in each educational group taken from the US Census Bureau's Current Population Survey (Ma et al. 2012). Because both men and women have their years of education inscribed on both the population surveys and on their death certificates, it is no problem (unlike in England and Wales) to calculate death rates by education for both genders. Table 2.3 shows what the result of this exercise looks like.

The table shows that the mortality rate for the least educated men, those with less than 12 years of education, fell from 695.5 per

Table 2.3   Mortality (age-standardized rate per 100,000) by years
of education in men and women aged 25–64 in 26 US states

Years of education	Men			Women		
	<12 yrs	16+ yrs		<12 yrs	16+ yrs	
	Rate/ 100K	Rate/ 100K	Relative Risk	Rate/ 100K	Rate/ 100K	Relative Risk
1993	695.5	279.9	2.5	346.1	180.8	1.91
2001	680.0	207.9	3.3	379.8	151.7	2.28
2007	657.1	184.4	3.6	385.3	129.0	2.56

Source: Drawn from Ma et al. 2012: Table 2

100,000 in 1993 to 657.1 in 2007, whereas for the most educated
men, with more than 16 years of education, it fell from nearly 280
per 100,000 to 184.4. This meant that the relative risk, which compares the two rates, increased from 2.5 to 3.6. It is rather alarming
to see that mortality rates among the least-educated women actually increased (from 346.1 deaths per 100,000 in 1993 to 385.3 per
100,000 in 2007). But we need to keep in mind the limitations of
using education as a measure of social position discussed here and
in chapter 1. The authors of this study did carry out some checks
against this problem and felt confident about their results (Ma et al.
2012). Figure 2.2, taken from the government report *Health United
States 2011*, uses different sources of data but shows a similar trend.
If we look at life expectancy rather than mortality, life expectancy at
age 25 in women with the lowest levels of education fell from 53 to
52 years (National Centre for Health Statistics 2012).

Health inequality in Europe

As we have seen, England and Wales (Scotland and Northern Ireland
have different official statistical systems) have a unique series of statistics on social position and mortality. Despite all the changes in both
measures and methods, it means that we can have a pretty good idea
of what has happened to this form of health inequality over a long historical period. This puts England and Wales in a more or less unique
position in respect to measuring health inequality over a long period
of time. But there have been efforts to compare health inequalities,
and how these have changed over a shorter period since the 1970s, in

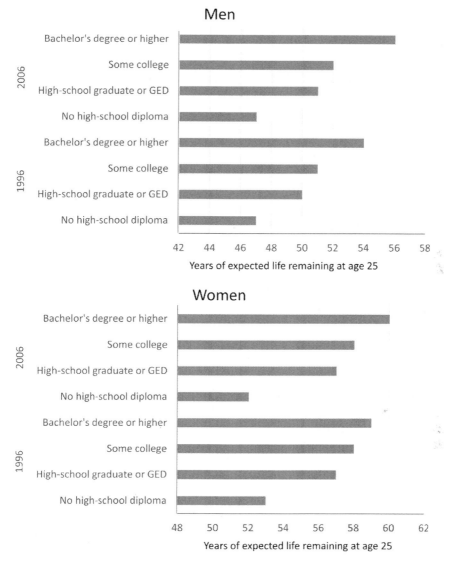

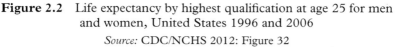

Figure 2.2 Life expectancy by highest qualification at age 25 for men and women, United States 1996 and 2006

Source: CDC/NCHS 2012: Figure 32

Table 2.4   Inequality in mortality in men aged 30−59 in European nations in 2000−2005

Country	Ratio of most to least advantaged occupational social class
Finland	3.42
Sweden	2.49
Denmark	3.47
E&W	2.12
Netherlands	2.04
France	2.73
Austria	1.74
Spain (Basque)	2.29
Spain (Madrid)	2.3
Italy (Turin)	2.21

Source: Toch-Marquardt et al. 2014

other nations in Europe. Most of this research has been undertaken by the group led by Johann Mackenbach at Erasmus University Medical Centre in Rotterdam. In 2014, this group produced a calculation of social class differences in mortality using a classification of social position that was as comparable as possible between the nations (Toch-Marquardt et al. 2014). It is not strictly comparable to the figures given in Tables 2.2 and 2.3 and Figure 2.1 because the age range is 30−59, rather than the full range of working ages.

Here, we are comparing between nations rather than over time, but the 'rate ratios' are the same and calculated in the same way as those for England and Wales in Table 2.2. You can see that the rate ratio for England and Wales is not quite the same as in Table 2.2, due to the different age range. This up-to-date comparison of health inequality shows the surprising result that mortality differences between the most and least advantaged occupational groups are not lower in the Nordic nations, which are thought of as being more egalitarian, than in Austria, Italy, Spain or even England and Wales. This poses one of the most interesting new questions about the causes of health inequality which will be discussed more fully in chapter 7.

Figure 2.3 gives the age-standardized mortality rates for the most and the least advantaged social classes so that we can see how this difference varies between nations. The first thing to notice here is that in the most advantaged social class there is not much difference between the mortality rates of different nations. The rather large differences in inequality as shown by the rate ratios are being caused by large dif-

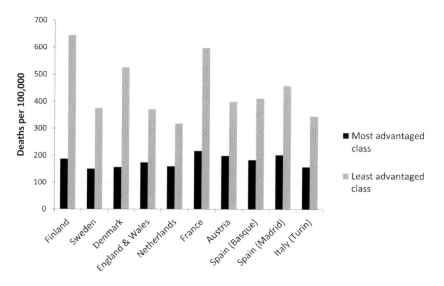

Figure 2.3. Age-standardized mortality in men aged 30–59 by occupational social class in different European nations

Source: Toch-Marquardt et al. 2014

ferences in what proportion of men in the least advantaged class die prematurely. This is highest in Finland, at more than 600 per 100,000 and lowest in the Netherlands, at 318 per 100,000. In fact, of all the nations Sweden has the lowest mortality among men in its *most* advantaged occupational class, whereas the low level of inequality in Austria is not due to low mortality among the least advantaged but to one of the highest levels of mortality among the most advantaged men.

This illustration of a comparative study shows another of the dimensions we can use when trying to understand health inequality. Historical trends give us ideas about what has changed over time; international comparisons give us ideas about what varies between nations. All of this helps as we try to understand why health inequality occurs.

Why health inequality?

Health care

One reason for the importance of the Black Report in Great Britain was that it showed, without any doubt, that the provision of health services to all citizens free at the time of need had not reduced differences in mortality risk between people in more and less advantaged social circumstances. There is now a large amount of evidence that health care itself has only a small impact on health at the population level, though it may have a large impact on the health of individuals who are ill. The work of McKeown (McKeown 1966), while itself controversial (Colgrove 2002; Link 2002; Grundy 2005), revealed many years ago that the greatest decrease in the killer diseases of the nineteenth and early twentieth centuries, such as typhus and tuberculosis, took place before the development of effective treatments. The number of doctors or of hospital beds or high-tech machinery in a nation does not seem to be important reasons for health inequality.

There are thought to be two main reasons for the ineffectiveness of access to medical care in lowering health inequality. The first of these is the importance of the social environment and lifestyles. Accordingly, this book will work through the evidence on the material environment, the psycho-social environment and health behaviours. The second reason is that the aetiology (causation) of the most common causes of mortality and disability in modern industrial societies almost always involves processes that take place over a very long period of the life course. By the time anything which looks like a recognizable disease appears (a heart attack, a visible tumour), it is often too late for cure. These diseases have to be combated by preventative measures extending over many years, such as protection from hazardous environments and lifestyles. So we will look carefully at new evidence on how processes that extend across the life course may be implicated in health inequality. An understanding of these issues is needed in order to devise more effective policies.

The Black Report's explanations

In 1980, the Black Report assembled a lot of data from official public health reports and created an overview of links between health and social position that had not previously been visible even to doctors working with individual patients. It was, however, part of a far longer tradition of public health commentary which had been used in political debates since the nineteenth century. Public health reformers had long used differences in the risk of death due to infectious diseases in arguments for and against the need for public investment in sewerage, water supply and sanitation. The emphasis in this work was on differences between poorer and richer geographical areas, between the country and the town, between market towns and industrial cities. Because these earlier 'sanitary reports' were read as part of a highly political debate over large amounts of taxpayers' money, their methods came under close examination. Did areas with dirty water have higher mortality just because they contained different sorts of people? Were the inhabitants of these areas condemning themselves by their feckless drinking habits and lack of domestic cleanliness?

Facts and figures ('data') on health differences between groups of people have always been debated because they have led to politically significant conclusions. As a result of this, the degree and even the very existence of differences in health between more and less advantaged people have been topics for strong argument. The findings of the Black Report in the United Kingdom were no different. Sanitation was considered indispensable by the 1970s, of course. There were two relevant political issues at the time the report was compiled. One of these was the doubt that had been raised over the effectiveness of a National Health Service, to which all citizens have free access. By 1980, British citizens had had access to health care paid for from general taxation for more than 30 years. It was a shock to find that health inequality not only still existed but also seemed (as we have seen) to have increased in a situation where everyone could get health care without payment at the time of an illness (Morris and Heady 1955). The second political issue raised was that of income distribution. Income inequality was still very much a fact of life in the welfare states of Great Britain and other European nations in the 1970s, despite progressive taxation and the provision of social services. However, income inequality had fallen from pre-war levels and was not thought to be large enough literally to affect the length of life. In the eyes of some commentators, the fact that it did so brought into question the usefulness of both the large amounts of public money spent on health services and of what was regarded by some as the very high taxes paid by the rich.

The Black Report and all the following studies during the 1980s put forward three different types of explanation for health inequality (Blane 1985; Smith, Bartley and Blane 1990; Davey Smith, Blane and Bartley 1994). One of these was based on a 'material' interpretation: that low income and its consequences could be the cause. The research relevant to this explanation will be discussed in more detail in chapter 6. The second explanation put forward was a 'cultural behavioural' one, which laid emphasis on the possibility that different cultures might be prevalent in lower income groups or less privileged social classes (discussed more fully in chapter 4). People in manual occupations and lower income groups were believed, for reasons that were not widely discussed, to share a culture that promoted behaviours such as smoking, eating an unhealthy diet and adopting low levels of physical activity. Why there might be class differences in such cultural practices was seldom asked. At the time, however, it seemed that if health differences could be attributed to culture, the troublesome issue of income inequality could be avoided.

The third possible explanation for the persistence of health inequality in a welfare state was 'selection'. This idea was somewhat similar to Darwin's 'natural selection'. People were regarded as gaining access to high incomes and privileged occupations by means of a kind of struggle involving 'the survival of the fittest'. One version of this, the simplest, held that people with poor health in childhood and adolescence were more likely to find themselves in the less privileged social classes as adults. So the son of a wealthy businessman, lawyer or doctor, if he were a sickly child, would end up as a miner or a bricklayer. The relationship of class to health was therefore nothing to do with conditions in the social classes themselves. Those in lower-paid, manual jobs were already more likely to be ill because they always had been. This version of the selection explanation is usually referred to as 'direct selection' (Fox, Goldblatt and Adelstein 1982; Wadsworth 1986). It may seem a bizarre idea that people in poor health from childhood or adolescence would be more likely to find their way into such occupations as mining, building or labouring (Fox, Goldblatt and Jones 1985; Power et al. 1990). For this reason, a more commonly held version of this explanation was that of 'indirect selection'. This was a more complex idea (Blane, Smith and Bartley 1993; Marmot et al. 1997; van de Mheen et al. 1998; Mackenbach 2010c). Could it be that people with lower amounts of 'potential' for good health found their way into the less privileged social classes? Did those with higher intelligence, better coping styles or more stable personalities gravitate towards the social classes with higher levels of skill, pay and prestige? As research has increasingly adopted a more individualistic approach to health inequality (Popay, Whitehead and Hunter 2010; Katikireddi et al. 2013) and a more structural-functional interpretation of inequality (as discussed in chapter 1), it is not surprising that this type of explanation has gained traction in the last decade. Structural-functionalism holds that it is 'functional' for society when people with greater intelligence and energy in early life gain access to higher-paid, higher-status or more skilled jobs, and these in turn have a higher 'standing in the community'. These people would also have the ability to manage their consumption, leisure and use of health services in a more health-promoting manner. The implications for political debates of the selection explanations were similar to those of the cultural-behavioural explanation: inequalities in income, housing, stress or hazardous working conditions were not responsible for health inequality.

Genetic explanations

The Black Report did not consider genetic explanations for health inequality, perhaps for two reasons. In the days before the sequencing of the human genome, there was far less interest in genetics than there is nowadays. Also, 40 years ago when the work was being done, memories of the Holocaust were perhaps fresher in people's minds, certainly in the minds of the report's authors who had fought in the Second World War. The idea that any important differences between human beings could be due to biological inheritance was linked in their minds to the policies of ethnic cleansing and to the slaughter of persons with disabilities carried out under Hitler. In the 1970s, few social scientists would have sympathized with the idea that illness was more prevalent in people who were socially or economically disadvantaged because of genetic inheritance. On the contrary, the defeat of Fascism had been accompanied by a commitment to provide better living and working conditions for less privileged people and by a widespread questioning of social inequality. The 'selection' arguments I have outlined above were the nearest to a genetic explanation for health inequality that were put forward. Even in this case, there was no claim that the illness that might cause people to be poorer and to live shorter lives was 'inherited'. Times have changed, however, which means that it is necessary at least to address the possibility that health inequality could be in some sense genetic in origin.

A more sophisticated appreciation of the application of genetics to the understanding of health inequality would have to take account of what it is that genes actually do. This cannot be attempted here, and in the last 10 years genetics has reached a far more complex view. For example, it is now no longer possible to talk scientifically about 'the gene for' characteristic X or Y. Rather, characteristics of individuals, even height for example, are now thought to be influenced by a wide range of different genes interacting with the environment. Holtzman has written a clear but comprehensive account of the problems involved in claiming that health inequalities are genetic (Holtzman 2002). To outline briefly one of its main points, let us take the idea that some characteristic that would fit a person to be a member of a privileged social group is 'influenced by a gene'. A gene has several alleles; if it is the gene for eye colour, there will be an allele for blue eyes, one for brown eyes and so on (although even this is now known to be an oversimplification). Each allele 'codes for', or influences, a protein, and it is this protein that in its turn influences the colour of a person's eyes. This 'influence' of the protein is itself complicated, and the form that the 'influence' takes is very variable, depending on what characteristic we are talking about. It may be that the protein works as an enzyme (facilitating some other chemical reaction), or it may act as a hormone or a transporter of other molecules. Sometimes all that an allele will do is make another gene do something different from what it would otherwise have done. So, even if you inherited an allele of one particular gene that meant you were not susceptible to a certain illness, you would only be less likely to contract this illness than other people who were *exactly* like you in all other respects. This is because what the allele does depends on all kinds of other genes and, in most cases, also on the environment. A striking example given by Holtzman is what happens to women who have the BRCA alleles that increase the risk of breast cancer. Of women with the high-risk allele born before 1940, 38 per cent got the disease, but as many as 69 per cent of those born after 1940 did so. Nobody knows why this is. But although the great difference between women with and without the relevant BRCA gene may be 'due to genetics', the difference in disease risk between women with the same gene but born at the earlier rather than the later time cannot be. The very size of the genetic difference itself seems to depend on some kind of change in the environment, or perhaps in lifestyles, that happened quite quickly.

The complexity of how genes actually work also makes it hard to argue that complex characteristics are more common in one social group than in another because of inheritance. If we look at a characteristic such as 'leadership potential' or 'intelligence', this would involve a large number of genes and very complex relations between them (Chabris et al. 2015). So even if a person's high income were due to some complex set of genetic influences, there would be very little chance of them passing all of these on to their offspring. The idea that health inequality is genetic needs not only 'favourable' psychological characteristics but also favourable health to be passed on from one generation to the next, which is even more unlikely (Keyes et al. 2015).

However, the notion that health inequality exists because, somehow or other, people with more money, power and status are just 'innately superior' to other people and therefore bound to be healthier is a very powerful one. It is now increasingly (if not altogether intentionally) written into the very definitions of social position used in research (see chapter 1). It reappears in various different forms throughout the body of research on health inequality and therefore will keep reappearing in this book, mostly in the form of arguments about 'selection'.

Contemporary social and environmental explanations

There are three theories for the persistence of health inequality that have developed since 1980, as more studies were carried out and as the debate became more international in its scope: the psycho-social model; the macro-social or 'political economy' model; and the life-course model. These will be dealt with in detail in later chapters. Of these, the *psycho-social model* relates to the psychological effects of the experience either of stressful conditions at work or home or of low social status (Schnall, Landsbergis and Baker 1994; Elstad 1998; Theorell et al. 1998). Some researchers, whose studies have laid emphasis on 'materialist' issues (such as working conditions), were not convinced that chemicals, fumes and other hazards were enough to explain health differences between more and less privileged workers. Large differences in health and life expectancy were even found in people working in office-based organizations with none of the classical industrial hazards (Marmot et al. 1991). According to this model, whether we are looking at circumstances in the present or in the previous life course of the individual, we need to give at least as much attention to the causes of psychological stress as we do to physical danger. Such stresses may include the social rather than the physical characteristics of the work environment. These include the amount of control and autonomy over the work a person has to do (Bosma et al. 1997), how routine the work is, how much support is available from co-workers (Johnson et al. 1996), and relationships to supervisors (Lynch et al. 1997). The extent to which individuals feel adequately rewarded for the amount of work they do has also been a focus of inquiry (Siegrist et al. 1990; Bosma et al. 1998; Landsbergis, Grzywacz and LaMontagne 2014). Other research has combined these two types of psycho-social risk factor (Wahrendorf et al. 2012; Burgard and Lin 2013). Perhaps it is not how much you earn at work which is important for your health, nor the physical conditions under which you earn it, but how your work conditions and relationships make you feel day to day. These ideas seem plausible to many people, simply on the grounds of their personal experience: it certainly is much worse to have to go in day after day to a workplace where things feel out of control and where people's relationships are unsupportive than one in which work is stimulating and a source of satisfaction

The *macro-social or political economy* explanations for health inequality pay less attention to the individual. I am including under this heading both the studies of income inequality by Wilkinson, Pickett and others and studies of health in countries with different levels of welfare generosity. These types of explanation pay more attention to whole societies and how they differ. Richard Wilkinson and his colleagues do not actually study health inequality between social groups at all. Rather, they study the relationship between inequality of income of individuals in a whole area (nation, federal states in the United States and other nations) and the overall health (life expectancy, rates of ill health) of the whole population in those areas (Wilkinson 1992, 1996; Wilkinson and Pickett 2006, 2009; De Maio 2012).

A type of political economy approach that is more relevant to this book is the work on health inequality in different 'welfare regimes', exploring differences between societies in social policies and institutions, which has been greatly expanded since 2003 (Bambra 2007; Beckfield and Krieger 2009; Brennenstuhl, Quesnel-Vallée and McDonough 2012). On the whole, countries where income differences between richest and poorest are smaller also provide more generous benefits to those unable to work. They also tend to have better public health, education, housing and transport provision. In countries with these kinds of policies, individuals with lower incomes are not thereby excluded from reasonable levels of education, health and social participation. We can investigate how important factors such as the provision of high-quality public services, generous welfare benefits and pensions might be in producing health inequality by comparing health differences in nations with different policies in these respects. The ideas underlying this work, and its rather surprising results, will be further discussed in chapter 7.

Perhaps potentially the most important 'political-economic' factor of all is the standard of publicly subsidized housing available to those with lower incomes. Unfortunately, there is relatively little research on the role played by housing quality in the causation of disease (Lloyd 1991; Eng and Mercer 1998; Mitchell, Blane and Bartley 2002). We will see later on that one of the great puzzles in the academic writing on this subject is why health inequality seems lower, at least in Europe, in the southern nations around the Mediterranean, such as Spain, Italy and Greece, than in Nordic nations with far more egalitarian welfare states (Mackenbach 2012; Mackenbach et al. 2014). These are not particularly rich or egalitarian countries. The most popular explanation for their lower levels of health inequality is the 'Mediterranean diet'. However, climate may have some relevance as well, in that cheaper housing will not expose its residents to cold and damp to the same extent as it does in northern regions (Blane, Mitchell and Bartley 2000; Mitchell et al. 2002).

Perhaps the most important innovation in health inequality research of the 1990s was the emergence of the life-course explanation. The life-course explanation for health inequality was not put forward in the original Black Report, but appeared more often in subsequent reports such as the Acheson Report (Acheson 1998) and the Marmot Review (Marmot 2010). It only became possible because of studies that were not available to the authors of the Black Report. The British Birth Cohort studies and other longitudinal studies followed the lives of people over long periods of time, sometimes from birth. There are five major longitudinal studies in the United Kingdom: cohorts of people born in 1946, in 1958, in 1970, and in the millennium year 2000, and a large group of people of all ages in 1991. The 'life-course approach' was not only a new type of explanation, but also made possible new explorations of the older ones. One of the most important aspects of the life-course approach was the suspicion that the chances of good or poor health were influenced by what happened to people in very early childhood and even before they were born (Halfon and Hochstein 2002; Chen, Martin and Matthews 2007; Gluckman et al. 2008). For the first time, researchers could actually investigate whether sick children were more likely to find themselves in less skilled jobs as adults (Wadsworth 1986; Power et al. 1990; Caspi et al. 1998; Case and Paxson 2011). It is possible to measure health in cohort members when they are children and to see if this predicts their social class membership, income and employment patterns as adults. It is also possible, though more difficult, to measure the factors which have been claimed as the basis for 'indirect selection'. We can see whether children who, although healthy, displayed troublesome behaviour were more likely to end up in less advantaged social and economic circumstances later on and showed less healthy behaviour (Fronstin, Greenberg and Robins 2005; Osler, Godtfredsen and Prescott 2008).

By definition, any selective process must take place over time. If we are to investigate Mackenbach's hypothesis that 'increased opportunities for social selection and may have made the lower social groups

Table 2.5 Models for understanding health inequality

	Cultural/behavioural	Psycho-social	Material	Selection
Cross-sectional	Bad diet, smoking, high alcohol consumption and lack of exercise are more common in less socially and economically advantaged groups, which causes health inequality.	People in occupations with less favourable employment conditions, or who experience disrespect due to low status or income, experience greater stress. Chronic activation of fight-or-flight increases risk of heart disease. Immunity may also be damaged with implications for cancer	Work hazards, poor housing and polluted environment expose people in less advantaged socio-economic positions to greater disease risk. Those with lower incomes may be forced to take greater risks.	The selection model cannot be tested in a cross-sectional study.
Life course	Adverse conditions and experiences in early life are strongly associated with risky adult health behaviours. The harmful effects of risky health behaviours can best be understood when behaviour is measured over time rather than at a single time point.	Adverse experiences in childhood make the individual more sensitive to later stresses (more likely to 'fight or flee'). Early adversity may reduce the individual's capability to relate to others at work and in the community.	Family poverty exposes children to physical risks such as damp, pollution and overcrowding from birth. Poverty is also now known to have an adverse effect on the development of the brain and nervous system.	Individuals with less favourable personal characteristics, such as intelligence, conscientiousness, coping skills, are left behind in the less advantaged social and economic situations. This is true especially in nations with a lot of social mobility. Lower personal skills result in riskier health behaviours.
Macro-social	Very little knowledge at present as to whether health behaviours vary between nations with different income distribution of welfare regime type	Better support for parents may reduce risk of adverse experiences in early life. Greater income equality may reduce anxiety and stigma in those with relatively low pay	Better provision of low-cost housing protects from hazards. Higher benefits protect living standards during unemployment, parental leave, etc.	More meritocratic education systems may increase health inequality.

more homogeneous with regard to personal characteristics like low cognitive ability and less favorable personality profiles' (Mackenbach 2012), then we are inevitably committed to longitudinal research. It is now generally agreed that material and psycho-social exposures, if they are indeed health hazards, are likely to operate over the life course. Perhaps the most important advance in the most recent research on health inequality has been the discovery of links between adverse childhood experiences (ACEs) and health behaviours in adulthood (Tubeuf, Jusot and Bricard 2012; Giesinger et al. 2014). Chapter 10 will discuss life-course research on health inequality in more detail.

We have seen that, combining the Black Report's explanations originating in the 1970s with explanations that emerged between 1980 and 2015, we can distinguish four types of influences that may be responsible for health inequalities between socio-economic groups. These may be classified as material, behavioural, psycho-social and selection. Each of these types of influence is now agreed to act over the life course. Macro-social models must also ultimately explain any observed differences between political and economic factors that differ between nations or other geopolitical units in terms of one or more of the three types of influence acting on individuals over time. These different explanations form the basis for understanding health inequality at the present time, at least in the more economically developed nations (see Table 2.5). Of course, the different types of explanation are not mutually exclusive. Nor are they likely to be identical for different health outcomes, although the health gradients for different diseases are remarkably similar. But we do need to have clear concepts and theories to guide research on health inequality in order to contribute to the design of effective policies to reduce it.

Further reading

Still the classic study of health inequality in the United States:
Kitagawa, E. M. and Hauser, P. M. S. (1973), *Differential Mortality in the United States: A Study in Socioeconomic Epidemiology.* Cambridge: Harvard University Press.

The original British reports that started the debate on health inequality:
Townsend, P., Davidson, N. and Whitehead, M. (1986), *The Black Report and the Health Divide.* Harmondsworth: Penguin.

3

Figuring Out Health Inequality

It is not the aim of this book to be a methods text. But there are a few simple basic ideas used in health inequality research that are very helpful to understand. Research in this area is constantly making comparisons between groups such as occupational social classes, status groups or groups based on education. When studies find that one group is less healthy than another, the next step is to try and figure out what are the differences between groups that might account for differences in health. This chapter will go through some of the most frequently used methods for comparing health in social groups in order to ascertain the causes of health differences. Of course, it would be surprising if there were a single explanation for such differences. Studies usually have to expect to consider more than one factor at a time. But it is not very difficult to reach a general understanding of how this is done. The examples given here are an attempt to show step by step some of the 'mechanics' of these methods. The mathematics needed to understand these methods is no more advanced than multiplication and division.

Over the last 10 years, research into health inequality has begun to use more complicated methods. Readers wishing to gain a better understanding of these are referred to the recommended texts at the end of this chapter. One good reason for methods to become more complicated is the enormous increase in the availability of life-course data, which are collected from the same people over many years, sometimes from birth to early old age. But that does not prevent anyone with an interest in health inequality from gaining sufficient understanding for all practical purposes.

Statistical explanation

What do we mean when we claim to have 'explained' something using statistics? In sociology, we often claim to have explained something if we can see how the motivations of all parties involved in some process or activity have led them to act as they did. This is Weber's notion of 'understanding' (*verstehen*), which is expressed in terms of being able to put oneself in the place of another social actor and see why this person did what they did. However, 'taking the role of the other' very often does not go far in helping us to understand the actual outcome of the actions of more than one person. We also need to understand the 'unintended consequences' of action. This allows us to see why the ultimate result of several different parties' actions can be something that none of them individually expected. In such cases, understanding in the sense of *verstehen* does not actually allow us to explain the outcome, only why each individual participant acted as they did.

Statistical explanations have nothing to do with understanding the motivations, intentions or feelings of the people involved. You have attained a degree of statistical explanation insofar as you have located a group of measures of some factors (often called 'variables') whose values can be used to predict the health outcome you are interested in. Imagine starting with no idea about who in a given population might have worse health, measured in terms of life expectancy, than anyone else. In statistical terms, you have no reason to expect anything other than that health is 'randomly distributed': any one person is as likely to be as ill or as healthy as any other. Then you observe that men and women have somewhat different levels of health: women have longer life expectancy. Gender then becomes part of a statistical explanation (although you may have no idea why). Further, you observe that people with higher income, higher education and higher-level managerial jobs all seem to have longer life expectancy. All these variables – gender, income, education and job type – become part of the statistical explanation. Once again, there is no requirement to understand why any of these characteristics might lead to longer or shorter lives, only that if you know a person's 'score' for any of them, you will have a better idea of how old they will live to be.

The next step is to find out whether your predictor variables are related to each other: do women live longer than men because they have higher incomes and are more likely to have managerial jobs? No: in fact women tend to have lower incomes and are less likely than men to have managerial jobs. So the explanations for gender differences in health will be different from the explanations for health differences between people with different incomes and types of work. Perhaps we then observe that people whose high incomes do not depend on their work alone but come partly from other people (in the form of inheritance, dividend and interest payments or the earnings of other family members) live longer than those who spend many years at work. In each of these steps, all we are doing is putting people into groups and seeing how similar the health of group members might be. Eventually, we would like to have a set of groups in which everyone's life expectancy was very similar. Then the characteristics of these groups would be a 'good explanation' in statistical terms. The longest-living people might be men or women who all had degrees and professional training, very high incomes, had spent their young adulthood in comfortable homes and with plenty of domestic help and their later working lives in a powerful professional or managerial job with a generous occupational pension. Let us say that members of this group lived on average to 90 years of age. If you, the researcher, knew how far any individual in your population departed from this 'perfectly healthy' paradigm, you would be able to predict with some confidence how much shorter that individual's life would be. This set of values, and the predictions they allow you to make, would be a 'statistical model explaining life expectancy'.

Having arrived at this very good statistical model, you would still quite possibly have no idea why this should be the case in terms of anyone's personal or biological experience. This type of understanding would need to be pursued by clinical and qualitative methods: using biological measurements, life-histories and in-depth interviews, and making an ethnographic study of different social settings. At the present time, there are very few studies of health inequality that aim at this form of explanation (Ostergren et al. 1995; Cable et al. 1999; Fassin 2000). Most research on health inequality so far has aimed only at statistical explanation, so that is the form I will concentrate on here.

Vital statistics: numerators and denominators

Much of the information used in debates on health inequality comes from the national statistical services of various countries. Many nations keep records of births, marriages and deaths – these are often called vital statistics. Most of the information on comparing mortality rates between nations, regions or social groups used in this book has relied on these kinds of figures.

In order to trace what is happening to its death rate, a country needs two pieces of information. The first of these is a record of all deaths in a given time period. The second is a good estimate of the population. These two figures make up, respectively, the numerator and the denominator for the death rate in that period. Death rates are a good measure to use in the study of health inequality because death is an objective fact that is substantiated and is not, unlike for example self-rated health, influenced by national or regional cultures. For this reason, studies using self-rated health will not be widely quoted in this book.

Dividing the numerator by the denominator and multiplying this by 100 gives the rate (in this case a percentage). But death rates are usually not expressed as percentages because luckily death is a fairly rare event before age 75, so these reports usually give rates per 10,000, 100,000 or even per million. Whatever is chosen as the basis for the rate, it is derived from this formula:

$$(\text{number of deaths (numerator)}/\text{number of people (denominator)}) \times [\text{e.g.}]\ 10{,}000$$

So that, if there were 500 people in the population and two of them died this would give a death rate per 10,000 for that year of

$$(2/500) \times 10{,}000 = 40 \text{ per } 10{,}000$$

If a death rate for a certain sub-group of the population is needed, it can only be arrived at if the relevant information has been included both at the time when the death was recorded and at the time when the population was recorded (often at national censuses). So if we want to calculate death rates by gender, social class, ethnic group or whatever, social class, gender and ethnicity must be recorded both at each census and on the death record. National official statistics seldom include death rates according to income or ethnic group because many people might object to having these recorded at the time of the death of a family member. Social class, however, as we have seen, is based on occupation, which is a less sensitive piece of information.

In order to obtain some idea of death rates in different ethnic groups or income groups, some countries carry out what are described as 'census-linked' studies. In this kind of study, some or all of the population's census information (which often does include all kinds of measures that it would be inappropriate to ask about at the time of a death) is linked to death records of the same people. In the simple 'rate method' (sometimes called the 'unlinked method'), all that is needed is the numbers of people in a certain group who died and the numbers of that group in the whole population. In the linked method, census information is linked to the death record for the same individual. In many Nordic nations, this can be done for the entire population, giving a very powerful data set (called a 'register') for investigating health inequality. In the United States and Great Britain, there are special linked studies such as the Office of National Statistics' Longitudinal Study of England and Wales (Fox and Goldblatt 1982; Drever et al. 1997) and the US Panel Study of Income Dynamics (McDonough and Amick III 2001; Duncan et al. 2002). Merely obtaining accurate death rates is therefore not as easy as it might appear. A lot of recent health inequality research has taken the form of studies comparing differences between nations in the death rates of different social groups (Mackenbach et al. 2008; Mackenbach 2012). The accuracy of all this work will depend on having good data for both numerators and denominators

Absolute and relative

In a lot of papers, you will see a distinction being made between 'absolute' and 'relative' rates. Confusion often arises over this distinction, even in quite experienced observers, and it is worth further thought. There are two common phrases in which the distinction occurs: 'absolute versus relative difference' and 'absolute versus relative risk'.

Absolute versus relative difference

The distinction between absolute and relative difference is important, for example, when trying to decide how important a certain form of health inequality is for policy purposes. 'Absolute difference' means the difference between the *numbers* (not the percentages) of people who get a certain illness, or who die, in various groups (defined according to social position, gender, ethnicity, area of residence or whatever the study is concerned with). 'Relative difference' usually means the *percentage* difference in illness or mortality between groups. A large absolute difference can exist at the same time as a small relative difference; this depends on how common a disease is in the population. For example, there are very large relative social differences in lung cancer, even larger than the relative differences in heart disease. Take a population of 100,000 people with a heart disease rate of 2 per cent and a lung cancer rate of 0.4 per cent, and two social groups, the 'more favoured' and the 'less favoured'. Because heart disease is so common, there could be 900 deaths in a more favoured social group and 1,000 in a less favoured group, which would be a relative difference of 10 per cent between the social groups and an absolute difference of 100 deaths. Compare this to lung cancer, a much less common disease. Here, if there were 200 deaths in the favoured group and 250 in the less favoured, this would give a relative difference of 20 per cent but an absolute difference of only 50 actual lives lost. In public health planning terms, it may be regarded as more pressing to prevent an absolute difference of 100 deaths which is only 10 per cent rather than an absolute difference of 50, even though it represents a 20 per cent reduction in inequality.

Absolute versus relative risk

Then there is 'absolute versus relative risk'. The term 'risk', or 'absolute risk', may be thought of just as the proportion, or percentage, of people with a certain condition. This is not a very correct term in many ways and not all statistical experts would agree with its use. For one thing, the percentage of people with a certain condition today may not be a good predictor of who will get it in the future, and one thinks of a risk as something that could happen in the future. In contrast, the term 'relative risk' refers to the comparison between the percentage of the population that has the condition and the percentage that does not. This figure is also often called the 'odds' So an absolute risk of 80 per cent is a relative risk (or odds) of (80/100)/(20/100), in other words, 4 to 1. Bookmakers on a racecourse would call these 'odds of 4 to 1 on': if 80 per cent of a certain group have disease X, we could say the odds of getting the disease versus not getting it in this group were 4 to 1 in favour of getting it. Later in this chapter, we take a closer look at the 'odds ratio' (OR) which divides these 'odds' for one group by the odds for another group as a way of comparing their levels of risk.

Standardization: what is it and why is it needed?

In order to make valid comparisons between two or more social groups, and attribute the differences to a social factor such as class position or status, official statistical reports take steps to ensure that the difference is not simply due to the different ages of the groups.

Suppose that people tend to move up the income scale as they grow older. In this case, one might see worse health in the top income group than at the bottom. More realistically, it sometimes happens that, as they become older, men doing manual work move from more strenuous jobs, such as mining, to jobs such as that of a night porter. The most commonly used illustration of this problem shows health inequalities not between social groups but between geographical areas. If you found that the state of Florida in the United States, or the county of Hampshire in England, had higher mortality than other areas, would you suspect that there might be a lot of hazards in the environment? It would be a mistake not to take account of the fact that many people retire to these areas, so that the average age of their citizens is higher than in most areas with heavy industry.

Indirect standardization: the standardized mortality ratio (SMR)

This correction for the possibility that a group that looks unhealthy is in fact just 'old' is called 'standardization'. The most common form, used in many of the older reports which contributed importantly to present understanding of health inequality, is the standardized mortality ratio (SMR), also called 'indirect standardization'. Nowadays, most statisticians find this a rather strange measure and it is seldom used in research papers. But several tables in regular government reports on health inequality which show figures for SMRs are used in this book, and it is useful to have an idea of what this measure can tell us. It is called a 'ratio' because it compares the death rate in any social class to what that rate would have been if the social group had exactly the same age structure as the whole population (so it is the ratio between the two rates). The easiest way to think of it is as comparing the death rate in each of the social groups with the 'average' for the whole population. The 'average' is set by convention to be 100. If we find that the most advantaged social class has an SMR of 50, therefore, we can say that this group has only half the average death rate. If the most disadvantaged class has an SMR of 150, we can say that it has a death rate 50 per cent above the average, taking account of age differences between the groups. We need to be careful when thinking about what these can and cannot tell us because the SMR only shows relative mortality, that is, the mortality in each class relative to the average for all persons in that year. So that if the SMR for heart disease in NS-SEC 7 is 80 in one time period and 160 in a later period, this certainly does not mean that heart disease in this social group has doubled! What it means is that in the earlier period a man in NS-SEC 7 was about 20 per cent less likely than average to die of heart disease, whereas in the later period he was about 60 per cent more likely than average to do so. It is not possible, using this measure, to compare one time period with another, only to compare each social group to the average within each time period. That is really all one needs to know about this measure. However, for the details of how it is calculated, see Table 3.7 in the Appendix to this chapter.

Direct standardization

A second form of standardization, called 'direct standardization', is now more commonly used and is found in reports on health issued by the World Health Organization and by many national governments. The SMR, as we have seen, is a ratio between the death rate in a group and what we may think of as the 'average for the population'. (This is not exactly what it does but there is no harm in thinking of it in this way.) Direct standardization gives us a standardized percentage (or rate per 10,000 or 100,000 and so on). It tells us what proportion of people would have fallen ill, died (or whatever other outcome we are interested in) in the whole population if that population had the same age structure as the social class in question. This method is useful for two main reasons. The first is that it can be read in just the same way as an ordinary percentage. When calculating SMRs for two or more different time points, at each time the 'average' death rate for the whole population for that time is 'reset' to equal 100, and all other groups are compared to this. If the SMRs for our rich and poor groups in 1981 were, let us say, 75 and 150, and in 1991 they were 65 and 170, this does not mean that mortality risk has fallen in the rich and risen in the poor. It only means that the risk for the rich has fallen relative to that for the whole population (the imaginary '100') and that for the poor has risen relative to the population. A directly standardized rate, on the other hand, does allow us to compare over time.

In order to carry out direct standardization, you need to have a 'standard population'. This can be taken from a number of sources. Nowadays, most European (including British) publications use a 'European standard population' or a 'world standard population' in order to make international health comparisons ('Britain is healthier than France, say experts'). American publications use either a world standard, when comparing the United States to other nations, or an American standard population for comparing between groups within the United States. It does not matter what country or what time point is included in the standard population, as long as all other groups at all other times are compared to the same one. In the example used here, the standard population will be taken as the whole population made up of the 'rich' and 'poor' social classes that we want to compare to each other. Once again, the object of the exercise is to correct for the possibility that disease or death rates look different between times or between groups because the age structure varies between groups or at different times. Because direct standardized rates are so commonly used, I will show the way they can be calculated here in full. Table 3.1 shows a table giving an example of direct standardization. In this imaginary population, there are two social groups, the 'rich' and the 'poor'. We want to see whether the poor group has a higher death risk than the rich group, after taking account of the fact that there are more older people in the poor group.

How to do direct standardization

1 Separate the population into age groups (10-year age groups for this example). In Table 3.1, you can see that the two classes have different age profiles. Although there are the same numbers in each age group in the population as a whole (80), in the poor class there are 50 people aged 55–64, compared to only 30 people of this age in the rich class. Because older people have a higher risk of death, there is a chance here that differences between rich and poor could be due to their age profiles.

2 Get the rate of mortality in each age group for each social class.

3 Calculate how many people would have died in the whole population of that age if everyone had the same risk as the people in each of the social classes.

4 This gives two numbers of deaths for each age group. In Table 3.1, the death rate of 15–24-year-olds in the 'poor' group is 13.3 per cent, and in the 'rich' group it is 8 per cent. Because there are 80 people in that age group in the whole population, if the whole population in age group 15–24 had the same death rate as the 'poor' class there would have been 10.6 deaths, and if the whole population aged 15–24 had the death rate of the rich class, there would have been 6.4 deaths. In age group 35–44, 15 per cent of the poor died, and 10 per cent of the rich. Because there are 80 people aged 35–44 in the whole population, there would have been 12 deaths in the age group if they had all had the same risk as the poor class.

Table 3.1 Example of direct standardization

Social group		Age					Total population	Total 'standard deaths'	Standardized rate
		15–24	25–34	35–44	45–54	55–64			
'Poor'	Number in age group	30	30	40	50	50			
	% died	13.3	16.7	15	16	20			
	# in whole age grp who would have died if rate same as 'poor'	10 (13.3% of 80)	13.4 (16.7% of 80)	12 (15% of 80)	12.8 (16% of 80)	16 (20% of 80)		64.8	16.2 (64.8/400)×100
'Rich'	Number in age group	50	50	40	30	30			
	% died	8	6	10	13.3	20			
	# who would have died in whole age grp if rate same as in 'rich'	6.4 (8% of 80)	4.8 (6% of 80)	8 (10% of 80)	10.6 (13.3% of 80)	16 (20% of 80)		45.8	11.5 (45.8/400)×100
Total number in both classes		80	80	80	80	80	400		

If the whole age group had the same death rate as the rich, there would have been eight deaths. And so on. The estimated numbers of deaths that would have taken place in the population if it had the same age profile as each of the social classes are called 'standard deaths'.

5 Next, add up all the 'standard deaths' for each class.

6 Express the numbers of standard deaths in each class as a percentage of the whole population. The directly standardized rate for the 'poor' class may be thought of as what the death rate in the whole population would have been if each age group had the same rate as that for people in the poor class, and the directly standardized rate for the 'rich' class may be thought of as the death rate for the whole population if the risk in each age group were the same as that for the rich class.

Observational studies and 'causality'

A great deal of ink has been used in the past five years on the tricky question of 'causality'. In part, this has been due to an epidemic of serious problems in the scientific literature. First, several results from the kind of study that was the norm in twentieth-century health inequality research turned out to be not just wrong (Ioannidis 2005), but possibly dangerously wrong. The most famous correction was perhaps the Women's Health Initiative in the United States (Investigators, Writing Group for the Women's Health Initiative 2002). For many years, it had been claimed that taking hormone replacement therapy (HRT) during the menopause had wider benefits than just the control of symptoms. It seemed that women taking HRT were less likely to die of heart disease and cancer, for example. Then someone noticed that women taking HRT were also less likely to die in motor accidents. This rang alarm bells; this was obviously not some biological effect of hormones. Perhaps the real story was about the kind of women (basically those from more advantaged sectors of society) who had easier access to HRT, not the biological effects at all. A clinical trial was undertaken where women were randomized into taking the drug or not, so that their social position or any other characteristics could not possibly influence the health outcomes of HRT. And what this trial showed was that there were in fact slightly higher, not lower, risks of heart disease in women taking a certain type of hormone replacement (Kuller 2003). The result of this randomized trial in the United States was official advice from the National Institutes of Health in 2004 that HRT only be used for moderate or severe symptoms and for the shortest possible time (Women's Health Initiative 2004). By early 2015, the leading centre for health evidence, the Cochrane Centre, stated there was no evidence that HRT could benefit the heart (Boardman et al. 2015). Although debate still goes on about the risks and benefits of different HRT regimes for women with severe menopausal symptoms (Manson et al. 2013; Nabel 2013), the WHI trial had shown the dangers of what are called 'observational' studies, where investigators merely compare people in different groups (like HRT users and non-users) without taking into account the possible reasons for group membership (like income). This means we cannot rule out the possibility that it is not group membership itself (users versus non-users of a certain drug, for example) which is beneficial or harmful but other ways in which the groups are similar.

It is generally accepted that causality can only be demonstrated in randomized trials, where the treatment is administered to half the study participants according to a kind of throw of the dice. Strangely enough, this in itself is because of the enormous power of social circumstances themselves to influence health. Trials need to be 'blinded', that is, the people not getting a treatment need to be given the equivalent of a sugar pill so that they do not know whether they are getting the active drug. This is an equally powerful demonstration of the importance of psycho-social factors: people who believe they are being treated often feel better even if they are not taking anything more than a dummy pill. And many trials are 'double-blinded' because, even if only the doctor giving the treatment knows which pill is real, this can often influence the way the patient feels.

Limiting claims of causality to randomized trials obviously produces very great problems for research on health inequality. There is absolutely no chance of allocating trial participants randomly to, for example, low and high income, smoking and non-smoking, or low and high educational attainment. But because so many of the most important questions in public health are of a similar kind, opinions on the value of studies other than clinical trials have recently softened somewhat. Doubt has also been thrown on the sacred character of trials by the discovery that not all are properly conducted or reported, and that their results do not always translate into the practice of medicine in real life. There have been large trials, for example, of intensive advice and support to try and change health behaviours (although no one could call these 'blinded'). But despite almost 40 years of such work, as we have seen, health inequality remains stubbornly high. Although people in general are living longer in industrial societies, the gaps between more and less socially and economically advantaged groups remain undiminished. It seems that we are dealing with enormously powerful social forces. And a lot of work remains in the effort to understand these.

Spuriousness and confounding

When a health outcome that looks as if it has been produced by one factor (say, a drug or treatment) turns out to have more likely been caused by another related factor (say, being rich enough to afford the treatment) we often call this a 'spurious' or 'confounded' result. Confounding is an enormous problem in any 'observational' study, that is, anything other than a randomized trial. And it has bedevilled research on health inequality throughout its history.

Confounding may have been a particularly big problem for research on the causes of health inequality because of the political sensitivity of this topic. A frequent move in these debates has been to claim that an apparent relationship between a health measure and a measure of the social and economic environment is not real, but is 'confounded' by something unconnected to social or economic inequality. 'Confounding' is often explained by telling stories about storks and babies. In a mythical society, outside observers notice that babies often arrive in the spring, at the same time as migrant birds such as storks. The observers conclude that the storks bring the babies – the arrival of storks is the 'cause' of the babies. What they do not take into account is that the members of this society deliberately plan the arrival of their babies to coincide with the warmer seasons of the year. So the season is (in one sense or another) the 'real' cause of both the variables; it is 'confounding' the arrival of babies and of storks. Throughout the rest of this book, there will be a number of examples in which some kind of personal characteristic, such as 'intelligence' or 'coping ability', is invoked as a type of confounder, and in which it is claimed that apparent relationships of social disadvantage and poor health are spurious. We might imagine quite plausibly that certain mental qualities could be the cause of a person attaining (or failing to attain) a certain social position or income, and also the cause of ill health. In these cases, it could be claimed that the relationship between social position or income and health was 'spurious with respect to' or 'confounded by' the personal characteristic.

Models of health inequality

In most academic papers (as opposed to official reports) on health inequality, use is made of statistical models. These models are the way in which researchers try to pinpoint the causes of health inequality. Are they really due to differences in environmental conditions, work hazards or types of lifestyle? It is always necessary to check whether groups of people with different work hazards or lifestyles might have other characteristics that could also be contributing to health differences between the groups. Statistical models are really just an extension of the methods we have seen used in age standardization. They look at the relationship between two variables (the one you think might be the 'cause' and the 'effect', or health-outcome variable) with every other relevant variable held constant. Would the relationship between social position (class, prestige or income) and blood pressure be the same if not just the ages of the different class or income groups were the same, but also their gender, education, diet and so on?

The studies of health inequality that are discussed in the rest of this book address competing explanations or models of how this inequality might be used. These hypothetical explanations contain several possible causal factors, and they need to be tested by the use of statistical models. If we combine age and income in a model, we can think of the result as the relationship of income to health after taking account of differences in age between people with different incomes. This kind of exercise is often referred to as 'holding age constant'. If we combine social class with intelligence in a model, likewise we can think of the result as showing the level of health in each social class 'holding intelligence constant', that is, 'if everyone in each class had the same level of intelligence'. This is a very simple way to understand statistical models of health inequality and it will not be enough to meet all cases. However, it is always worth bearing in mind when first considering any study. Introducing another variable into a model in this way is often referred to as 'adjustment'. But the principle is the same as 'standardization'.

The odds ratio (OR)

The outcome measure in many studies of health inequality is some kind of qualitative or categorical measure, such as the presence or absence of an illness, so that we have 'the percentage (or rate) of ill people' in richer and poorer groups combined, for example.

Table 3.2   Odds ratio: depression by gender

	Depressed?		
	Yes %	No %	Odds
Women	28	72	0.39:1
Men	22	78	0.28:1
Odds ratio			1.38

Source: Office of Population Censuses and Surveys (1997); author's analysis

This percentage is regarded as reflecting the risk, or probability, of illness in each individual member of the group. The conventional way to compare these probabilities in statistical models is to use a measure called an odds ratio (OR). Statistical models that present their results in terms of odds ratios are called 'logistic models'. This is the method used at any time when the result of a study can only be represented in terms of categories such as 'ill' and 'healthy', or 'large' and 'small'.

The OR is just what it says it is: the ratio of two sets of odds. Rather as in gambling, one might say that the odds of having good health are '10 to 1 on' in a rich class, versus '2 to 1 on' in a poor class. Here, the ratio of the two odds would be 5:1; you are five times more likely to have good health if you come from a rich than from a poor class. In Table 3.2, 22 per cent of men as opposed to 28 per cent of women are depressed. The odds of being depressed in men are 22/78 = 0.28 to 1, while the odds of being depressed in women are 28/72 = 0.39 to 1. Dividing 0.39 by 0.28 gives 1.38. This is the OR and we can think of it as saying that women have 1.38 times the risk of depression in this population as men do. When calculating an odds ratio, one group has to be given the odds of 1. It does not matter which group is chosen, but this will often be the group with the lowest risk, so that the ORs for all the other groups are greater than one. In research papers, the most favoured, lowest-risk group is referred to as the 'baseline', with all the others having ORs greater than 1, to show how much greater their risk is. In Table 3.2, men are the baseline category.

This method was devised to help in finding the cause of outbreaks of foodborne diseases. The epidemiologist would compare the rate of disease in people who had been exposed to whatever she thought was the relevant risk factor (a type of food, say) with the rate in those who had not been exposed. So another way to think of the data presented in the table is in terms of 'exposure' and 'disease' (see Table 3.3). If the odds of illness are significantly higher in those who ate the suspect

Table 3.3   Exposure and disease: odds ratio

Exposure	Disease Yes%	No%		Odds
Yes, did eat suspicious food	A % of people who ate suspicious food and became ill	B % of people who ate food but did not become ill	A + B = 100% All who ate suspicious food	A/B: odds of getting ill if you ate the suspect food
No, did not eat food	C % of people who did not eat the food but became ill	D % of people who did not eat the food and were not ill	C + D = 100% All who did not eat the food	C/D Odds of getting ill if you did not eat the suspect food
Odds ratio				(A/B)/(C/D) Compares odds of getting ill for those who ate suspect food to the odds of getting ill for those who did not

food than in those who did not, then the evidence against the food is increased.

Statistical adjustment

In most studies, odds ratios are not calculated in exactly the same way as in this illustration. The 'causes' of health inequality are nothing like food-poisoning bacteria: they are far more complex. As a result, we need to check whether any apparent relationship has been biased by factors other than the measure or measures of social inequality that are used in any study.

When it is proposed that some variable which is not a result of social disadvantage or privilege is the 'true cause' of an instance of health inequality, we have seen that this variable is often referred to in epidemiology as a 'confounder'. Although there is some confusion and debate around the question of confounding in studies of health inequality, for the moment we just need to be clear about what it is usually supposed to mean. In other disciplines, the same idea is referred to in different terms, for example, 'spuriousness'. The way many studies check for confounding or spuriousness is by statistical adjustment. This is essentially the same thing as 'holding constant'. As we have seen, standardization 'holds age constant'. Just as in the directly standardized measures age is held constant, statistical adjustment is a way to 'standardize' or hold constant a range of other factors besides age in more complex statistical models. Adjusting, standardizing and holding constant are basically the same exercise. We want to see if a relationship we think we have discovered (say, between social class and health) is still there when other factors are taken into account. And, roughly speaking, this is done by re-examining the relationship within groups whose members resemble each other in terms of a third (fourth, fifth and so on) factor – that is, within groups where the value of the other factors is 'constant'. If the original relationship disappears within the sub-groups with constant values of the other factors, the original relationship is regarded as having been 'explained away'.

The classic example of a confounder in epidemiological studies in the past has been smoking. If any relationship between an illness and, let us say, social class position can be shown to disappear when smoking is adjusted for, then it would be said that the apparent relationship with social disadvantage was not real but due to confounding. If we take the concrete example in Table 3.4, we see that working-class men are more at risk of suffering our 'disease' (21.1 per cent have it) than middle-class men (only 14.4 per cent). In fact, you can even work out the odds ratio, which is (21.1/78.9)/

Table 3.4   Social class differences in disease before adjustment for smoking

	Disease		
Social class	Yes	No	All
Managers & professionals number	49	290	339
%	*14.4*	*85.5*	
Routine workers number	83	310	393
%	*21.1*	*78.9*	
All	132	600	732
Odds ratio		1.58	

(Artificially constructed data.)

Table 3.5 Social class differences after adjustment for smoking

	Smokers		Non-smokers		Total numbers
	Disease		Disease		
Social class	Yes	No	Yes	No	
Managers & professionals number	25	70	24	220	339
%	26.3	73.7	9.8	90.2	
Routine workers number	70	190	13	120	393
%	26.9	73.1	9.8	90.2	
Odds ratio		0.97		1.0	732

(Artificially constructed data.)

(14.4/85.5) = 1.58. So it looks as if working-class men have around half as much risk again of suffering the disease.

However, what happens if we 'adjust for smoking'? The way to see what happens when statistical adjustment is carried out on these kinds of data is by dividing the population up into smokers and non-smokers and looking at the disease rates within each social class group.

We can see from Table 3.5 that when you divide the sample into smokers and non-smokers, the odds of having the disease in working- versus middle-class people are little different from 1:1, that is, there is no excess risk in the working class. This is the easiest way to think about statistical adjustment: it is what happens when the original relationship you thought you saw is re-examined in those who do and those who do not have the possible 'confounding' factor. In this case, we repeat the relationship of socio-economic position to ill health in those who do and those who do not smoke. What would be presented in a research paper on health inequality would not usually be the odds ratios for the two different groups but a single 'adjusted odds ratio'. We can think of this as the additional risk to a working-class over a middle-class person if both classes were equally likely to smoke. The adjusted OR is more or less an average, that is, calculated by adding up the ORs from the two social groups and dividing by two. This is not quite what happens: in fact, more weight is given to larger groups than to the smaller ones. But when you see an 'adjusted odds ratio', it does no harm to think of it in this way. In Table 3.5, it is easy to see that the adjusted OR would be around 1, that is, there are no differences in health between social classes once smoking has been held constant.

Showing only a single 'adjusted odds ratio' would not have allowed us to see an important fact about the relationship of class and smoking to health in this example, however. Because I have shown the relationship separately for smokers and non-smokers in each social class, we can see how the appearance of an excess risk was due to the fact that more working-than middle-class people smoke, as well as that the disease is more common in those who smoke. While about 26 per cent of both groups have the disease among the smokers, only around 10 per cent have it among the non-smokers. And while 95/339 = 28 per cent of the middle class are smokers, 260/393 = 66 per cent of the working class smoke. Such a clear case of confounding is in fact rather unusual, and the example given here is a contrived and artificial one, not using real data. But it serves to show in detail what people are thinking of when they say 'health differences between group A and group B were explained away by adjustment for smoking'.

In this example, once the social groups were divided according to smoking, the odds ratios were reduced to 1:1, that is, there was no remaining difference between the groups. In this case, we would say that the social difference was entirely due to smoking. But what more often happens is that the social 'difference is reduced, but only partly: it does not disappear altogether. It is useful to be able to have some idea of how much of the social difference can be explained in terms of smoking. Let's take an example where the odds of poor health are still greater in routine workers even after adjustment for smoking, but not 1:1, as in Table 3.6.

In many papers, you will find that the amount by which the relationship between two variables expressed as an odds ratio is reduced after adjustment for a third factor is calculated by this formula:

(Unadjusted Odds Ratio − Odds Ratio for adjusted model)/
(Unadjusted OR-1)

The result of this calculation is often called 'percentage (or "proportional") reduction in odds'. In the artificial example given in

Table 3.6   Odds of poor health before and after adjustment for smoking

Social class	Odds of poor health	Odds of poor health adjusted for smoking
Managers & professionals	1 (baseline)	1 (baseline)
Routine workers	2.2	1.7

Table 3.6, if you want some idea of how much of the unadjusted excess risk of disease might be regarded as 'due to smoking', you can calculate this by:

$$(2.2-1.7)/(2.2-1) = 0.42$$

This reveals that around 42 per cent of the relationship between social class and this disease was due to smoking. This kind of calculation is not without its critics but is now widely used in research papers.

Linear regression

So far, we have considered examples where the measure of health or illness has had only two values: dead versus alive; ill versus healthy. For these kinds of outcomes, it is necessary to use the odds ratio. But there are many interesting health measures that can be represented in terms of a continuous score or measure, such as blood pressure, height or weight. When this is the kind of health measure we are looking at, ordinary linear regression models can be used. In mathematical terms the equation for an ordinary regression is:

$$y = a + bx + e$$

In a linear regression model we are not looking at the percentages of people in different boxes in a table. Rather, we observe the 'average score' on an outcome variable y for people with a certain 'score' on a possible causal or independent variable x. These two amounts, the values of x and y, can be plotted as in Figure 3.1. The regression equation describes the amount of change in the outcome measure y (weight, let us say) for a single unit change in the exposure measure x (such as the number of calories eaten per week, for example). In the equation above, a represents the starting point or 'intercept' (let us say, in this example, the minimum weight in the sample of people we are analysing). The b refers to the amount of change in weight per each unit change in the independent variable. This is referred to as the regression coefficient. The equation tells us that weight in any one person will be equal to the minimum weight for everyone plus b times the exposure measure x (x could be calories eaten). The term e is an error term, which we do not need to think about in any detail, except to remember that in any real-world study, all the measures we take are subject to various types of error. These errors inevitably influence our conclusions about the effect that each 100 calories will have on a person's weight.

How are real numbers substituted for y, x and b? In this case, we

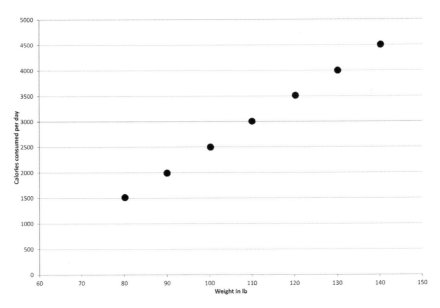

Figure 3.1 Relationship between weight and calories consumed

would have studied the intake of calories of a large number of people, measured their weight and drawn a diagram in which each individual's combination of weight and calories was plotted. The best way to think about the results is in terms of a plot on a graph, with calories consumed per day up the side and weight along the bottom, as in Figure 3.1, where we can see that weight goes up steadily as calories increase. The value of b (which may be referred to as the regression coefficient or the parameter estimate) is discovered by measuring how much each additional 500 calories increases weight; in this case, it is by 10 lb. The 'minimum' weight or starting point for someone who eats only 1,500 calories a day is about 80 lb.

So we can now rewrite the equation as:

$$\text{weight of individual } i = 80 + 10x \text{ (number of 500-calorie meals)} + \text{allowance for mistakes}$$

so that someone eating 2,500 calories would weigh about 100 lb.

Of course, all these figures are the result of averaging out the relationship between food intake and weight in a whole sample of people, maybe thousands. A graph like Figure 3.1 taken from real research data would show lots of little dots representing each individual, scattered around the straight line. So if we try to use the equation to predict how much any individual weighs, it will not give the exact answer. The line that relates the points in the graph is only a 'best estimate', and for this reason researchers often talk about 'fitting a regression line (or curve)'. For the same reason, the *b* that gives us the relationship between calories and weight is known as an 'estimate' (or 'parameter estimate'). All we can say is that, on average, a person will weigh 10 lbs more for each additional 500 calories they eat each day, but some will weigh far more than this and some far less (as many of us know to our regret). Also, the relationships we can calculate from this kind of procedure are no more than estimates, although we try to get as close as possible to the observed data. This kind of exercise is known as 'modelling'. This means simply that we are doing our best to arrive at a kind of sum or equation that reasonably closely describes all the individual scores on the variables that have been collected in the research.

Mediation: the pathways from inequality to illness

Many studies of health inequality take the general form of social class or socio-economic status or some other measure of social position on the one hand, and a health or disease measure on the other. Having found that, let us say, those with a less privileged social position more often have the disease, the studies then proceed to carry out a number of statistical adjustments: for age, for psychological factors, for certain behaviours such as smoking and so on. As more and more health inequality studies now use longitudinal or life-course data (see chapter 10), researchers have been forced to consider more carefully the distinction between a 'confounder' and a 'mediator'.

In order for a factor to be a confounder, it must itself influence factors it is claimed to confound, without being influenced by them. In the case of storks and the babies, it is the season that 'causes' the arrival of both. Neither the storks nor the babies can sensibly be regarded as causing spring to arrive. Smoking, in contrast, is not this kind of factor (nor is diet or exercise). These are not very usefully thought of as causes of being in a particular income group or social class. On the contrary, it looks very much as if smoking itself is in some sense caused by socio-economic disadvantage. Disadvantage for some reason makes it harder to give up smoking and therefore means that smoking-related diseases are more common in disadvantaged people. So it is more logical to think of smoking as being on the pathway, or 'mediating', between social position and health.

In many ways the term 'adjustment' is rather misleading. You will often see it used in research papers and reports on health inequality. But it is more helpful to think in terms of building up explanations by adding variables, according to whatever theory we may have as to the causes of a health difference between social groups, tracing pathways between a measure of social circumstances and a measure of health.

Simple models can go a long way in testing these kinds of ideas about the reasons for health inequality. But as our understanding becomes more sophisticated, it is sometimes an advantage to use more complex methods. This is particularly important for analysing pathways between social and economic circumstances and health over time. Some researchers are beginning to use methods such as path models and growth models. Readers with a special interest in these will have to consult the appropriate literature. But, in these examples, I have tried to provide a straightforward account of the most common types of statistical method used in studies of, and arguments about, health inequality. It does not require advanced statistics to understand this logic, nor to evaluate contributions to the debates in the literature. But reading about health inequality in an informed and critical way is made much easier by a grasp of these basic techniques. I have tried to emphasize the importance of the logic of each form of argument. Even the most sophisticated statistics can be wasted if hypotheses and the terms in which they are tested are not clearly thought out.

Further reading

Basic statistics and data analysis:
Bryman, A. (2012), *Social Research Methods*, 4th edn. Oxford: Oxford University Press.

Personally, I have found it far easier to learn about statistics through practical use in data analysis, which is the approach taken in:
Field, A. (2013), *Discovering Statistics Using IBM SPSS*. London: Sage.

Appendix: How to Calculate a Standardized Mortality Ratio (SMR)

Say we have two social groups or classes, the 'rich' and the 'poor'. The groups are of equal size, 200, but in the rich group 25 deaths have been recorded in the past 10 years, while in the poor group 35 deaths have been recorded. Does this really mean that the poor are at a higher risk – that is, is there evidence here for health inequality?

What if it is just a matter of poorer people being older? Calculating an SMR can check this.

1   Suppose we start with a population made up of 400 people, with two classes: there are 200 people in the rich class and 200 in the poor class. Over a period of time, 13.5% of all these people die (or become ill). This rate is made up of 16.5% of the poor class and only 10.5% of the rich class. But we know that the poor class contains rather more older people than does the rich class. How far is this health inequality between rich and poor classes just a result of their different ages?

2   Separate the total population (rich and poor together) into age groups. (This is usually done in groups of 5 or 10 years: in this case, we take 10-year age groups.)

There are two classes: rich = 200 people and poor = 200 people, that is, a total of 400 people: 80 each in age groups 15–24, 25–34, 35–44, 45–54 and 55–64.

3   Calculate the death rate for each of these age groups – say, 10% in age groups 15–24 and 25–34, 12.5% in age group 35–44, 15% in age group 45–54 and 20% in age group 55–64.

4   Now take each of the social classes and divide them into same-age groups. Suppose the poor class has an older age profile:

30 people aged 16–24
30 people aged 25–34
40 people aged 35–44
50 people aged 45–54
50 people aged 55–64

and imagine that the rich group has a younger age profile, so that you have:

50 people aged 16–24
50 people aged 25–34
40 people aged 35–44
30 people aged 45–54
30 people aged 55–64

(This is a far more extreme example of age differences between social groups than would ever be found in reality but it makes a vivid example.)

5   Work out how many people in each class would die in each of these age groups if the percentage dying was the same as in that particular age group in the whole population. This gives an expected number of deaths in each age group in each class.

6   Add up all these deaths (some will be fractions). This gives a total
    expected number of deaths. The result would look like this:
    For the poor group:

Age group	Death rate	Deaths expected in age group
16–24	10% of 30	= 3
25–34	10% of 30	= 3
35–44	12.5% of 40	= 5
45–54	15% of 50	= 7.5
55–64	20% of 50	= 10

Total expected deaths 28.5

For the rich group:

Age group	Death rate	Deaths expected in age group
16–24	10% of 50	= 5
25–34	10% of 50	= 5
35–44	12.5% of 40	= 5
45–54	15% of 30	= 4.5
55–64	20% of 30	= 6

Total expected deaths 25.5

7   This shows the way indirect standardization works. Even though
    the number of people in each of the social classes is identical
    in this example, there would be more 'expected' deaths among
    the poor than the rich. There is an 'expected' difference purely
    because the death rate in older people is higher and there are
    more older people in the poor group. In order to see if there is
    'really' a higher risk in the poor group, we need to compare the
    actual numbers of deaths in each group with the numbers that are
    expected on the basis of age alone.
8   The next step in calculating the SMR is therefore to compare
    the number of deaths you would have expected to see in the two
    classes because of their age distributions with the number that
    has actually occurred.
9   Divide the number of people who actually died, i.e. the 'observed
    deaths' in the poor social class (in this case that happens to be 33)
    by the expected number (28.5), and multiply this by 100.
10 This is the SMR for the poor groups: Observed deaths = 33

$$\text{SMR for poor group = observed/expected} \times 100$$
$$\text{i.e. } 33/28.5 \times 100 = 115.8$$

11 Do the same thing for the rich group: we saw that 21 deaths took place in this group, resulting in:

$$\text{SMR for rich group = observed/expected} \times 100$$
$$\text{i.e. } 21/25.5 \times 100 = 82.4$$

If the number of observed deaths in each social group was exactly equal to the expected number, then all groups would have an SMR of 100. So one way to think of the SMR is that it tells us how much the death rate for a social group falls above or below the death rate for the whole population. In this case, the rate for the rich was about 18 per cent below that, and the rate for the poor was about 16 per cent above it. (Table 3.7 gives this example.)

Table 3.7   Example of indirect standardization: standardized mortality ratio

Age	Number of people			Observed deaths		Death rate in each age group	Total number of deaths	Overall death rate	'Expected' death rate*	
	Poor	Rich	Total	Poor	Rich	Both classes	Both classes		Poor	Rich
15	30	50	80	4	4	10	8		3	5
25	30	50	80	5	3	10	8		3	5
35	40	40	80	6	4	12.5	10		5	5
45	50	30	80	8	4	15	12		7.5	4.5
55	50	30	80	10	6	20	16		10	6
all	200	200	400	33	21		54	13.5	28.5	25.5

Note: SMR for each class is equal to observed/expected × 100, i.e. for the poor, it is 33/28.5 × 100 = 115.8; for the rich, it is 21/25.5 × 100 = 82.4.

*Number of deaths if rate for poor and rich were the same.

4
Explanatory Models I: Behavioural and 'Cultural' Explanations

As we saw in chapter 2, it has become conventional to categorize three types of explanation for health inequality, behavioural, material and psycho-social, and to regard these as acting over the life course. Although a satisfactory explanation will probably end up combining these types of influence, I believe we need to understand each individual model of explanation rather better before we can make sense of attempts at combination. Some of the literature, increasingly in the last five years or so, attempts to set some of the approaches, particularly behaviour (smoking, diet, exercise) and psycho-social stress, against each other in a competitive manner. I do not think this has been very helpful, but it can be understood in the context of the turn towards 'functionalist' approaches to social inequality, discussed in chapter 1.

One of the explanations put forward in the Black Report for the existence of health inequality was what it called the 'behavioural/cultural explanation'. It was described in this way:

> emphasizing unthinking, reckless or irresponsible behaviour or incautious life-style as the moving determinant of poor health status. . . . Some would argue that such systematic behaviour within certain social groups is a consequence only of lack of education, or individual waywardness. . . . Others see behaviour which is conducive to good or bad health as embedded more within social structure − as illustrative of socially distinguishable styles of life, associated with, and reinforced by, class. (Townsend et al. 1986: 110, 114)

Both individual research reports and official surveys have repeatedly documented persistent differences between social groups in various types of consumption and leisure activities that are related to health. Most prominent among these are smoking, alcohol, leisure-time exercise and the amount of fats, sugars and salt in the diet.

Smoking displays a clear 'social gradient': the less advantaged a person's social position, however it is measured, the more likely it is that he or she will smoke. One could repeat this for a large number of different 'risky behaviours', and for different measures of social position and circumstances (occupational class, income or status) and find the same thing (Lantz et al. 2010). The less advantaged the employment conditions, and the lower the income or status, the more likely it is that a person will engage in what are considered to be 'risky' forms of behaviours, such as consumption of refined white bread and high-fat meat, and the less likely it is that they will engage in health-promoting behaviours, such as jogging or eating five portions of fruit and vegetables a day.

'Individualized' behavioural explanations

The Black Report, along with a large number of subsequent studies, used the term 'behavioural/cultural explanation' to refer to the role played by smoking, eating, alcohol and exercise in producing health inequality. In practice, most research using a behavioural model of health inequality focuses on 'behaviour' rather than 'culture'. In general, most research also takes a rather less considered approach than that of the Black Report, in that it tends to leave undeveloped any theoretical perspective on why behaviour might vary systematically between social classes, income or status groups. It has only been in very recent research on health inequality in the life course that a clearer theoretical framework has begun to emerge (Giesinger et al. 2014; Jusot et al. 2013).

Underlying much research on health behaviour as an explanation for health inequality is what Goldberg has called an 'individualized behavioural model' (Goldberg 2012). It rests on an assumption, discussed in chapter 1, that people with lower status and income are less endowed with some types of personal characteristics (Bosma, van de Mheen and Mackenbach 1999; Pulkki et al. 2003; Mackenbach 2010c; see also chapter 10). Implicitly, these can often be read as versions of 'intelligence', 'coping skills' or personal resilience. Following (sometimes unconsciously) the ideas of functionalism, the individualized behavioural model posits that people with low levels of these attributes have not done well enough in school to acquire the better

types of job that carry advantages with them. Why should such attributes be linked to risky health behaviours? Once again, the implicit
assumption is that people have worse working conditions, less money
and lower status because they did badly at school and so are not able
to grasp the health education messages put out by governments and
health professionals, or do not have the self-discipline to obey them
(Mackenbach 2012). People with less social and economic advantage
may also be thought of as having less self-control ('external locus of
control') or may have a shorter time perspective that makes them
unable to grasp the longer-term health consequences of things that
give them short-term pleasure. Although these ideas are seldom
explicitly tested in research, they underlie some influential work.

In the individualized behavioural explanatory model, the link
between social position and behaviour is due to adverse personal
characteristics of individuals, which also influence their position in
the social structure. Social position does not 'cause' behaviour; the
two have their common basis in personal characteristics. The model
can be expressed in terms of a testable hypothesis. If it were true,
and if we had data on 'locus of control' (to take one of the potential
underlying explanatory characteristics), social position and risky
health behaviours, we would expect to end up with data similar to
that presented in Table 4.1.

Here, we can see that there are 100 people divided equally into
two social classes, one advantaged, the other disadvantaged. There
are also 50 people with an 'internal locus of control' and 50 with an
'external locus of control'. No one with an internal locus of control
engages in risky behaviours, while 50 per cent of people with an
external locus of control do so (5/10 in the advantaged and 20/40
in the disadvantaged class). In the advantaged class, however, 40
people have an internal locus of control compared to only 10 people
in the disadvantaged class. The fact that more people in the disadvantaged class (20/50 compared to 5/50) engage in risky behaviours
is entirely due to there being more people with an external locus of
control in that class (and vice versa). In percentage terms, the rate of
risky behaviour in those with an external (50 per cent) or an internal
(0 per cent) 'locus of control' is exactly the same in each class. So
the difference between the classes depends solely on the different
numbers of people with an internal locus of control in each class.
We could relabel the column for locus of control with a range of
other psychological characteristics – conscientiousness; fatalism; or
even 'intelligence'. The argument would take the same shape. If an
individualized behavioural explanation for social inequality in risk

Table 4.1   Hypothetical relationship between social position, locus
of control and health risk behaviour if the 'direct behavioural model'
is accurate

Locus of control	Advantaged social position			Disadvantaged social position			
	Risky behaviour			Risky behaviour			
	No	Yes	All	No	Yes	All	Total
Internal	40	0	40	10	0	10	50
%	*100*	*0*		*100*	*0*		
External	5	5	10	20	20	40	50
%	*50*	*50*		*50*	*50*		
	45	5	50	30	20	50	100

(Artificially constructed data.)

behaviours is true, then the differences between the social classes will
be due entirely to the distribution within these classes of people with
different psychological characteristics.

This example is so crude as to seem almost ridiculous. But it does
have a purpose: it makes explicit the shape of the kind of argument
that is used in research into behaviour as a cause of health inequality. The psychologically 'superior' people were *always* going to have
better health, and they were *always* going to end up in more favoured
social circumstances. In this simplest and clearest version of the
individualized behavioural explanation, people with, shall we say, an
external locus of control, are just more likely to be or become socially
disadvantaged and more likely to smoke, drink a lot or take little exercise. The few unlucky ones with a high locus of control who end up in
a disadvantaged social position are still leading healthy lives; there are
just not enough of them to influence the general level of behaviour in
that social class as a whole.

There is not very much evidence that social position is linked to
the degree to which health education messages are understood. A few
studies have found that most people in all social classes understand
perfectly well that smoking is not good for health (Blaxter 1990;
Shewry et al. 1992). But differences in understanding do not explain
the differences in smoking itself. Nor does social position seem to influence the likelihood of trying to quit (Kotz and West 2009). Perhaps
the most important example is Blaxter's analysis in her classic, *Health*

and Lifestyles, of the role of class differences in beliefs about healthy behaviour (Blaxter 1990). Blaxter defined social advantage and disadvantage in terms of whether people's occupations were manual or non-manual. She was able to show that class differences in attitudes toward healthy eating, for example, explained less than 1 per cent of the differences between manual workers and non-manual workers. In other words, the reasons why the non-manual workers had a healthier diet were not defined by differences in knowledge or understanding between them and manual workers about what a healthy diet was or how important it was. In this study, the strongest anti-smoking beliefs were in fact held by men who did smoke (who were also more likely to be in the less advantaged manual social class). So in this case there was no chance whatever that differences in understanding of health risks could be responsible for social differences in smoking.

Some recent research has set out to test the extent to which 'personality characteristics' might be responsible for risky health behaviours and thereby for health inequality. What evidence is there that some of the differences in health between groups with unequal amounts of social and economic advantage might be a result of characteristics like hostility, introversion, extroversion or conscientiousness? A study in France found that 'neurotic hostility' explained some of the relationship of occupational social position to mortality risk (Nabi et al. 2008), and another study of a sample of the US population was consistent with this (though using different measures of personality type) (Chapman et al. 2010). Several studies, not surprisingly, have found that people with more 'conscientious' personalities are less likely to smoke or to be overweight, but this does not explain social inequality in these health risks (Gallacher 2008; Chapman et al. 2010; Chapman, Roberts and Duberstein 2011; Pluess and Bartley 2015).

Behaviour as a result of 'culture'

The Black Report did not adopt the 'individualized behavioural' type of explanation outlined in the last section. This is presumably why the authors used the hybrid term 'behavioural/cultural'. However, no social anthropologist or cultural psychologist could accept 'unthinking, reckless or irresponsible behaviour or incautious lifestyle' as a valid description of 'culture'. The authors of the report, and many who have followed them, seem to have regarded social differences in health-related behaviours as somehow being a consequence of disadvantaged position in the social structure and of low income. They do not seem to have viewed either the risky behaviour or the social disadvantage as a consequence of either beliefs or personality characteristics. However, ideas about cultural distinction may in fact help us to understand one of the pathways to health inequality.

Experts in the study of culture have defined it in various ways. As long ago as 1871, the anthropologist E. B. Tylor defined it as 'that complex whole which includes knowledge, beliefs, art, morals, laws, customs and any other capabilities and habits acquired by man as a member of society' (Tylor 1871, cited in Berry et al. 1992: 165). Often included under this very wide umbrella are shared rules (norms), governing the activities of a social group, and traditions. Some 80 years later, Kroeber and Kluckhohn sum up their definition as 'traditional . . . ideas and especially their attached values' (Kroeber and Kluckhohn 1952, cited in Berry et al. 1992: 166). This is an 'ideational' model of culture: culture seen as a system of meanings that exists in the heads of people within a community. The alternative 'behavioural' model of culture sees it as composed of behaviour which occurs regularly in institutional domains within communities such as religious, familial or political institutions (A. Singh-Manoux, personal communication). Under this heading could be included Bourdieu's concept of the habitus as a collection of learned behaviours that are shaped over the life course by exposure to a certain social environment. Fassin has vividly described the relation of life circumstances to behaviours and their outcomes as 'l'inscription de l'ordre social dans les corps ou . . . l'incorporation de l'inégalité' [the inscription of the social order on the body, or . . . the incorporation of inequality] (Fassin 2000: 135). This notion of 'embodiment' has more recently become a popular one in social epidemiology (Krieger 2005).

Culture as social distinction

The most important research that throws light on links between culture and health behaviour is that of Bourdieu. In order to understand this, we need to go back to the distinction between class and status in chapter 1. This allows us to take a much more consistent theoretically based approach to understanding social differences in health behaviours, one which takes into account the importance of identity discussed in the Introduction. In the words of a reviewer of Bourdieu's influential book *Distinction*:

Les goûts sont classants: ce sont des marqueurs fins de la position sociale, la culture dominante étant la culture des classes dominantes.

Dès lors, ils jouent un rôle stratégique dans la lutte pour le classement. [Tastes are 'classifying': they are fine markers of social position, where the dominant culture is that of the dominant classes. For that reason they play a strategic role in the struggle for status.] (Review of *La Distinction*, Parienty 2005)

Bourdieu pointed out that a wide range of activities, including the choice of leisure pursuits and diet, forms part of the strategies by which individuals display or claim membership of higher status groups and distance themselves from groups of lower status (Bourdieu 1984b, 1984c). Thus, using the concepts of status and culture, we can see what might be a powerful reason for associations of social position with health behaviours.

In order to test this idea, the best measure of social position might be either the Cambridge scale or the Oxford social-status scale, both of which are based on friendship choices. These would give us indicators of shared culture and habitus, over and above whatever people might say about how important they believe diet or smoking to be for health, and how far they believe they can control their own health. Perhaps social differences in diet, smoking and so on are really more like choices of decorative style or fashion. It may be that people in certain social milieux simply do not think it is 'people like us' who smoke or who do not to go to the gym. So there may be powerful reasons for adhering to certain kinds of behaviours which have nothing whatever to do with people's knowledge or beliefs about health. In Hindu culture, for example, vegetarianism is a sign of being a member of the highest Brahmin caste. It is such an important symbol of social status that social groups aspiring to higher-caste status adopt vegetarianism and give up wearing leather (Shatenstein and Ghadirian 1998). This is a strategy called 'Sanskritization' (Srinivas 1956). In French society, Bourdieu points to the ways in which discussions of taste in food or music are subtle ways in which people seek to establish social status, and thus express relationships of dominance. The effects are so profound as to make it very hard for young people from less culturally advantaged backgrounds to fit into the social life, or even the intellectual life, of elite Paris universities and technical colleges.

There is a small amount of evidence that measures of status do indeed have a stronger relationship to health behaviours than measures of social class based on occupation (Bartley et al. 1999; Sacker et al. 2000a). The findings of these studies give some support to the idea that shared culture or lifestyle may be an influence on social differences in health (Chandola 1998). Even if differences in expressed attitudes to health do not seem to have much effect on health-risk behaviours (everyone knows it is bad for you to smoke), it may still be that other forms of cultural differences between people of different social status are important. Social differences in the adoption of a healthy lifestyle do not have to be a result of explicit beliefs about health itself. They may simply be part of what is viewed as appropriate behaviour for 'people like us'.

'Cultural shift'

There is a sophisticated version of the behavioural/cultural theory which has emerged from a major comparative study of health inequality in the European nations (Kunst 1997a; Mackenbach et al. 1997). I will call this the 'cultural shift' explanation. It focuses on the differences between countries in the overall prevalence and social patterning of certain kinds of health-risk behaviours. There is a group of Southern European nations with relatively large income inequalities but overall good health, with small health differences between more and less advantaged social groups (Kulhánová et al. 2014; Mackenbach et al. 2014). The research that first discovered this pattern observed that the diet followed by the majority of people was a healthy one. 'Having a healthy diet' was not some special kind of lifestyle in these societies, so eating fruit, salads and olive oil was not seen as a particular lifestyle choice and therefore was not associated with social advantage or disadvantage. Similarly, in nations where there was generally a low level of alcohol use (or at least of 'binge drinking'), inequalities in alcohol-related deaths were low. It seems as if there may be a kind of 'national sin' that differs from country to country. Citizens who find themselves in difficulties are most likely to fall into whatever this particular 'sin' may be, with a resultant impact on the causes of disease responsible for health inequality. These include heavy alcohol consumption with resultant deaths from acute poisoning and accidents in Finland; high-fat, low-vegetable diet leading to heart disease in the United States; smoking and lung disease in Great Britain; and chronic high-alcohol consumption with resultant high incidence of cirrhosis in France. The wide availability of guns in the United States may also be thought of as one reason for the very high mortality from homicide of young men in the poor inner-city areas which makes a major contribution to overall health inequality in that nation. These comparative studies also found that, to some extent, social-class health behaviours differ between nations, as one might expect from the observed differences in health inequality (Federico et al. 2013). Many more middle-class people smoke in France or Spain than in Sweden, for example. The middle-class obsession with a healthy lifestyle has not as yet been as widely adopted in France, Spain, Italy, Greece or Switzerland as it has been in Sweden, Norway or Britain.

There are therefore two elements to the cultural shift theory. One might be regarded as 'cultural': the idea of adopting a lifestyle of no smoking, low-fat food and leisure exercise as a way of expressing social distinction has simply not yet penetrated Spanish, Italian or Greek society. If everyone consumes olive oil, it is useless as a way of displaying one's high status and is meaningless as a symbol of identity. The second element is concerned simply with the material realities of local existence. In countries where fruit and vegetables are cheap and plentiful, they form part of everyone's diet and are affordable for all. One does not need to have intelligence, coping skills, self-control and so on to decide to eat tomatoes, garlic and olive oil in Spain or Italy. Nor is such a lifestyle a signal of wealth or status. In all Southern European nations, there is a high level of smoking throughout all social classes, and inequality in heart disease in these nations is low. Because heart disease is one of the most common single causes of mortality in men of later working age in most European nations, this means that overall health inequality is low or absent in these nations. And it is also in the Southern European nations that a 'healthy' diet and moderate alcohol consumption are seen more or less equally throughout all social classes. According to this theory, health inequality would therefore only emerge in the Southern European nations if their less socially advantaged populations developed a fondness for foods with a high fat and sugar content, and began to drink alcohol in the more northern 'binge' pattern, at the same time as those in more advantaged social circumstances abandoned smoking.

It cannot be stressed too carefully that this is at present no more than a theory. We do not currently have any information over time on representative samples of the populations of, say, Italy or Spain to see if their citizens in less advantaged social positions are less likely to suffer heart attacks than their northern neighbours, even if they were to 'binge' drink and eat burgers. We do not know if a salad-eating Swedish stockbroker has the same life expectancy as a steak-and-chips-eating Greek one (Kulhánová et al. 2014).

Perhaps the best evidence we do have about the relationship of changes in culture to changes in health inequality comes from a study of health behaviours in British and Japanese men of different occupational grades (a measure of their social position) (Martikainen et al. 2001a). Japanese men in less privileged socio-economic positions, as indicated both by employment grade and education, were more likely to smoke and had higher fibrinogen (a substance that makes blood more likely to clot and cause heart attacks) and blood pressure. This was similar to the gradients seen in a comparable sample of British men. However, social differences in other risk factors for heart disease were quite different to those found in Britain. In Japan, the more privileged men in the higher occupational grades were more likely to have high body mass, and an unhealthy body shape with a lot of fat around the middle, than their lower-grade peers were. And this was all the more true for the younger Japanese men.

The authors of this paper surmise that, in the younger Japanese men, a northern/western lifestyle or cultural pattern was emerging, taking the form of a liking for meat and other high-fat foods not found in the traditional Japanese diet. Whether this could be regarded as a 'cultural shift' is an interesting question: the paper is an epidemiological study which does not include information on values or beliefs. Did these younger Japanese executives pick up signals about the status implications of lifestyle as they had increased contact with western colleagues? And had they adopted these behaviours as an expression of being both high status and 'modern'? Certainly, beef is a very expensive commodity in Japan, and consuming large amounts would operate as a signal of wealth. If so, and if the 'cultural shift' theory has some truth in it, the next thing we would expect to see would be a diffusion of high-fat food eating from the more to the less privileged social layers in Japan (although the price of beef would possibly have to fall before this could occur). If this were to happen, the high-status lifestyle could be expected to shift again towards jogging and salad, accompanied by an increase in social inequality in heart disease among Japanese men. Whichever interpretation may be closer to the truth in this case, it illustrates the need for better understanding of the links between social forces – such as globalization – and lifestyle. In practice, however, it does not seem that inequalities in cardiovascular risk factors have increased among Japanese men in the subsequent years (Fukuda and Hiyoshi 2013; Silventoinen et al. 2013).

Evidence against the 'cultural shift' explanation has also come from the repeated studies of health inequality in industrial nations (Kunst and Mackenbach 1994a, 1994b; Mackenbach et al. 2014). The small inequalities accorded to social class or education (often used as a proxy measure of social position for the sake of convenience) in Italy and Spain have not in fact increased over time. It had been thought that as Northern European health-behaviour patterns – more smoking and less healthy diet in less advantaged social groups – spread to Southern Europe, health inequality would increase. This has not in fact happened. The authors of the most recent study comment that:

> Barcelona, the Basque Country, Madrid and Turin have been able to strengthen their favourable positions because differences in mortality decline between the low and high educated often were smaller than in other countries. . . . Further study of downstream and upstream determinants of inequalities in mortality in Southern Europe may help to better exploit this 'good practice' for mutual learning. (Mackenbach et al. 2014: 9)

So 25 years after the first European comparative study of health inequality, differences in mortality between people according to social position are still less in Spain and Italy (Schröder et al. 2004; Federico et al. 2013; Mackenbach et al. 2014) than in Northern European nations. But the reasons for this are still not understood.

How important is behaviour for health inequality?

A lot of recent work seems to have more or less abandoned analysis of the 'cultural' aspect of social inequalities in health-related behaviour in favour of older explanations such as selection by personal characteristics (Mackenbach 2012). Fewer researchers ask 'What are the differences in cultural practices and beliefs between groups that help us understand differences in health-related behaviours?' than 'How do the kind of people who take risks with their health end up in less social advantaged situations?' But there is still room for a major debate on how important behaviours are, however they arise.

We have already seen that many commentaries on the success or failure of new policies have highlighted behaviours. This is partly because the policies themselves have concentrated on health education and behaviour change. Popay and colleagues have written about the tendency for policy to be affected by a 'lifestyle drift', in which verbal statements admitting the possible importance of economic inequality, low incomes and other material factors were nevertheless accompanied by actual policies solely concerned with behavioural change (Popay et al. 2010). Such a policy environment is rich ground for researchers to appear to have an impact on policy by showing that, after all, health behaviours are the most important cause of health inequality, and thereby provide a kind of retrospective justification for what governments are doing in any case. There are rather striking differences within the work of some of the leading research teams between their earlier papers, which tended to emphasize the material and psycho-social factors mediating health inequality between social groups (van Rossum et al. 2000; Van Lenthe et al. 2002; Kivimaki et al. 2006a; Skalicka et al. 2009), and their later papers (Stringhini et al. 2010; Mackenbach 2012; Toch-Marquardt et al. 2014), which tend to either show empirically or to assume a much more important role for behaviours.

Van Rossum and colleagues used longitudinal follow-up data from a large study of London civil servants, the Whitehall I study, to show that only around a third of the differences in mortality risk between those with the highest income and status and the best working conditions (the 'administrative grades') and those in the least advantaged occupations, such as catering staff and messengers, was explained by differences in health-related behaviour (van Rossum et al. 2000). This was quite surprising at the time but was accepted for many years. A series of studies carried out by Lantz and colleagues in a more representative (all different kinds of occupations, not just civil servants) sample of the American population found similar results (Lantz et al. 1998, 2001), as have studies in Norway (Skalicka et al. 2009), the Netherlands (van Oort, van Lenthe and Mackenbach 2005) and the United Kingdom (Ramsay et al. 2009). Even smaller estimates of the importance of behaviour were found in two other multinational European studies (McFadden et al. 2008; Gallo et al. 2012).

But these low estimates of the importance of health behaviours for inequalities in mortality came to be increasingly challenged. A Finnish study estimated that behaviours explained around 54% of social inequality (using education as the measure of social position) in Finnish men, and 38% in women, in the 1980s (Laaksonen et al. 2008). In Australia, Beauchamp et al. found that health behaviours explained more than 70% of the excess risk of mortality from heart disease in those with low educational level (Beauchamp et al. 2010). An important innovation, made possible by the existence of longitudinal follow-up studies observing both behaviours and health over many years, was made, ironically, by the Whitehall II study team. They reported that when smoking, diet and exercise were re-measured several times over a 24-year period, these explained 72% of the relationship of social position (measured by occupational grade in the London civil service) to mortality (Stringhini et al. 2010). This much stronger effect of behaviour when measured several times, rather than just once at the beginning of a study, was repeated by Whitley and her colleagues in Scotland (Whitley et al. 2014). Using a different method in the United States, Nandi and colleagues reached a very similar conclusion (Nandi et al. 2014). Another American study, using repeated 'time-varying' measures of behaviour, could only explain 24% of mortality differences between social groups if measured once but 39% if measured repeatedly (Mehta, House and Elliott 2015).

These recent, much larger estimates of the importance of health behaviours to health inequality have not gone unchallenged. The authors of the Whitehall II paper, which was the first to use measures of behaviour taken at several different times ('time-varying coordinates'), themselves pointed out that their study participants are taken from a single, though large, organization and are not representative of the British population (Stringhini et al. 2010). A subsequent study led by the same author and with a similar sample belonging to a single company but carried out in France showed completely different results. Here, the use of time-varying measures of behaviours only explained around 17 per cent of the inequality in mortality between the most and the least advantaged occupations (Stringhini et al. 2011), despite the presence of somewhat greater health inequalities to be explained. This was a very important result which did not receive the amount of attention it deserved. Social differences in behaviours are not as great in France as they are in the United Kingdom, but this does not mean that inequality in the risk of death is lower. If you take two different samples and find that inequality in mortality risk is bigger in one than in the other, but health behaviours, even measured in detail, explain less where inequality in the health outcome is greater, this does throw some doubt on the universal importance of smoking, drinking, diet and exercise.

Why are risky behaviours unequal?

Even when we used to think that around 30 per cent of the difference in mortality risk between people in more and less socio-economically advantaged situations was a result of different health-risk behaviour, many researchers were unhappy that the argument would stop at that point. The same is just as true if we now believe behaviour to be a lot more important. Why do health-risk behaviours vary so much between people according to their social position (at least in many nations)? If we want to study health inequality as a way to reach explanations that will inform policies to improve health in the whole population, we need answers to this question. Over the past 40 years, health education efforts to change behaviours have been pretty successful among more prosperous people with higher status and incomes and better working conditions. This is regarded as an important reason for the widening social gradient seen in chapter 2. For a striking illustration of the effectiveness of health education, you only have to look at old films, for example, of the NASA operations centre during the Apollo (moon) programme. There sits the legendary flight director Gene Kranz with the traditional cigar lit to celebrate a successful mission. People smoked in theatres, cinemas, even courtrooms. Health promotion policies, and more recently stronger and stronger limits on the legality of smoking in public spaces and workplaces, have led to its widespread abandonment but far less success in narrowing the social gap in smoking.

As Figures 4.2 and 4.3 show, especially for men, the gap between the proportion of smokers in non-manual and manual occupations

Figure 4.1   Smoking represented as a celebration of success and status
Source: NASA

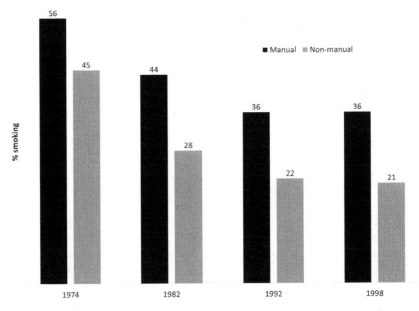

Figure 4.2   Trends in social inequality in smoking in Great Britain,
1974–1998: men

Source: Evandrou and Falkingham 2002: Table 3

(as they were classified in Great Britain at that time) grew over the 24-year period to 1998 from 11 percentage point to 15 percentage points in men and from 7 percentage points to 10 in women. The biggest increase in the social difference took place between 1974 and 1982, which was also when the biggest fall in smoking overall also occurred. (These comparisons cannot be extended beyond 2000 due to the change in the measurement of social class.)

Health education and health promotion have traditionally been based on the 'individualized behavioural model' (Goldberg 2012), discussed at the beginning of this chapter. We can see that these efforts have been effective in reducing at least one risky behaviour, smoking (there is more doubt about diet, alcohol and exercise), but not in reducing social differences in smoking. It is far more important to understand why this happens than to engage in 'beauty contests' over the relative importance of behavioural versus material or psycho-social factors. But first we need to understand the evidence relating to these other aetiological pathways and then how this might be placed in the context of the new advances in life-course research (see chapter 10).

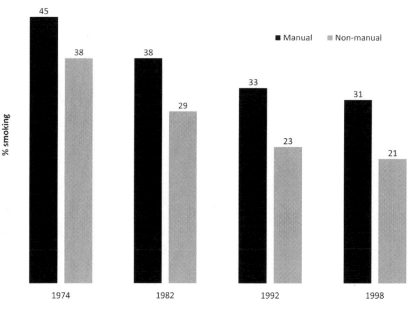

Figure 4.3   Trends in social inequality in smoking in Great Britain, 1974–1998: women

Source: Evandrou and Falkingham 2002: Table 3

Further reading

The classic study of the relationship of lifestyles to health:
Blaxter, M. (1990), *Health and Lifestyles*. London: Tavistock.

Contains useful chapters on this topic from a US perspective:
Amick III, B. C., Levine, S., Tarlov, A. R. and Chapman Walsh, D. (1995), *Society and Health*. Oxford: Oxford University Press.

Most interesting recent papers:
Dunn, J. R. (2010), Health Behaviour vs the Stress of Low Socioeconomic Status and Health Outcomes. *JAMA* 303(12): 1199–1200.
Goldberg, D. S. (2012), Social Justice, Health Inequalities and Methodological Individualism in US Health Promotion. *Public Health Ethics* 5(2): 104–15.
Jones, I. R., Papacosta, O., Whincup, P. H., Goya Wannamethee, S. and Morris, R. W. (2011), 'Lock-in' among middle-aged and older men: a Multiple Correspondence Analysis of the British Regional Heart Study. *Sociology of Health & Illness* 33(3): 399–419.

5

Explanatory Models II:
Psycho-Social Factors

The health differences between social classes revealed by the Black Report and subsequent studies were not until very recently claimed to be mainly caused by health behaviours. And they always seemed to be too great to be explained, at least in modern welfare state societies, by 'purely material' factors. Members of the most insecure and routine occupations (NS-SEC7 in terms of the official British classification) earn very much less than lawyers, doctors and managers. But until widespread appearance of food banks in the United Kingdom in the early 2010s, it was not generally thought that the wages of a labourer were so low as to mean that he or she would be unable to buy enough food to avoid under-nutrition. Working people with very low incomes usually receive various kinds of state help, for example tax credits and rent subsidies, and their children receive free school meals and so on. These issues will be more closely examined in the next chapter. For the moment, let us accept that literal starvation or exposure are unlikely to be fully responsible for the excess risk of death of more than 2½ times in the least advantaged social classes compared to the most advantaged seen in chapter 2 (Table 2.2) (White et al. 2007). One of the most widely researched alternatives has been the psycho-social model, which argued that we may need to include what are described as psycho-social risk factors. These include social support, control and autonomy at work, the balance between home and work, and the balance between efforts and rewards (Hemingway and Marmot 1999).

In most of the psycho-social literature, the focus is on how feelings which arise because of inequality, domination or subordination may directly affect biological processes. In various guises, this kind of explanation for social inequality in health has been a pervasive influence on health inequality research. Rather than emphasizing physical hazards, or behaviour alone, the psycho-social model focuses on the way social inequality makes people feel, and how these feelings may themselves alter body chemistry.

The biology of stress: fight, flight and defeat

The original ideas behind this line of research were based on the existence of two types of response to external threats shared by both humans and other animals (Brunner 1997). The most well-known of these is the so-called 'fight-or-flight' response. The body receives alarm messages from the brain that can be thought of as activating one or other of two 'response circuits': the sympathetic-adrenomedullary and the hypothalamic-pituitary-adrenocortical axis. Both of these circuits involve the adrenal gland (hence 'adrenaline'), which sits close to the kidney. The adrenomedullary circuit involves a structure within the adrenal medulla, one of the inner layers of the gland, whereas the cortical circuit involves the outer layer or cortex.

It is the sympathetic-adrenomedullary circuit that is perhaps nearer to popular ideas of the fight-or-flight response. This reaction involves the sympathetic nervous system, which, in balance with the parasympathetic nervous system, is responsible for much of what goes on in a routine and subconscious way in the body. They govern how fast the heart is beating, responses to changes in outside temperature (shivering, sweating) and the pH (acidity) level of the blood, for example. Sympathetic nervous stimulation releases adrenaline from the adrenal medulla, and at the same time the ends of the sympathetic nerves themselves release noradrenaline. This prompts the release into the bloodstream of fibrinogen, a substance that helps blood to clot more easily. At the same time, the heart rate and blood pressure rise, and the small blood vessels (capillaries) nearest to the skin narrow sharply. This prevents excessive blood loss from a wound, but it also has the effect of raising blood pressure.

In the human evolutionary past, the argument goes, violent activity would follow the arousal of the fight-or-flight response (Brunner 2000; Steptoe and Willemsen 2002). Adrenaline remains in the blood for only a few minutes. Then vigorous physical activity (fighting or running away) burns off the excess. Once this was over, if the person survived, the parasympathetic nervous system would quickly return the body to a more normal state. However, under modern conditions, feelings of fear or anger must often be subdued.

Examples often given include those of being caught in a traffic jam or bullied by a superior at work. There is little prospect of being able to respond physically to these events. Even when escape is effected, this is done without physical effort. And endurance of prolonged stress over long periods of time is thought by some to eventually 'reset' the blood pressure to a chronically high level.

The second stress circuit is the hypothalamic-pituitary-adrenocortical (HPA) axis. One of the most important links in this chain of effects is the release of cortisol. Hormonal messages travel from the hypothalamus to the pituitary gland (which are more or less next to each other at the base of the brain). The pituitary gland in turn secretes into the blood a hormone that stimulates the adrenal cortex, which then proceeds to release cortisol into the blood. Cortisol and other related hormones called glucocorticoids regulate several aspects of human metabolism under normal circumstances. For our present purposes, the most important of their actions is to increase the amount of energy we can expend by mobilizing reserves of sugars and fats in the bloodstream. If the stressful situation does result in violent activity, these will be burned off, as they would have been in our evolutionary past. But in the traffic jam, this does not happen. As a consequence, in susceptible people, fats and sugars build up in the blood, and a porridgy substance ('atheroma', derived from the Greek word for porridge) is deposited, which begins to narrow the blood vessels. Fibrinogen (which, as we have seen, will have been increased by the fight-or-flight response to the same stress factor) then encourages the formation of small blood clots that may become stuck in these narrowed vessels. If this happens in one of the blood vessels that feed the heart muscle, the muscle becomes starved of its blood supply. The heart may then beat irregularly, accompanied by severe chest pain – a heart attack.

The glucocorticoids are also thought to affect mood directly. There is a rare disease called Cushing's syndrome, in which the body produces far too much cortisol, whose sufferers experience profound feelings of threat and depression regardless of their social environment. This has led some researchers to look for, and to find, links between depression and later heart disease (Rugulies 2002; Van der Kooy et al. 2007; Gan et al. 2014). Cortisol also has the effect of damping down inflammation. In general, the glucocorticoids may be thought of as 'diverting' some of the body's 'energies' from routine tasks, such as watching out for infections and abnormal cell growth and repairing damage to body tissues, towards mobilizing energies for short-term reactions. Once again, this is a useful process for meeting short-term extreme threats. The problems arise when people are constantly under threat with no obvious way to fight or run away. The ability to fight infections and even some early cancers may then be reduced.

Stress-induced damage to the metabolism and the immune system has been described as a result of excessive 'allostatic load' (McEwen 1998, 2013; Dowd et al. 2008). The term 'allostasis' means, literally, 'the ability of the body to keep itself stable' during changes in the external environment, such as alterations in temperature and diet. The 'allostatic load' model of psycho-social causes of ill health focuses on what may happen when there are too many changes in too short a period of time, so that the body's attempts to respond result in overload and exhaustion. The idea would lead us to expect, for example, that an objectionable boss would be harder to bear in an environment that was also too hot, cold, or noisy, or when the individual also had a poor diet.

Failures of these processes of allostasis have been associated in one way or another with the aetiology of heart disease. It is known that people with high blood pressure are more likely to have heart attacks. The same is true of people with high levels of fibrinogen in their blood (Fibrinogen Studies Collaboration 2005; Woodward et al. 2009). Some evidence can also be found that allostatic overload is more common amongst less socio-economically privileged people. Several studies have shown that people in less advantaged social positions have higher blood pressure and higher fibrinogen (Brunner et al. 1993; von Känel et al. 2001). It has also been observed that men who report feeling insufficiently rewarded for their effort at work have high fibrinogen levels (Siegrist 1995) and those with an 'over-committed' work style have an impaired capacity for fibrinolysis (breaking down blood clots once they have formed) (Vrijkotte, van Doornen and deGeus 1999). These observations have led to the hypothesis that stressful experiences associated with lower levels of power and advantage in both the workplace and society at large may result in a tendency of the blood to clot too easily and thereby to an increased risk of heart attack.

Cortisol released under stress conditions, as we have seen, also increases the levels of certain fats in the blood. The most common types of 'dangerous blood fats commonly measured in studies are triglycerides and low density lipoprotein cholesterol (LDL). Studies have shown that stressful situations can also produce an increase of these fats in the blood (Friedman et al. 1958). Other studies have shown that indicators of more chronic anxiety, such as a high heart rate, are related to raised blood pressure and also to higher levels of triglycerides in the blood (Myllykangas et al. 1995). Social epidemiologists have concluded that there might be a causal pathway by which stressful social circumstances produce emotional responses, which in turn bring about biological changes that increase the risk of heart disease. The people participating in the experiments that showed these biological effects were not poor, although the study participants have tended to be white-collar workers such as accountants (Friedman et al. 1958) and civil servants (Ferrie et al. 1995; Carroll et al. 1997), neither of whom are at the bottom of the income distribution.

Types of psycho-social factor

Social support

I have outlined the biological justification for using a psycho-social explanation for health inequality because it is easier to evaluate the plausibility of different kinds of psycho-social factors as explanations for health inequality with this in mind. Research at the time of writing has tended to concentrate on three spheres of life: the home, the workplace and the community.

Social support was perhaps the original psycho-social factor to be examined in the literature on the social causation of ill health. As a possible reason for health inequality, it is less widely studied on its own. It is more often coupled with other kinds of stress and regarded as a 'buffering factor'. That is, when other stresses take place (such as an increase in stress at work or even the loss of a job), social support is thought of as a defence against the ill effects of the event (Steptoe 2000; Vahtera et al. 2000). In the case of stressors such as the traffic jam or the bullying boss, there is a reasonably plausible sequence of social, psychological and biological events hypothetically linking the event to a disease outcome. The fight-or-flight response raises blood pressure and fibrinogen, then, if the threat does not recede, cortisol raises blood fats and sugars. If threats are very prolonged or repetitive, these high levels of blood fats and fibrinogen increase the risk of blocking the coronary arteries, and the effect of cortisol on immunity may weaken other aspects of the body's defences. An inclusive theory of psycho-social causation would need to look in a similar way at the different types of psycho-social stressors and ask what kinds of processes were likely to be at work (Steptoe and Kivimäki 2013). In practice, this is not very easy to do.

Studies on this question relate various possible stressful events to health outcomes and, if any of these relationships looks strong (in statistical terms), a report is written. Because of the problems already mentioned, there are few studies of, for example, fibrinogen in people with low social support (Seeman et al. 2014; Yang, Schorpp and Harris 2014). Biologically speaking, we might expect that people with few supporting friends or relatives who experience a threatening event might have a larger increase in the levels of blood fats and sugars (that is, a 'worse' response in terms of the HPA circuit) than those with greater support. If social support helps them by making the resolution of the stressful situation easier, the initial fight-or-flight response is less likely to progress to 'defeat' with activation of the HPA axis. There is evidence from longitudinal studies which relate social circumstances to later illness and mortality that social support may be protective (Rosengren et al. 1993; Greenwood et al. 1996). But this kind of study, which relates a psycho-social factor to a later health event, does not necessarily guarantee the operation of what we have been thinking of here as a psycho-social pathway. We do not know if later disease was the outcome of the biological processes set out in the theory of psycho-social causation. The findings from studies of animals isolated from their fellows have been more positive. The blood vessels of isolated monkeys have been shown in one experiment to have become more thickened by fatty deposits (Shively, Clarkson and Kaplan 1989). But some studies of humans have reported no relationship of social support to biological cardiovascular risk factors, such as blood fats and blood pressure (Jönsson et al. 1999; Dowd and Goldman 2006).

In most long-term studies, it is observed that people with good relationships with family and friends, and who participate in the community (for example, by going regularly to church), have longer life expectancies than those who are more isolated (Berkman and Syme 1979). This is impressive evidence: it is not just that cheerful, sociable people *say* they feel better. However, that is not proof of the existence of a psycho-social pathway in the sense discussed here. People who have good supportive relationships with others may differ in many health-relevant ways from those who do not. And there may be a number of mundane reasons why supportive relationships act to avert health disasters, by making it more likely that a person receives timely treatment, for example, or is nagged more persistently to 'look after themselves' and adopt healthier behaviour. Be that as it may, social support is one psycho-social factor that has been most consistently found to be related to health. Other research also shows that those in more advantaged social positions tend to receive more social support, especially from outside of their immediate family (Marmot et al. 1991; Power and Matthews 1997; Matthews, Stansfeld and Power 1999; Cable et al. 2013).

Psycho-social work hazards I: job demands, work control and job strain

A number of studies have addressed the question of whether a combination of high demands on the worker with little control over the tasks undertaken, the skills used or the pace of work might be related to the risk of heart disease. Demands and control are usually measured according to a set of questions based on the work of Robert Karasek, an architect who initiated this idea in the early 1980s (Karasek et al. 1981). The combination of high demands and little control over the work situation is also called 'job strain'. One could imagine that reactions to job strain might well include some variety of the 'fight, flight and defeat' sequence as described above. Consistent with the earlier discussion of the fight-or-flight response, studies in the 1950s showed that one of the occupations most at risk of heart disease at a young age was that of bus driver (bus drivers being constantly stuck in traffic jams). The early studies, however, merely looked to see if people who scored highly on an index of demands and low on a measure of control were more likely to develop or die of heart disease. They did not, on the whole, investigate the degree of physiological reaction (changes in blood pressure, blood fats, etc.) to job strain.

The results of the studies to date are somewhat inconsistent. Many do show a relationship between psycho-social risk and disease. Others do not. Theorell (Theorell 2000) has reflected that the negative studies tend to be those with a very long follow-up, using outdated measures of demand and control, studying older people or populations with little variation in work conditions, or studying people who already had heart disease. Most well-designed studies do show a higher risk of heart disease over a period of up to around five years when demands are high and control is low. In the Whitehall II study, for example, objectively measured low job control (no measure of demand was included in this analysis) made it about 50 per cent more likely that a person would develop heart disease in the following four to seven years (Bosma et al. 1998). The relationship between job control and heart disease was an important reason for the occurrence of more heart disease in the lower-ranked civil service grades. Disease was more common in low grades because so many more people in these grades had low control. Men and women in lower grades who had high control were not at high risk of heart disease; men and women in higher grades with low control were at higher risk. This does not yet prove that there is a psycho-biological pathway at work. For that, we would have to see that people with high work demands and/or low work control also showed signs that psycho-biological processes were operating, such as high fibrinogen and triglycerides in their blood and high blood pressure.

In many (Landsbergis et al. 1994; Pickering et al. 1996; Netterstrom et al. 1998; Schnall et al. 1998) but not all (Steptoe et al. 1995) studies, high job strain is related to high blood pressure. As with social support, there are in fact very few studies that follow the whole process through (Siegrist, Klein and Voigt 1997). What we would need to see would be that men and women with high job strain (high demands and low control) showed a tendency to have high blood pressure, a 'risky' lipid profile and higher than ideal levels of clot-making fibrinogen (perhaps with lower than ideal levels of clot-busting fibrinolytic factors). Then we would need to see that it was the people with high job strain *and* the suspect physiological changes who developed heart disease. For this pathway to be the 'reason' for social inequality in heart disease, we would have to see that people in less-privileged class, status or income groups were more likely to develop heart disease both *because* they had low job control and *because* people with low job control had higher physiological risk factors. The increasing amount of linked social and biological data measured at different points in the life course may increase the ability of researchers to test these ideas (see chapter 8).

In theoretical terms, the concept of job strain, involving as it does control and autonomy at work, creates a link between sociological theories of class (as discussed in chapter 1) and health inequality. Measures of social class, such as the Erikson–Goldthorpe schema and the NS-SEC, use the degree of autonomy at work and the amount of control over one's own or other people's work activities as criteria for deciding which occupations fall into which classes. The theory of psycho-social causation therefore helps us to make sense of the observation that some social classes have better health than others (Kunst and Roskam 2009). And, exactly as would be expected from the literature on job strain, it is found that the classes with greater autonomy and control, on the whole, experience better health (Dollamore 1999; Sacker et al. 2000). Some evidence is emerging that this is *because* members of the occupational social classes who tend to have more work autonomy have lower blood pressure and fibrinogen or a less risky combination of fats in their blood (Chandola, Brunner and Marmot 2006), but studies disagree on this (Dowd and Goldman 2006). Although some tendency in this direction has been observed, the relationships could mostly be explained by the fact that men and women in less autonomous social classes also have lower status, lower incomes and riskier health behaviours (Bartley et al. 1999). Recent evidence has also failed to find evidence that high blood pressure is the reason why people with high job strain are at higher risk of heart attacks (Kivimäki et al. 2007). It has not been shown that people in occupations with greater autonomy have lower levels of stress hormones in their blood, or better health, regardless of their status in the wider community, their income or their health behaviours.

Psycho-social work hazards II: effort–reward imbalance

Johannes Siegrist and colleagues in Germany have developed the concept of effort–reward imbalance (ERi) in relation to health. A number of studies have shown that workers who experience high effort combined with low rewards in the form of pay, security, approval from superiors and chances of promotion do tend to have higher blood pressure and fibrinogen, and a more adverse blood fat profile (Siegrist 1995; Siegrist and Peter 1996; Peter, Geissler and Siegrist 1998). These workers also have an increased risk of developing heart disease and strokes (Siegrist et al. 1992; Peter et al. 1998; Kivimaki et al. 2002). In part because of the determination of Siegrist (a sociologist) to carry out studies that followed through the full social to biological pathway, the 'full' psycho-social model is perhaps better tested in relation to ERi than in relation to job strain. This does not necessarily mean that ERi will turn out to be a 'superior' or stronger factor in the aetiology of heart disease or a better explanation for health inequality more widely conceived. That remains to be studied.

Theoretically, ERi can be related to the concepts of prestige and status as well as to that of social class. Job security is one of the major forms of 'reward' whose lack acts as a risk factor in Siegrist's model. It is also a criterion for social class membership, according to the Erikson–Goldthorpe schema and the NS-SEC. However, the notion of a mismatch between the amount or intensity of work and its rewards does not enter into class theory. It is explicit in the studies of ERi that one of the most stressful things about this imbalance is the feeling that progression in one's job does not match the amount of effort one has put into it. It is not so much control over what is going on in the work environment that matters in this approach, but the feeling of lack of recognition of one's efforts. Thus, ERi may be regarded as taking us beyond the fight-or-flight model into the territory of status. Rewards for work done, in the form either of increased income or of promotion, may be significant to the individual because of what they allow him or her to feel about their place in a social hierarchy. The question of which is more important − material goods, relationships and conditions of employment or status in the social hierarchy − is an important but as yet unanswered question in health inequality research. Even if we had an answer to this question, much work would need to be done to investigate the extent to which the link between social circumstances and health involves the psychobiological pathways described in this chapter.

The challenge is to show that associations between certain work conditions and disease or mortality exist *because* people in more advantaged classes or status groups have higher levels of blood pressure or lower levels of dangerous blood fats (Siegrist 2000b). Ideally, we would need a study in which a group of healthy people (with normal blood pressure, blood fats, fibrinogen and so on) in different socio-economic positions were followed up over a period of time. Those in the less advantaged socio-economic positions should be more likely to experience higher job strain and lower rewards relative to their efforts at work; in these people blood pressure and blood fats should rise, and ultimately more of the less advantaged than of the more advantaged should have developed heart disease (Steptoe and Willemsen 2002). Outlined like this, it may sound a simple matter to test the psycho-social model of health inequality.

In practice, there are a number of reasons why it is a lot less simple than it seems. Not least important of these is cost. Collecting blood samples from large numbers of people is expensive, and this kind of exercise now needs to be approved by formally constituted ethical committees in many nations. Many of the sorts of social changes that would reduce stress caused by social inequality would be regarded as desirable, regardless of whether they improved health. There is therefore some real doubt as to whether it is ethical to carry out invasive tests to prove the link of poverty or low social status with health. Processing the blood to establish the levels of fats, fibrinogen and so on then involves further substantial additional costs. The second major difficulty for this kind of study is that it is in fact rather difficult to find reasonable numbers of people in different social positions who all have equally good health to begin with. Some of the reasons for this are obvious, and they will be considered in chapter 8 in the context of how social inequality affects the whole of the life course. A sufficiently healthy group of people from all social classes would tend to be rather young. Nowadays, it is becoming increasingly unusual to develop heart disease before the age of 60. This leads to the third problem, which is that, in order to observe a large enough number of heart attacks (let alone deaths from heart disease), the study would need to sample a lot of people, most of whom would remain perfectly healthy and not provide any 'outcome data' at all, or at least not for a very long time.

How important are psycho-social factors?

In country after country, study after study, what we see is not a group of very poor people at the bottom of the income distribution or the status order who have poor health while everyone else is fine. Instead, what we see is a steady gradation from the very top to the very bottom. It is not only that men and women in the UK NS-SEC1 have better health than those in NS-SEC7. Earlier research, using the less well validated Registrar General's social class schema, had also found that those in most advantaged RGSC I, with a car and a mortgage, had a higher life expectancy than those in RGSC I with only one of these (Wannamethee and Shaper 1997), while those in RGSC I owning two cars have better health than those with only one car (Goldblatt 1990). However many fine gradations of socio-economic advantage anyone has been able to measure, these have so far all tended to show similar gradation in health, a phenomenon that has been called the 'fine grain' of health inequality (Davey Smith, Bartley and Blane 1990; Davey Smith, Blane and Bartley 1994). It has been claimed for the psycho-social model that a gradation of stress, or of effort−reward imbalance, fits this observed pattern of health inequality better than a model of material hazards or income deprivation.

The Whitehall studies in the United Kingdom compare the health and mortality risk of London civil servants in different employment grades (Marmot et al. 1978, 1991; Marmot and Brunner 2005). They range from messengers and security staff in the lowest grade, through clerical staff in the middle, to senior administrators in the highest. The British civil service being a rather hierarchical organization, employment grade is an even more accurate measure of prestige than of employment conditions or income. For example, if you write a memo to several civil servants, you must arrange the names of the addressees in strict grade order so as not to give offence. In the Whitehall studies, the observed patterns of health-related behaviour did differ between grades, but this did not explain the whole of the fourfold difference in the risk of death between lowest and highest grades over a seven-year period (Marmot 1989; van Rossum et al. 2000).

In a comprehensive study on this topic, Lynch and colleagues studied the associations between income and mortality in a population-based sample of 2,272 Finnish men over 10 years (1984–93). Compared with the highest income quintile, those in the bottom quintile were more than three times as likely to die from any cause during the period of the project. Behavioural risk factors, such as smoking and obesity, formed part of the explanation for the income–health relationship, but psycho-social risk factors were also needed in order to fully explain the difference. This study showed two important things. One was that the link between income and mortality could be understood in terms that did not relate to starvation and exposure – persons on lower incomes were at higher risk of heart disease (in part) because they were heavier, not lighter, and because they smoked. In a modern welfare state, lower income seems to be a health hazard because it encourages certain patterns of consumption. The other important finding was that the researchers needed to include psycho-social variables such as social support and relationships at work to achieve this 'total explanation'. Behavioural variables alone, such as smoking, were not found to be sufficient (Lynch et al. 1996).

As the literature in this area has grown, there have been several attempts to synthesize it by carrying out systematic reviews, which take steps to ensure that all studies of sufficient quality are included, and 'meta-analyses' that combines results from many individual studies to find whether, on average, there is an effect, and how strong that might be. One of the earliest of these concluded that evidence of a relationship of psycho-social factors with serious disease such as heart disease was strongest for depression and lack of social support (Hemingway and Marmot 1999). Later reviews, using sophisticated methods, concentrated more on psycho-social factors in the workplace (Kivimäki et al. 2006b; Kivimäki et al. 2012) and resulted in more robust evidence of the importance of job strain (Kivimäki and Kawachi 2013). These led to some controversy, however, as to the accuracy with which the size of the psycho-social effect had been measured (Choi et al. 2013; Landsbergis et al. 2013), and the relative importance of psycho-social versus behavioural pathways. One estimate was that, while people with high job strain had around a 25 per cent greater risk of heart disease, having an unhealthy life style increased the risk by more than 150 per cent (Kivimäki et al. 2013). Does this mean that health policies should ignore psycho-social factors and continue to concentrate on lifestyle messages? We can easily see how well these results fit into the new paradigm of the importance of individual risk behaviours caused by personal weaknesses and the functionalist model of social inequality. To address this question, a life-course approach to health inequality is needed, which is introduced in chapter 10.

Further reading

Brunner, E. J. and Kivimäki, M. (2013), Epidemiology: Work-related stress and the risk of type 2 diabetes mellitus. *Nature Reviews Endocrinology* 9: 449–50.

Matthews, K.A., Gallo, L.C. and Taylor, S. E. (2010), Are psychosocial factors mediators of socioeconomic status and health connections? *Annals of the New York Academy of Sciences* 1186: 146–73.

Steptoe, A. and Kivimäki, M. (2012), Stress and cardiovascular disease. *Nature Reviews Cardiology* 9: 360–70.

Steptoe, A. and Kivimäki, M. (2013), Stress and cardiovascular disease: an update on current knowledge. *Annual Review of Public Health* 34: 337–54.

6

Explanatory Models III: Materialist Explanations

What is the materialist model?

The materialist model was the one accepted by the authors of the UK Black Report at the end of their extensive analysis of the evidence that existed at the time. They identified the importance of 'the . . . diffuse consequences of the class structure: poverty, work conditions . . .and deprivation in its various forms in the home and immediate environment, at work, in education and the upbringing of children and more generally in family and social life' (Black, Morris and Townsend 1982: 134). Yet, despite the importance given to it by this pioneering document, there is less research using the materialist model than any of the others. Much of the evidence for the existence of material causes of health inequality comes from studies which show that health is worse and life expectancy lower in people who have, or may reasonably be assumed to have, relatively low incomes (Aittomaki et al. 2012). In the Whitehall II study of health in employees of the British civil service, for example, average pay in the lowest civil service employment grade in 1985, when the second Whitehall study began, was around £3,061 per year compared to around £62,100 in the highest grade (Marmot et al. 1991). Household income predicted mortality in the province of Manitoba (Mustard et al. 1997), and individual income showed a graded relationship to mortality risk in Canada (Tjepkema, Wilkins and Long 2013). Differences in mortality risk between those with higher and lower incomes in the United States have been demonstrated (Kitagawa and Hauser 1973; Murray et al. 2006; Galea et al. 2011) and are thought to be increasing (Ma et al. 2012). Wealth, as well as current income, is strongly linked to health in American citizens (Robert and House 1996). Studies with information on both individual income and health or mortality are not very common, but the observation of the link between income and health is made in the vast majority. Other studies have made similar links between measures of health (usually mortality) and average income in small areas such as neighbourhoods of the Canadian province of Winnipeg (Roos and Mustard 1997), US census tracts (Stockwell et al. 1994; Stockwell, Goza and Roach 1995; Anderson et al. 1997) and postal areas (Davey Smith et al. 1998b), parishes in European nations (Osler et al. 2002) and boroughs in European cities (Reijneveld 1995). Even AIDS, not for a long time regarded as a disease of poverty in industrialized nations, has been shown to have an 'income gradient', with highest occurrence in the poorest postal zones of Los Angeles, medium rates in the middle-income zones and lowest rates in the zones with highest average incomes (Simon et al. 1995).

An impressive feature of many of these studies is that illness and mortality are not just high among 'the poor' but average for everyone else. Rather, the risk of illness and premature death shows 'the gradient': stepwise increases with each step down the income ladder (whether this is individual income or an average for the area of residence) (Marmot et al. 1997; Waldron 2013). The existence of the gradient poses one of the greatest puzzles for researchers trying to understand health inequality. When trying to explain an income gradient, the challenge is to look for convincing reasons why income should be related in this graded way to health and life expectancy. Townsend and his colleagues, who wrote the Black Report and originated the idea of a 'materialist explanation for health inequality', did not equate a materialist explanation with one that concentrated on income or wealth. One reason for this was that the Black Report authors did not have access to information on income, as this was seldom asked in British surveys and never in the census. The Black Report was possible because of a unique series of official British reports on health inequality, using census data, which allowed changes to be traced over the whole of the period from 1921 to 1971 as shown in chapter 2. No other nation has data of this kind, which allow us to see what has happened to health differences between similarly defined social groups (the RGSC) from the 1920s and throughout the affluent period that followed the end of the Second World War. The series was put together using data from the censuses that take place every 10 years in England and Wales. Because there were no questions on income, the 'material' factors identified by the Black Report were expressed in terms of social class, housing and car ownership.

The second reason why the authors of the Black Report may not have concentrated on income is that it would not have explained health differences between classes or status groups very well, even if it could show that it was all due to income. Obviously, a certain number of dollars, pounds or euros in wages or salary cannot literally affect the body. Income and ownership of goods, in most cases, do not give us a direct plausible causal pathway. One way to approach this puzzle from a 'materialist' perspective is to look at the ways in which income serves as both a cause and an indicator of exposure to physical hazards. In what ways might income cause people to be more at risk of exposure to danger in their everyday lives? Even if income is not a cause of such exposure, what might it tell us about a person's life that is relevant to understanding the ways in which it may involve risks to their health (Martikainen et al. 2001b)?

Measuring material risk

Poor health and high mortality are found in almost all studies of geographical areas characterized by poverty (Gorey and Vena 1995; Anderson et al. 1997; Pickett and Pearl 2001) and the levels of pollution that often go alongside poverty (Mackenbach, Looman and Kunst 1993; Pearce et al. 2010; Yap et al. 2012). However, taken one at a time, factors that can be clearly identified as material do not seem to have much effect on health. There is a clear paradox here. When we look at income, social class or area of residence, those in the poorest circumstances have between a 40 per cent and 150 per cent greater chance of illness and death in most studies. But when we look at hazards such as cold and damp housing, work hazards and inadequate (as opposed to 'unhealthy') diet, the effects are nowhere near this great.

In chapter 2, we saw that death rates have fallen steadily over the period 1931–2011. What produces the level of health inequality we see in the United Kingdom today is the fact that this fall has been greater in the more privileged social classes. This raw fact is perhaps the most important reason for continuing to pay attention to material factors. Few people would argue that life in professional or managerial social classes was more psychologically stressful, or that levels of social support were lower, in 1931 than in 2011. If anything, an anecdotal impression of trends in stressfulness in the different types of occupations that make up social classes would lead one to believe that professional and managerial jobs in the 2000s were less leisurely and more stressful than in the 1930s. There are no particular grounds here to anticipate a widening of the health gap between professionals and managers, on the one hand, and workers in more routine occupations, on the other, if this were to have been produced by differences in levels of stress. As far as social support is concerned, both academic and popular commentary on social and family trends regrets the decline in the stability of marriages and of community relationships. The falls in mortality we observe are not therefore likely to result from improvements in community or family solidarity.

In contrast to these trends in stress and social support, some commentators argue that changes in the social distribution of smoking are more consistent with the large-scale trends in mortality (Doll and Peto 1981), although not all agree (Williams and Lloyd 1991; Vartiainen et al. 1998). Here, we need to discriminate between changes in the differences between social classes and changes overall. Table 6.1 shows the trends in mortality from all causes between 1931 and 1991 in men in the different RGSCs, broken down into different age groups.

The most striking thing seen in this table is what happened to men at the end of their working lives at ages 55–64. Whereas mortality rates at these ages in classes I and II fell very sharply, in social class V they hardly fell at all. The second interesting feature of the table is the enormous improvements in mortality risk among the young age groups between the recession year of 1931 and the post-war censuses of 1951 and 1961 (there was no census from which to obtain the denominator for the mortality rates in 1941 due to the Second World War). We can also see that during the increase in smoking in all social classes between 1931 and 1951, overall mortality in men in RGSC I and II continued to decrease. The generation who took up smoking in the First World War would have been aged about 18–25 in 1914, reaching the 48–55 age group 30 years later in 1958. By this time, many of them would have been affected by the carcinogenic substances in their cigarettes. But mortality in RGSC I and II men of this age in 1961 was actually 32 per cent lower than in 1951 (792 per 100,000 in 1951 versus 535 in 1961), and mortality in RGSC II men was 23 per cent lower (706/100,000 versus 545/100,000). In contrast, mortality in RGSC V men rose by almost 7 per cent, from 1,041/100,000 to 1,119/100,000 (Blane, Bartley and Davey Smith 1997). Although smoking became relatively less common in middle-class men than in working-class men between the 1950s and the 1990s, death rates did also fall in working-class men during this time, just not as quickly. The cause of death most definitely linked to smoking – lung cancer – did not fall at all. It is argued that tobacco

Table 6.1   Trends in health inequality, England and Wales, 1931–1991: annual deaths per 100,000 in each Registrar General social class in men aged 25–64

Age	Year	Registrar General's Social Class			
		I	II	IV	V
25–34	1931	288	283	360	374
	1951	147	112	172	224
	1961	82	81	119	202
	1971	65	73	114	197
	1981	54	62	106	204
	1991	39	57	96	187
35–44	1931	439	468	609	667
	1951	241	232	291	417
	1961	166	177	251	436
	1971	168	169	266	394
	1981	114	131	233	404
	1991	101	111	195	382
45–54	1931	984	1,021	1,158	1,302
	1951	792	706	725	1,041
	1961	535	545	734	1,119
	1971	506	564	818	1,069
	1981	398	462	728	1,099
	1991	306	314	545	916
55–64	1931	2,237	2,347	2,340	2,535
	1951	2,257	1,957	2,105	2,523
	1961	1,699	1,820	2,202	2,912
	1971	1,736	1,770	2,362	2,755
	1981	1,267	1,439	2,082	2,728
	1991	953	1,002	1,620	2,484

Source: Blane, Bartley and Davey Smith 1997, by permission of Oxford University Press

takes a long time to produce tumours in the lungs, so that we will only see the effects of lower levels of smoking on lung cancer rates around 20 years after smoking habits have changed. In contrast, the physiological effects of smoking mean that it may have a shorter-term effect on heart disease. For example, the carbon dioxide in cigarette smoke makes the blood less efficient in carrying oxygen around the body from the lungs, which can place strain on the heart. The main reason to attribute changes in health inequality to smoking is because of these effects on heart disease, although it does not play as great a role as it does in lung cancer and other serious lung diseases. Moreover, during the 1970s and 1980s, mortality from many causes unrelated to smoking fell at a similar rate to mortality from heart disease.

The main impact on the overall improvement in life expectancy during the early twentieth century was in fact the decrease in deaths from infectious diseases. Although the advent of effective antibiotic treatment was part of this change, the most important change was the decrease in the numbers of people who developed serious infections, or complications resulting from less serious ones, in the first place. In fact, until the arrival of HIV/AIDS, the disappearance of infectious disease as a dreaded cause of death was so total that it was more or less forgotten. This is perhaps one reason why at present we find it difficult to understand why life expectancy improved so much more for people in more privileged social circumstances. Access to foods that are free from contamination and homes that are sufficiently warm, dry and hygienic to protect people from serious infection are now taken for granted. But this is a relatively recent phenomenon. Even as late as the 1950s in the United Kingdom, many families shared kitchens and bathrooms and had lavatories outside the home. By the 1970s, this was very unusual (Wadsworth 1991).

Hygiene and infection are probably only a small part of the causation of the diseases that produced health inequality in the last quarter of the twentieth century and that contribute to its continuation in the twenty-first. I say 'probably' here because it may transpire that infections suffered during childhood have more to do with chronic diseases later in life than we believe at present. To understand the material influences on health inequality in the early twenty-first century, we need to look for factors other than infections. However, these factors must be linked to disease risk in the same way as biological hazards such as bacteria and viruses; they must be 'biologically plausible' factors in the chain of causation. Income and wealth may be related to illness in part because they are linked to both the type of job a person does and the type of home in which they live.

Work and environmental hazards

Evidence of the relationship of individual work hazards to actual diseases is rather difficult to gather. Cancer-causing chemicals in the workplace (occupational carcinogens), for example, are estimated by some studies to be the cause of 40 per cent of cases of lung cancer but by other studies to cause less than 1 per cent. The 'average' amount, as far as one can tell from scattered studies, seems to be around 5–6 per cent (Blane, Bartley and Davey Smith 1997). Fumes and dust might be estimated to cause around 10 per cent of deaths from lung diseases such as chronic bronchitis and chronic obstructive airway disease. Industrial accidents are easier to identify: between 2008/9 and 2012/13, for example, an average of 164 workers were killed by work accidents each year (Health and Safety Executive 2014). This is about 2.5 per cent of all accidental deaths and gives the low average rate of 0.56 per 100,000 workers.

Living environment and housing are other places where the body comes into contact with health hazards (Doniach, Swettenham and Hathorn 1975; Gardner, Winter and Acheson 1982), and where the extent to which this happens is partly determined by the amount of money available to the individual. For example, in England and Wales in the late 1980s, accidental deaths of children were 4½ times more common in socio-economically disadvantaged families than in the most advantaged homes (Roberts 1997). Damp and mould in the home have been linked to infections and asthmatic symptoms in children and older people (Martin, Platt and Hunt 1987; Platt et al. 1989; Gunnbjörnsdóttir et al. 2006; Webb, Blane and de Vries 2013). Residents unable to afford sufficient heating is one reason why the death rates in older people are very much higher in winter than in summer (Eng and Mercer 2000; Mercer 2003). Cold raises the blood pressure and cholesterol level: this means that low temperature is a biologically plausible hazard for heart attacks (Lloyd 1991; Mitchell et al. 2002). Areas of residence will also influence how much people are exposed to fumes and dusts from factories in their neighbourhood (Lloyd 1978), and to the noise and pollution of passing traffic. Air pollution is estimated by one study to be responsible for perhaps 2 per cent of all cancer deaths. There is no study that tries to put a figure on how much air pollution affects the rate of mortality from other lung diseases such as bronchitis, emphysema or asthma.

Adding up the results of the few studies that can be used to estimate the size of the effect of this type of material factor on health, it would appear that it is not responsible for more than 25 per cent of all deaths at the most. Moreover, this estimate includes aspects of work relationships, such as control at work, which have been included under the psycho-social rather than the material explanatory framework. Warmer, drier, cleaner homes and workplaces, fewer hours of work and more holidays resulting in less exposure to what hazards there are, seem to be plausible explanations for trends in mortality over time, but they do not seem very important for present-day health inequality. One reaction to this has been to pay more attention to the other types of explanation, such as behavioural and psycho-social, set out in chapters 4 and 5.

However, some caution is needed when considering the nature of the evidence in studies of material factors. Many of the causes of death most obviously linked to industrial hazards, such as certain kinds of lung disease and some cancers, make their victims eligible for compensation from owners of their workplaces. Death certificates are legal documents that may be used in court cases. Studies comparing what is written on death certificates to what can be seen at an autopsy have shown, for example, that between half and three-quarters of deaths due to diseases such as pneumoconiosis (caused by coal dust), asbestosis and mesothelioma (another disease that is caused by asbestos) were misclassified (Newhouse and Wagner 1969; Hammond, Selikoff and Seidmann 1979; Cochrane and Moore 1981). Deaths and injuries caused by cars, vans and trucks being used to transport goods and workers are not recorded as industrial accidents. For these and other reasons, it is reasonable to think that quite a few deaths that result from workplace hazards are not classified as such in official statistics.

Research on environmental hazards to health has advanced more than that on work hazards (Evans and Kantrowitz 2002; O'Neill et al. 2003; Evans and Marcynyszyn 2004). A particularly promising scientific initiative recognizes the ways in which the social structure exposes certain groups to combinations of material and psycho-social adversities. Evans and Kim point out that:

> Income and class tend to sort individuals into different settings that are often accompanied by systematic differences in environmental quality. Housing and neighbourhood quality, pollutants and toxins, crowding and congestion, and noise exposure all vary with SES [sic]. Persons lower in SES also experience more adverse interpersonal relationships with family members, friends, supervisors, and community members. . . . Thus, the convergence of exposure to multiple physical and psychosocial risk factors accompanying disadvantage may account for a portion of SES gradients in health. (Evans and Kim 2010)

Some of this innovative thinking has been crystallized into a new measure of environmental disadvantage, the Multiple Environmental Deprivation Classification (MedClass) (Pearce et al. 2010; Shortt et al. 2011).

Can there ever be a 'pure material' model?

A 'purely material' model of health inequality is not, in fact, very easy to sketch out. What would such a model look like? It would mean that we could account statistically for most of the difference in illness and death between social class or status groups in terms of greater or lesser exposure to physical hazards. Someone of a higher class or status would only be at greater health risk if they were more exposed to direct material risk factors: if they were not, they would not experience this risk. In the home, these could include cold, damp, infestation, overcrowding and insufficient calories and nutrients in meals. Low income can also lead to direct hazards when it results in a person only being able to afford to live in an area with high levels of pollution, traffic and other accident dangers. Blane, Berney and Montgomery have commented that 'social class . . . in relation to health, is manifest in crucial ways through differential exposure to environmental hazards; such exposure resulting from class differences in money and power' (Blane, Berney and Montgomery 2001).

People who work in jobs where they are exposed to accident hazards or to dangerous substances, as well as extremes of temperature, also tend to be paid low wages. This link between income and employment conditions will produce a correlation between low income and hazard exposure. However, we cannot say in exactly the same way that low income 'causes' the hazard exposure in the same way that low income may directly 'cause' people to have poor housing. The relationship of income to housing takes place in the sphere of consumption (what we buy with our money once we have earned or otherwise obtained it). The relationship of employment conditions to income takes place in the sphere of production (how we obtain our income). One does not 'buy' a job (generally speaking) in the same way as a house. If we want to understand how the relationship of income to work hazards might be part of a materialist explanation of health inequality, we need to adopt a more complex definition of 'materialist'.

Blane, Bartley and Davey Smith have defined materialist explanations as those which refer to 'experiences arising as a consequence of social structure and organization, over which the individual has no control' (Blane, Bartley and Davey Smith 1997). This definition has obvious links to Weber's concept of 'life chances', which are distributed according to one's bargaining power in the labour market. The person with a humble background, no influential contacts and few qualifications or credentials is less able to claim a safer, cleaner, better-paid job. In this model, 'good' jobs are things that people compete for, and the ability to win one of them is related to resources which have been acquired over the lifetime of the individual. It follows that a person well placed to compete successfully for a good job is also likely to have experienced other benefits earlier in their life course. The multifaceted nature of social inequality has also been captured in the concept of 'fundamental cause' (Link and Phelan 1995).

The puzzle of the gradient

One of the issues facing a materialist model of health inequality is that studies show that there are differences in health and life expectancy between the most advantaged groups and those just beneath them. as well as between those who are poor and those who are 'getting by' (Waldron 2013). We need to remember that we are thinking about life expectancy, that is, about being healthy enough to keep going over a long period of time. Official statistics for England and Wales show that, in the mid-2000s, the least socially advantaged men, those in routine occupations, lived on average to about 75 years of age, while the most advantaged, those in higher management and professional jobs, lived to about 81. The figures also show that men in the middle of this particular ranking of social advantage, the intermediate occupations, lived to about 79 years, and those in lower-ranked technical occupations lived to about 77. There is a similar pattern in women (see chapter 1 for a fuller explanation of these social classes).

So we have to ask ourselves, what is it about having a *slightly* more advantaged occupational position that makes you *a little* healthier? One possibility is to go back to the definitions of social class in terms of power and life chances as well as employment conditions and money. The amount of money a person earns at any one time may be regarded in two ways. It buys things, some of which may be important for health. But both money and employment conditions also act as indicators of where that person is in the structure of power, and thereby of opportunities and life chances in society. It may be that we need to examine more closely the 'fundamental cause' of power that influences what happens to someone from day to day. There are major differences in the ability of people in different positions in the social structure to avoid a wide variety of potential hazards. These range from having to take a dangerous job to having to live in a polluted area. And the ability to protect oneself from them may arise in a number of ways, from having parents who are comfortably off during youth and early adulthood to having a reasonable income during retirement. The answer to the puzzle of the gradient may lie in understanding how these different sorts of advantages combine across the whole of the life course.

As an example of the ways in which differences in power may, in the shorter term, help to explain the gradient in the shorter term, imagine a very senior manager earning £200,000 a year and a middle manager earning £70,000 a year. Both of these women live in good housing, can afford healthy diets and have office jobs without day-to-day problems of damp, dust or chemicals. But the very senior manager, by having many people working under her, may avoid even the very occasional hazardous task more easily than the senior manager. For example, an old cupboard needs to be moved out of an office. Imagine that the manager earning £70,000 is present in the office to supervise the task, while the one earning £200,000 has a delegate to do this, and blue asbestos dust flies off the cupboard. Given what we know about the causation of asbestos-related lung cancer, this single exposure will be enough to shorten the life of the senior manager. Because there are few early deaths among those earning either £200,000 or £70,000 per year, a few extra, produced in this way, will considerably increase the relative risk of the senior managers (the difference between one and two deaths is 100 per cent, whereas the difference between 50 and 51 deaths is only 2 per cent). So differences in power may give rise to differences in exposure to fairly unusual events and yet produce significant differences in health outcomes between groups of people who would all be thought of as 'privileged' in financial and occupational terms.

The cost of a healthy life

It is obvious, then, that the amount of 'purely material' health advantages an income will buy is not determined by that money alone. Many processes enter into determining what money will buy, and most of these processes take place at the level of whole communities, political and economic units, or even globally. Communities differ in the degree to which social inclusion, recognition as a member of the community, depends on money. In any situation that could be characterized as 'social' (apart from some kind of catastrophic situation in which the only relations between people were those in which money was exchanged for food and shelter), relationships are an inherent part of survival. The money left over for material survival to some extent therefore depends on the 'costs' of maintaining relationships. At the very lowest level, people usually need clothes or some form of bodily adornment in order to be allowed to interact with other people. Even where it is warm, and clothing is not a material necessity for avoiding hypothermia, these adornments will have a cost. This cost will affect what is available for food and shelter. Of course, in the vast majority of situations, what is necessary for social acceptance and participation is far more complex (and expensive) than in my extreme example. Morris and his colleagues have investigated the minimum cost of a healthy lifestyle for a young man in the year 2000, taking into account the costs of social participation (Morris et al. 2000, 2007).

This research group did not just look at the cost of survival, but at the cost of a lifestyle that would, on current best evidence, enable a person to live to a ripe old age. In a society where it is common to live to 75, health research cannot rest at finding out how much income a person needs to live to 40. In any case, everyone doing health inequality research knows that they need to explain the gradient in life expectancy. Morris and colleagues devised an 'evidence-based healthy lifestyle', using available research in the same way as a hospital doctor would (ideally) decide on the best treatment for a patient. The budget therefore included the cost of five portions of fruit or vegetables a day and two portions of fish a week. Because exercise was also included in the healthy lifestyle, the diet had to include 221 calories more than the minimum for a person in a sedentary job (2,771 calories a day), to provide enough calories for swimming and cycling. The healthy foods cost £14.05. Because the researchers recognized the importance of avoiding social exclusion, they also costed in TV rental, a small amount for books, telephone, some musical entertainment and the costs of participating in work-based social events, altogether costing £13.78 per week, and they also included £11.42 for meals outside the home. Then there was £33.70 for things like clothing, shoes, toiletries and fares (including £3.22 a week saved for a holiday trip) and pension contributions. Housing costs were assessed for a dwelling clean enough to avoid respiratory diseases caused by mould and digestive disease caused by dirty food-preparation conditions. But Morris and colleagues admit that at present there is hardly any research that makes it possible for us to put a minimum price on a healthy home. So they adopted the average expenditure on housing for young men in national surveys, admitting that this is probably too cheap, as many homes that people who spend an average amount on rent live in will be damp or dirty: this comes to £46.80 per week.

We can see from this that the 'bare minimum for physical survival' is difficult to separate out from the costs of social participation. It is also hard to know how to evaluate housing costs in terms of 'survival' since rents depend on market forces. So if we add up the 'purely material' elements of the budget – the food eaten in the home at £14.05, plus heating at £5.41 – this is really a fairly small proportion of the total costs. And these are the only items we can really regard as bottom-line 'material' necessities for physical survival. Even if we added the costs of clothes (£8.51 per week) and shoes, this only increases the price of survival to around £27.97. Compare this with the cost of the socially, rather than biologically, necessary costs of £11.42 for meals out and £26.97 for other necessities of social participation. And of course one could argue over how 'necessary' new clothes and shoes are: it would be possible to survive by patching up old ones or relying on second-hand shops. The single item that takes up the highest proportion of the total is the cost of rent. This shows why it is necessary to look at the wider economy and society in order to gain even the simplest or most 'materialist' understanding of how individual circumstances affect health. These questions will arise in chapter 7 when we look at the relationship of health to the economic structures in different societies.

Morris and colleagues' work has been criticized for its allowance of money for such items as meals out, holidays, books and a telephone. There are two answers to this criticism. The first relates back to the previous chapter: it is that there is quite a lot of evidence (though this has its critics as well) that social integration and social participation are necessary for good health (Holt-Lunstad, Smith and Layton 2010). The second answer is that people will in fact sacrifice food and heat in order to pay for things like social occasions, holidays, hairdos and presents for their families. In the real social world, it would take the most draconian dictatorial policies to force people to spend money only on 'absolute necessities'. In fact, there is very little research on this subject. We do not know in any detail what people on low incomes go without in order to maintain levels of social participation. In one study, food and clothing of other family members was sacrificed so that fathers could run their cars. In another, low-income families with children had money to spare where the father did not demand the conventional 'meat and two vegetables' for his meals, although the alternative meals were at least as healthy in nutritional terms. But everyone's personal experience tells him or her of many ways in which 'we cannot live by bread alone'. The economist Amartya Sen has put it this way:

> Relative deprivation in the space of incomes can yield absolute deprivation in the space of capabilities. In a country that is generally rich, more income may be needed to buy enough commodities to achieve the same social functioning such as 'appearing in public without shame' . . . [T]he deflection of resources involved in pursuing these social functionings also drains the financial means that are potentially usable for health and nutrition. (Sen 1992: 115–16)

Recognizing this fact may give us the most helpful version of the 'materialist' explanation for health inequality. Quite simply, 'direct material deprivation' comes about when people do not have enough money to pay for social participation *as well as* food and heat. Not because there is not enough money in an absolute sense, but because psychological and social survival compete with biological need.

Commodification

Some societies have policies that, to some extent, make it less likely that a period without work will result in a person falling below the income needed for a healthy life. A large literature appeared during the late 2000s and early 2010s that dealt with the idea that health inequality might be in part due to 'commodification', that is, the extent to which people were treated as mere 'work units' and their ability to work as 'commodities' like apples or milk. Commodities only have the value they can be sold for, so there must be a demand for them. If too many apples or too much milk is produced, these commodities are left and soon decay and go bad. If the energies of working people are treated as a commodity (think of the term 'labour market'), then, at the most extreme level, when there is low demand for workers, people too may be left to rot. Likewise, the level of wages a person can command will depend on the demand for their labour, not on what they need to keep healthy (or even alive). At times when many people are applying for few jobs, wages may be this low even for doing such work as is available.

During the Industrial Revolutions that took place in western nations between 1750 and 1850, new industries sprang up very quickly. For many ordinary folk who lived as peasants from their labour in the farms and fields, wages in the new industrial cities seemed high. Agricultural work had always been a very hard life for most people, and land reforms also made it harder to make a living. However, once in the industrial cities, families had no access to even tiny bits of land to keep a few hens and grow a few vegetables for hard times. The new industries were subject to sharp slumps when unemployment was rampant and wages were often barely sufficient. Living standards fell below what was needed to maintain a family. In the early years after the Industrial Revolution, the cities were famous for sucking workers in from the countryside and then 'wearing them out'. In 1905, the president of the Section of Industrial Hygiene of the British Medical association told a meeting that 'a Londoner of the fourth generation did not exist . . . [meaning that] . . . after the third intermarriage among London-born people the union was sterile or the infants did not survive' (Langley Browne 1905: 929). To help with family finances, children started work at a very early age, before growth was complete. Women took only a minimum time off when pregnant and could not stay at home long after giving birth. Industries depended on recruiting new people from the countryside once production picked up again and labour power was back in demand (Langley Browne 1905).

In Britain, one result was a serious lack of sufficiently healthy young male recruits for foreign wars. During the Boer War, the state of health of young working-class men was so bad (they were short, underweight and had little strength) that a Committee on Physical Deterioration was convened (HMSO 1904). New policies were enacted to try and make sure that pregnant women were better nourished and babies had better care. Health visiting as a profession was born. Laws were passed against the adulteration of food. These policies, which had their counterparts outside Great Britain, particularly in Germany under Prime Minister Bismarck, eventually grew into what we now know as the welfare state (Pierson and Castles 2006). The idea was that the health of workers should be improved, partly by provision for women who were pregnant and had young babies, and partly by provision of some kind of income ('benefit') for unemployed men. As a result, the living standards of people unable to work for various reasons became to some extent 'de-commodified'. People gained access to a limited amount of income even when they could not work due to illness, or when there were no employers willing to employ them. The notion of de-commodification was elaborated by Esping-Andersen (Esping-Andersen 1990). He developed a measure, which was (roughly) the proportion of the average wage of a worker, which was replaced by various benefits granted to those unable to work (through unemployment, long-term illness, maternity leave, old age). He then classified nations according to this 'de-commodification index'.

In the past 10 years or so, a great deal of research has examined the extent to which overall population health might be improved and health inequality lessened in countries with a higher de-commodification index. The research has already been touched on and will be further discussed in chapter 7. But the idea of de-commodification is in fact one of the clearest examples of a materialist model of health inequality. Linking this idea to the last section on the cost of a healthy life, we can see that in theory it should be easier to maintain a healthy life in a more de-commodified economy for people who, for whatever reason, are not able to spend most of their time in employment. But because the assumption is a clear one, it has also been subject to testing, which in turn has revealed a more complex reality.

Further reading

Evans, G. W. and Kantrowitz, E. (2002), Socioeconomic status and health: the potential role of environmental risk exposure. *Annual Review of Public Health* 23: 303–31.

Evans, G. W. and Kim, P. (2010), Multiple risk exposure as a potential explanatory mechanism for the socioeconomic status–health gradient. *Annals of the New York Academy of Sciences* 1186: 174–89.

Morris, J. N., Deeming, C., Wilkinson, P. and Dangour, A. D. (2010), Action towards healthy living – for all. *International Journal of Epidemiology* 39: 266–73.

7

Macro-Social Models

Income inequality and population health

Some of the most publicly influential work relating social inequality to health does not actually analyse differences between social class, status or income groups at all. Rather it studies differences in health (usually mortality or life expectancy) between whole areas (nations, US states, English counties, etc.) with more or less unequal income (Wilkinson 1996; Lynch et al. 1998; Wolfson et al. 1999). It needs to be emphasized that these studies are not talking about 'health inequality': a surprising number of people seem to confuse the two. Health inequality exists between groups of individuals in a single society. The work on health and income inequality looks at the health of whole populations in different geopolitical units. So while health inequality studies analyse differences in health between social classes, status or income groups, studies of income inequality and health examine differences in health between nations (Wilkinson 1992), US states (Mcisaac and Wilkinson 1997; Wolfson et al. 1999), Canadian provinces (Ross et al. 2000) and districts or regions in the United Kingdom (Ben Shlomo, White and Marmot 1996). The macro-level environment in these areas is defined in terms of the degree of inequality in income, measured in various ways. But all the measures attempt to summarize the differences in income between the richer and poorer people in the area. Where there is less difference in income between rich and poor residents in an area, many studies (though not all) find higher life expectancy overall. Even if you compare two regions with similarly low income, such as the Indian state of Kerala and the Philippine Islands, for example, you find that where differences between rich and poor are lower (as they are in Kerala), life expectancy is higher.

What, then, is the connection between these studies that relate income inequality to overall levels of health and 'health inequality' as we have been discussing it? How can our ability to build conceptual models linking dimensions of inequality to health outcomes be used to understand the ecological studies of health and income distribution? So far, the chapters of this book have unpacked some ideas about how to understand studies relating class, income or prestige in a single country to health differences between individuals and groups. We have considered the strengths and weaknesses of arguments based on health-related behaviour, on stress and its physiological effects and on 'materialist' theories. A case can be made for each of these, and for different combinations according to what form of inequality is being examined and what health outcome is being investigated.

This chapter will attempt to integrate two influential programmes of research and argument, that dealing with income inequality and that dealing with welfare regimes, into the framework that has been built up. It will argue that this might be done in two ways. A psychosocial model would regard health differences between more and less unequal nations as due to the different levels of stress experienced. A model emphasizing the importance of welfare state institutions would regard the key as residing in the different levels of provision of social goods, such as education, health services, public housing and welfare benefits, and the level of 'de-commodification'. We can combine the consideration of income inequality with that of the extent of de-commodification in different societies to gain further understanding of some of the processes underlying health inequality.

Considerable controversy has surrounded the work of Wilkinson and colleagues on the relationship between income inequality and health. The controversy has taken three major forms. The first source of disagreement is whether or not the relationship between income distribution and health actually exists. The second disagreement is over what might be regarded as causing the relationship (if it does exist). The third disagreement is over the policy implications of different possible causal explanations.

Is income distribution related to population health?

The research on the deleterious influence of income inequality not only on health but also (and even more strongly) on other forms of social pathology has been very well summarized in Wilkinson's book, *Unhealthy Societies*, and Wilkinson and Pickett's highly influential *The Spirit Level*. Readers are strongly advised to consult these very well-expressed and persuasive accounts (Wilkinson 1996; Wilkinson and Pickett 2009). The key idea is that, after a certain level of average income per person is reached in a society, additions to this average do not seem to improve that society's health any further. This is not the same as the effects seen in the studies we have been considering of the social and economic position and circumstances (such as income, social class based on occupation, or prestige) of individuals. As far as studies are able to tell us, the health of individuals within a country seems to be better the more prestige they have acquired, and the more favourable the conditions under which they are employed. 'Average' levels of health within social classes, income or status groups within a country, similarly, are better the higher the average income in the group. There is no limit above which further improvement in health does not take place. By contrast, when you compare countries (as opposed to comparing groups of people *within* countries), it seems from many (if not all) studies that population health, as measured by life expectancy, does not continue getting better the higher the total amount of money earned by everyone in the country. Figure 7.1 shows the well-known Preston Curve that relates the annual income of the average person in a nation to the average life expectancy of that nation. Beyond a level of around $7,000 per year, income is no longer related to life expectancy.

However, in many studies it appears that even above $7,000 per year average per capita income, countries (and other geopolitical units, such as American states) *do* have higher life expectancy if their total amount of income is more evenly distributed. These differences in income distribution are measured in studies in several different ways. One of the ways most often used to summarize the relationship between individual incomes is the so-called Gini coefficient. Without going into the complex construction of this measure, we can look at a similar measure, the coefficient of variation, which just divides the mean (average) income in a population by its standard deviation. The standard deviation gives the average amount by which each individual's income deviates from the average for everyone (this is not exactly how statisticians would calculate a standard deviation in a study, but it explains the general idea.).

Table 7.1 gives an imaginary example of two populations with the same average income, but with a wide range of difference between each individual income and the average. It shows how these two dif-

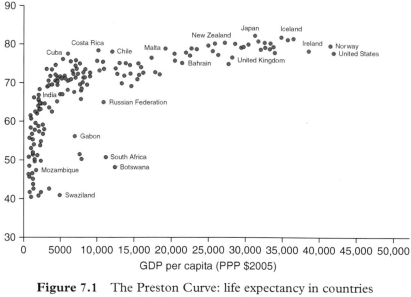

Figure 7.1   The Preston Curve: life expectancy in countries
with different levels of income

Source: Oxfamblogs.org

ferent populations have different coefficients of variation. Each population has five members, and the average income in both populations is $5,800 per year. The large difference between the two 'coefficients of variation' is produced by the fact that in Population One there is a far greater difference in earnings between individuals. This produces larger differences between the incomes of each individual person and the mean for them all (whether the difference between the mean and each individual's income is plus or minus can be disregarded in this kind of calculation). There are a number of other ways in which studies have measured income inequality, often by comparing the size of the top and bottom sections of the population (the highest-earning 10 per cent versus the lowest, for example), such as the nicely named Robin Hood Index. But the idea is always the same – to capture the degree to which earnings differ between members of a population.

Figure 7.2 shows that there is some relationship between income inequality and life expectancy as measured in 85 nations in 2012. This graph needs to be regarded with caution as it is understandably a lot more difficult to measure both income and life expectancy accurately in some nations than in others. I have omitted some nations that were in a state of conflict.

Table 7.1   Coefficient of variation measuring degrees of inequality in income for a more and a less unequal population

	Income	Variation of individual from mean		Coefficient of variation
More unequal population				
Person 1	9,900	4,100		
Person 2	9,300	3,500		
Person 3	5,700	100		
Person 4	2,100	3,700		
Person 5	2,000	3,800		
Mean income	5,800			
Sum of individual variations			15,200	
				2.62
Less unequal population				
Person 1	6,600	800		
Person 2	5,500	300		
Person 3	5,700	100		
Person 4	6,300	500		
Person 5	4,900	900		
Mean income	5,800			
Sum of individual variations			2,600	
				0.45

Many participants in the debate on income inequality and health have agreed that it is important to see whether income distribution is still related to health after taking account of individual income. If countries with large differences in income between richest and poorest simply contain more poor people, then it is not surprising that health is less good. But at least in its original form, most people understood the income distribution studies to be saying that the same income was 'healthier' if the person receiving it lived in a less unequal country or area.

Why might income distribution be related to population health?

If there is evidence that living in a more unequal social environment is bad for health, why might this be? Can we approach this question using explanatory models similar to those we have used in previous chapters on health inequality between social groups within countries?

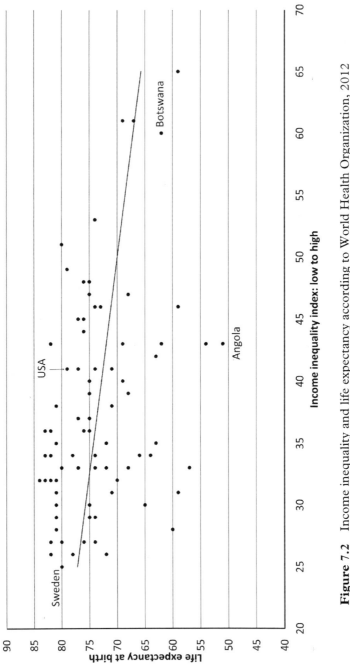

Figure 7.2 Income inequality and life expectancy according to World Health Organization, 2012

Sources: Income inequality, World Bank World Development Indicators; Life expectancy, World Health Organization

Behavioural explanation Can we similarly relate the behavioural explanation for health inequality to a behavioural explanation for the effect of income distribution? It is not possible for any relationship of income distribution to population health to be due to selection (Wilkinson and Pickett 2007). It is not very realistic to envisage that health differences between Japan and the United States (which are considerable) could be created by sick Japanese people migrating to the United States or healthy Americans going in the other direction. This means that the implicit selection model which, we have seen, lies behind the 'behavioural' explanation for health inequality is not plausible when we look at differences between countries. A behavioural explanation for these differences has to hypothesize a pathway from psychological states of mind to health-related behaviours. People who are made to feel inferior may be less motivated to protect their own health, and the stresses on them may induce cravings for unhealthy forms of consumption.

Might income inequality fit in with Bourdieu's theory of lifestyle as a way of expressing social superiority? This is harder to imagine. There does not seem any obvious reason why expressing claims to superiority might be less important in a society where income was more equally distributed. People might just as well put more emphasis on lifestyle where income differences were less, if they were determined to display their status in some way or other. However, we have no systematic studies on whether in fact there are different patterns of health-related behaviours in countries with higher or lower levels of income inequality. Using statistics from the World Bank it is possible to draw Figure 7.3 and Table 7.2 which combine information on income inequality (measured by a Gini coefficient) and smoking rates in men. There is no tendency for the two to be correlated (correlation 0.06). These figures need to be regarded with caution as the graph is limited by the availability of data on both measures.

Psycho-social explanation Even those who agree that there is plenty of evidence for a relationship between income distribution and health differ in their beliefs as to why this might be the case. Several of the leading researchers in this area have adopted a psycho-social explanation. This has been summarized well in a paper by Lynch and colleagues, despite the fact that their intention is to disagree with it. They write:

> Wilkinson has argued that income inequality affects health through perceptions of place in the social hierarchy based on relative position

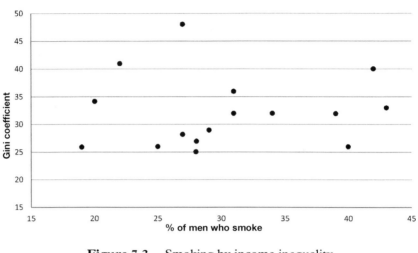

Figure 7.3   Smoking by income inequality
Source: Data from Table 7.2

Table 7.2   Smoking and income inequality

	% male smoking	Gini coefficient
Canada	20	34
Czech Republic	40	26
Estonia	43	33
Finland	27	28
France	39	32
Iceland	19	26
Italy	31	36
Japan	34	32
Mexico	27	48
Netherlands	29	29
Norway	28	27
Slovenia	28	25
Sweden	25	26
Switzerland	31	32
Turkey	42	40
United States	22	41
United Kingdom	22	38

Source: Data from World Bank World Development database

according to income. Such perceptions produce negative emotions such as shame and distrust that are translated 'inside' the body into poorer health via psycho-neuro-endocrine mechanisms and stress-induced behaviours such as smoking . . . . Perceptions of relative position and the negative emotions they foster are translated 'outside' the individual into antisocial behaviour, reduced civic participation and less social capital and cohesion within the community. In this way, perceptions of social rank – indexed by relative income – have negative biological consequences for individuals and negative social consequences for how individuals interact. Perceptions of relative income thus link individual and social pathology. (Lynch et al. 2000)

In individual members of less advantaged social groups, the psycho-social conditions in those groups induce 'stress', and this in turn affects the body (as described in chapter 5). In countries or areas with more unequal income distribution, two things seem to be happening (according to this theory, at least). First, there are similar effects on people with less than the highest level of income. Because they feel 'relatively deprived', this leads to negative emotions, which in turn set off bodily stress reactions (see chapter 5).

Secondly, there are effects on levels of 'social capital' in the more unequal societies. Much of the research puts forward the idea that where people feel very unequal, they are less likely to participate in community organizations (Kaplan et al. 1996; Kawachi et al. 1997). They are less likely to get together to improve their local environment for example. Unequal societies are more competitive and less cooperative in many ways. There is less trust between people and more criminal behaviour (Kawachi and Kennedy 1997; Wilkinson and Pickett 2009). This has an effect on everyone, not just on those with less money. Everyone is more at risk in an unsafe environment, with more pollution and traffic hazards, for example, where public participation in pressure groups is lower. Consumers are less able to ensure that the standards of safety in goods are high. And the fear of crime is well known to have a strong effect on the quality of life, even when people are not in fact at great risk.

Perhaps one of the most persuasive aspects of the psycho-social explanation for health inequality is that it appears to make sense of both work on income inequality and that on health differences between social groups using the same set of basic ideas. This is because we need to be able to account for the 'social gradient' in health that is so widely observed. The gradient means there is a significant health difference between the most privileged group within a society and the second-most privileged, not just between the poor or deprived and everyone else. If we look at a single country, we do not only find differences between 'the poor' (or the most disadvantaged people in terms of money, status and class) who are 'sick' and everyone else who are 'healthy'. What we find is a 'gradient'. People with two cars live longer than people with only one. Similarly, Wilkinson and his supporters point out that it is not only the health of people living in material poverty that is responsible for differences in the overall health of populations: income distribution seems to influence *everyone*'s chances of good health. Therefore, it is argued, there must be something about what you possess relative to what other people possess that affects your health. And the second-richest or second-most privileged group, as well as the 'bottom' group, may feel 'relatively deprived' in relation to the top group.

What is perhaps most controversial about this psycho-social explanation for the health differences between more and less unequal societies is the emphasis that has been placed on people's perceptions of their relative status in a social hierarchy. There is something rather depressing about this idea that not being a 'top dog' in some kind of fixed hierarchy could be so psychologically catastrophic as to have an effect on life expectancy itself. Do people really care so much about not having a bigger car than their neighbours that their immune defence systems collapse in protest? In the research on psycho-social work conditions that was described in chapter 5, we saw evidence for a psycho-social effect resulting from feeling out of control and being subjected to a lot of pressure from superiors. The research into social networks and social support shows that isolation and loneliness (themselves 'psycho-social risk factors') are harmful to health. This does not seem quite so challenging to our images of ourselves as adult human beings as the idea that the mere perception of relative social status may be a health risk. Do people really die of envy? Or is their position on the ladder of income or status also a measure of other kinds of hazard?

In order to help us understand the difference between the purely psycho-social and more materialist explanations, Lynch and colleagues use the striking image of people on a long-haul flight. In the back are the economy-class passengers in cramped seating while in the front is the more luxurious accommodation for business and first-class passengers. At the end of the trip, the economy passengers will probably be feeling less healthy than the others. Is this, Lynch and colleagues ask, purely because they so resented the relative luxury of the first-class passengers (Lynch et al. 2000)? This is what would be implied by the 'relative deprivation' psycho-social explanation for the relation of health to income inequality. Or is it more plausible to regard the health differences as being the result of the greater physical space in first class (we now realize that sitting in cramped conditions can be literally fatal)? Another way to look at this example is to ask whether we would expect the average health of all the passengers to improve if everyone sat in equally cramped conditions? No one would then feel 'relatively deprived', after all. In this example, one's commonsensical reaction would be to say that, of course, it would not help anyone to make all the passengers equally cramped. The health advantage to the first-class passengers would be lost, with no gain for the economy-class passengers. But the example also connects with another important point: the experience of inequality may depend on what else is going on. To extend the image, what would happen if no one on the plane had a cramped seat, everyone was comfortable and able to move around easily, but some passengers still had more space than others?

Maybe there really is no such thing as a 'merely relative' income difference. In many areas of life, the cost of things that everyone needs is influenced by the incomes of the wealthiest. The income of a short-order cook in London or Chicago might be a lot more than that of a small farmer in Kerala. But in the rich but unequal cities, that income might only be enough to buy housing of a quality that would harm the health of anyone who had to live in it. High property values could force a person earning only a little less than the average income for that society into damp, unhygienic conditions in a polluted area where traffic noise made sleep difficult. In a less unequal society or area, a person in the same position in terms of income distribution might be able to do better in terms of the quality of shelter her money could buy. One study has shown no relationship of income inequality to health in different areas of Denmark, where housing policies mean that richer and poorer citizens are far less segregated in terms of where they live than is the case in the United States (Osler et al. 2002). The relationship of any given amount of money to what the body has to endure is bound to depend on what that money will buy. And where a lot of people have a lot more money than you do, at least some of the things you need tend to be more expensive.

We saw in chapter 6 that a large proportion of the cost of the 'healthy life' in Morris and colleagues' study was taken up by rent. Housing is perhaps the most important influence on health to be very greatly affected (or at least potentially affected) by income distribution. But one could extend the general idea in other directions. If a family on an average income must devote 40 per cent of its income to paying the rent or mortgage, there is that much less money left to pay for a healthy diet, sufficient heating, maintenance of the home and health-promoting leisure activities. Where transport is poor, residents in areas where few shops sell fresh food (almost always poor areas) will either have unhealthy diets or spend a huge proportion of their budget on running a car. In some poor areas of the United Kingdom, families need to devote almost 30 per cent of their total income to run a car. By the time they have spent 40 per cent of their income on housing costs and 30 per cent on a car, not much is left. High property values often go along with high levels of income inequality because there is a group of people who have large amounts of money to invest in property which they do not live in but use purely as a profit-making venture. In countries with low levels of taxation on the wealthy, there may not be much finance available for public transport. Insights of this kind enable us to see that high levels of income inequality have consequences for health without needing to explain the relationship purely in terms of relative deprivation and the emotions that this may arouse.

'Neo-material' explanation   The so-called 'neo-material' explanation was one of the early challenges to the 'Wilkinson hypothesis'. As we saw in chapter 6, the attraction of a materialist theory is that it pays attention to how social and economic conditions can literally have an impact on the body. The neo-materialists looked for reasons why, in more equal societies, people may have experiences of a kind more favourable to good health across a wide range of situations. The neo-materialists also argued that these more favourable experiences are brought about by different policies towards the provision of public services, such as education and health care (Coburn 2000). The really important differences between countries might therefore be to do with public services, rather than with how people perceive their relative position in some kind of income or status hierarchy. The most impressive evidence in favour of this position comes from a study of health differences between Canadian provinces (Ross et al. 2000). The researchers found that there was evidence for an effect on life expectancy of income distribution when comparing US states, quite independent of average income. But they did not find the same effect in Canada. They argue that the reason for this is that public services such as health are far more highly developed in Canada, so that receiving such services does not depend to the same extent on individual income. This might suggest that only where income inequality is an indication of poor provision of services will it be related to health.

The implication of the neo-material explanation is that we ought to find health differences between countries with different levels of service provision. It may not surprise you by this time to learn that, once again, we have very few studies that have tried to test this idea with real data. It is certainly true that, since the end of the Second World War, most industrialized nations have greatly improved the provision of public services and that, during this time, we have also seen very great increases in life expectancy. However, improvements in health have not necessarily been greatest in those nations with better services. In the United Kingdom, between 1980 and 1997, public services were reduced, with absolutely no overall slowdown in the increase in life expectancy. There was, as we saw in chapter 2, some increase in the difference in life expectancy between the most privileged and the most disadvantaged social classes during that time, which continued roughly until 2003 (after which it becomes harder to see what happened). This trend is not unique to a time of rising income inequality but seems to have persisted for as long as we can see from the available statistics, at least in Great Britain. This kind of trend produces some difficulties both for the psycho-social version of the income inequality hypothesis and for the neo-material version. The 1950s and 1960s in Great Britain were times of great expansion of public services and some narrowing of income differences, but health inequality did not decrease.

Welfare regimes and health

It was mentioned in chapter 6 that one type of 'materialist' theory of health inequality could be based on the concept of commodification. To summarize: in a very strict market economy, people only have access to money if they 'sell' their labour power for a wage. When their labour power is in less demand, either because there are few jobs or because they have some form of work-limiting ill health, pay will be lower. When there is no demand for labour power at all, the individual will have no access to money. Labour power is a commodity, subject to the laws of supply and demand. The modern welfare state grew up as a response to the fact that this kind of labour market is wasteful of human life in ways that created problems for the owners of industry and for the military, and led to great conflict between the social classes.

The work of Gosta Esping-Andersen (Esping-Andersen 1990) allowed researchers to measure the degree to which labour power was 'commodified' in different European democratic societies during the 1960s and the 1970s. He developed an 'index of de-commodification' which was a measure of the proportion of the average worker's wage which was replaced by various different benefits available to those unable to work due to unemployment, ill health and old age. It is a relatively straightforward idea that, in societies where people have enough income to maintain the cost of a healthy life even when unable to work, health inequality should be lower.

In Esping-Andersen's work, there are three types of welfare regime.

1 A liberal regime in which benefits are the same for everyone, but are low and very restricted. Nations in this category include Australia, New Zealand, the United States and Great Britain after 1980.
2 A conservative or corporatist regime. Most people in this type of welfare state contribute to a social insurance scheme for unemployment, sickness and health care. They will receive different amounts of benefit according to their scheme, which often depends on their occupation. Germany and France are typical.
3 A social democratic regime. Here we find the highest level of de-commodification, in that anyone unable to work is entitled to relatively generous benefits. These nations also tend to have less inequality of income because taxes need to be very high to fund the welfare provision. Norway and Sweden are typical.

Are welfare-regime types related to health?

Researchers on health inequality set about to examining the not unreasonable hypothesis that nations with higher levels of de-commodification would have lower levels of health inequality (Mackenbach et al. 1997, 2008; Lundberg et al. 2008; Muntaner et al. 2011)

Throughout this book, frequent reference has been made to these international comparative studies. They have been one of the major achievements of social epidemiology research in the past 12 years. And the main finding has been, repeatedly, that welfare-regime type has little or no influence, either on levels of health in whole populations or on health inequality.

Figure 7.4 shows that life expectancy of men in 2009 was highest in conservative Switzerland. Social democratic Sweden did no better

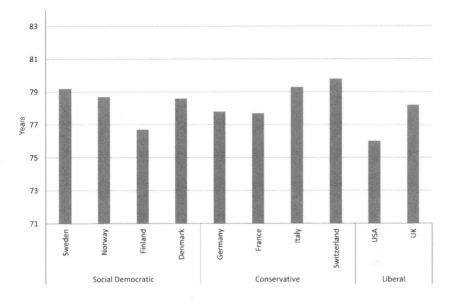

Figure 7.4 Male life expectancy in different welfare regimes, 2009
Source: Data from World Health Organization

than conservative Italy. Liberal United States does badly on many measures of health, but liberal United Kingdom is not very different to Norway and Denmark.

And how about health inequality? The team that has carried out the great majority of this comparative work published their findings on health inequality by welfare regime, and how this has changed over a 10-year period in 2014 (Mackenbach et al. 2014). As Figure 7.5 clearly shows, they found the persistence of the 'Mediterranean paradox' (see chapter 4) in that inequality in mortality was lowest in the 1990s in areas of Spain and Italy (data were not available for either nation as a whole), and this remained the case in the 2000s. Not only that, but the social democratic Nordic nations saw a greater increase in health inequality over this period of time than did the Mediterranean nations. In 'liberal' England and Wales, inequality was not only low to begin with but actually decreased. The graph, striking as it is, needs to be read with caution. This kind of study is extremely difficult to do. The authors have had to use education rather than a measure of social class, income or status, due to the availability of information for the different nations.

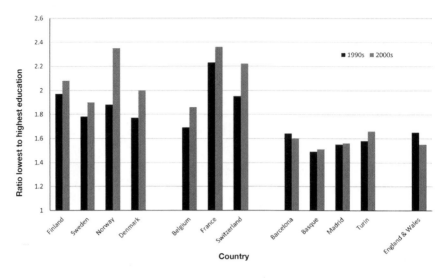

Figure 7.5   Inequality in mortality in men, 1990s and 2000s
Source: Compiled with data from Mackenbach et al. 2014

There has been a lot of speculation about the reasons for this 'public health puzzle' (Bambra 2011). Huijts and Eikemo (Huijts and Eikemo 2009) propose three possible reasons:

1 People in less advantaged social positions (or presumably with less education) in Nordic nations may feel a greater amount of stress because they realize they have failed to take advantage of all the opportunities that such generous policies afford.
2 More advantaged social groups may be better connected, even in the most egalitarian environments, and thereby better able to benefit from, for example, the health-care and education systems
3 Generous services and support for babies and children may allow 'sicker' individuals to survive childhood. These survivors then spend their adult lives in relatively socially and economically disadvantaged situations and die early.

The explanation offered by Mackenbach, which I have cited quite often already, is that the more generous welfare states have higher levels of social mobility. This results in greater 'sorting' of those with more favourable personal characteristics (intelligence, conscientiousness, etc.), through educational attainment, into more advantaged occupations. These same personal features also influence health behaviours and thereby life expectancy (Mackenbach 2010c).

Diderichsen has made an important point about the role of welfare regimes (Diderichsen 2002). De-commodification by welfare policies only applies to income available to people who are not able to work. These policies have no influence on the kinds of conditions to which the individual may be exposed when at work. The Nordic nations may have generous income replacement, but this is combined with quite vigorous 'active labour market policies' that, through training and rehabilitation, encourage as many people as possible to work. Participation in work in Sweden, for example, is very high, even among people with some degree of long-term illness (Burstrom and Whitehead 2000). It may be, therefore, that more attention should be paid to differences between social class or education groups on exposure to stresses and hazards at work.

Future research in this area will need to concentrate more on specific policies than on the broader notion of 'de-commodification'. Not only more specific policies (such as minimum income benefits) but also the stage of the life course at which they apply may be more important (Lundberg et al. 2008; Berggvist, Yngwe and Lundberg 2013; Nelson and Fritzell 2014). As pointed out by Clare Bambra (Bambra 2011), we also need a more theoretical approach. The lack of differences between welfare regime types may be telling us something about the inadequacy of our existing behavioural, material, psycho-social frameworks for analysing health inequality.

Macro-social factors in the life course

What if populations passing through periods of increasing (or indeed decreasing) inequality of income (or provision of services), or between periods of different levels of welfare provision, carry with them the 'embodiment' of earlier experiences? This would mean that, for example, the effect of decreases in income inequality on British citizens in the 1960s would have depended to some extent on what people experienced as children in the recession of the 1930s. Likewise, the effects of increasing inequality in the 1980s would have depended on people's experiences as children and young people in the 1950s and 1960s. Anyone aged about 40 or over in the 1980s would have experienced high levels of security of employment, free health care of a high standard and public housing provision of a mixed but often reasonably good standard for most of their adult lives. So the effect of shorter-term social and economic changes in middle-aged and older people (who contribute most to the mortality statistics) might not be expected to be that great. They often had considerable 'reserves of health resources' to fall back on. And not only 'health' resources. For example, many tenants of public housing were enabled to buy their homes at very low prices and to sell them on at considerable financial gain. In cities, people who did this and moved away from the more central areas were able to improve their housing, environment and living standards.

If the effects of possibly detrimental economic changes depend on what has happened earlier in the life course of population groups, what would we expect to see? One possible result could be that older groups would be less badly affected, as they had spent more of their life course in the more favourable environment. And in the United Kingdom, that is precisely what we did see. Life expectancy in men aged 18–34 actually fell during the 1980s, at the same time as overall life expectancy rose. Because death is a rare event in such young people, their mortality rate has little effect on the overall trends. But the different impact of rising inequality on younger and older men is consistent with what might be called a 'life-course political economy' of health.

Such an approach might lead us to look more closely at the ways in which both income inequality and the sorts of public policies that often accompany such inequality affect the ways in which people are able to build up and protect their health resources, and to deal with such misfortunes that do arise. Education, for example, is regarded by the neo-materialists as an important aspect of social provision. A life-course approach adds to this. It reminds us that education plays at least two roles in building health resources: it enables people to gain access to safer, better-paid and more secure jobs; but it also gives access to cultural resources. It may be that there are certain critical periods in the life course, at which having adequate publicly provided support is particularly important. It has been suggested that examples of such critical periods might include the move from home to school, the time of school examinations, the move from school to work, setting up a home of one's own, the transition to parenthood, the onset of physical changes that accompany ageing and exit from paid work (Bartley, Blane and Montgomery 1997). At each of these transitions, the quality of services may make a difference between a temporary instability and a long, descending spiral of disadvantage.

An example of this kind of process, in which a small deficit of income at a critical period determines health over the longer term, is the causation of neural tube defects, such as spina bifida, in children. This kind of birth defect has a sharp social gradient. How could a 'life-course political economy' model explain this? The neural tube is formed very early in the development of the embryo and is detrimentally affected by a lack of vitamin B. Many women will not even be aware that they are pregnant at this time. In households where money for a healthy diet is short, even for these few weeks, the damage will be done. The only way to be fully protected from the risk of neural tube damage to one's developing baby is to have fully adequate nutrition at all times during the reproductive years. Levels of income provision for unemployed families cannot therefore be set on the basis of allowing enough calories for physical survival without allowing for food of sufficient quality to ensure adequate intake of vitamin B. Take another example from the classic research on social inequality in mental health by Brown and Harris (1976). It is known that depression in mothers of young children is more likely when there is a less close relationship between the mother and her partner. It is also known that maternal depression is related to children's health and school progress. In families where income is low, employed partners often begin to work longer hours of overtime when children arrive in order to cope with the additional costs. This, in turn, makes it more likely that the relationship between parents may become less close and confiding, increasing the risk of maternal depression. The low basic income offered by many jobs thus triggers a sequence of adverse events that may influence the health of at least two generations. Not just health, but also 'health resources', as children who have experienced stress in the household during their early years are then themselves at higher risk of educational failure, unemployment and lower psychological well-being when they become adults.

These ideas bring us on towards the emerging field of life-course research, which is described in chapter 10.

Further reading

Lundberg, O., Yngwe, M. A., Bergqvist, K. and Sjöberg, O. (2014), *The Role of Income and Social Protection for Inequalities in Health, Evidence and Policy Implications. Final Scientific Report of DRIVERS Project.* Stockholm: Centre for Health Equity Studies.

Wilkinson, R. and Pickett, K. (2009), *The Spirit Level.* London: Penguin.

Wilkinson, R. G. (1996), *Unhealthy Societies: The Afflictions of Inequality.* London: Routledge.

8

Gender and Inequality in Health

This chapter will outline the way in which the different aetiological models – material, psycho-social and behavioural – can be used to address two questions. The first of these is: what are the reasons for the health differences between men and women? This question has been very fully researched, and there are many good papers and books dealing with it (Macintyre, Hunt and Sweeting 1996; Arber and Cooper 1999; Lahelma et al. 1999; Annandale and Hunt 2000; Rogers et al. 2010). So here I will only touch on whether gender differences in health could be illuminated further by the explanatory models that have been outlined in previous chapters. Would it help the understanding of health differences between men and women to distinguish psycho-social, material and behavioural theories?

The second question is whether health *inequalities* between social groups are less or greater in women than in men. Because women live longer than men do in industrial societies, relatively less attention has been paid to health differences between women in different socio-economic circumstances. Analysing health inequality in women has also raised many of the problematic issues of theory and method that have been discussed throughout this book. How is the socio-economic position of women best measured? Do women in a given occupation belong in the same social class as, or have similar status to, men in that occupation? Do the stresses of the home affect women in the same way as the stresses of work affect men? Or do domestic responsibilities protect women's health? Only after we have dealt with these issues can we advance further in understanding health inequality in women and the ways in which this differs from that found in men.

In recent years, understanding of sex and gender has become more complex. An increasing number of people change their gender, in terms of their appearance and inner identification as 'male' or 'female', or even their 'sex' by surgical alteration of their bodies. The relevance to health inequality takes us back to the discussion of identity in the Introduction. There, I surmised that the increasing freedoms that accompanied modernization may have been accompanied by additional risks to health, or at least by an increase in the importance of having the protection of a high income and status. The same may well turn out to be true for the increasing freedom to choose one's gender. I argued that it was not possible to put the genie back in the domestic bottle by forcing women back into the home in order to provide guaranteed emotional support and healthy meals. And it may be that the same will soon be true for the ability to choose and change gender. Because health risks to trans-gender people are known to be high, these risks, as for all other excess health risks to non-dominant social groups, must be better understood in order to be prevented.

Gender 'inequalities' in health

Much has been written on why it might be that, in industrial societies, women live longer than men but appear to experience more ill health (Nathanson 1975; Verbrugge 1976, 1980; Waldron 1976; Oksuzyan, Brønnum-Hansen and Jeune 2010; Emslie 2014). Higher mortality in men is found in all studies of industrial nations.

In England and Wales in 2013, women's life expectancy at birth was just under 83 years, compared to men's life expectancy of just under 79 years. In the United States in 2013, the figures were 81.2 years for women and 76.9 years for men (Xu et al. 2016). Men have higher mortality from the most common single causes of death. In 2010, adjusting for age differences between the two populations, men in the United States suffered 168.5 deaths per 100,000 from circulatory disease (heart disease and stroke) and 141.3/100,000 from all forms of cancer, compared to 108.5 and 102.3 for women. In the same year in the United Kingdom, the male death rates from these causes were 153.5 per 100,000 from circulatory disease and 156.3 from cancer, while the female rates were 94.5 and 115.1 respectively (World Health Organization 2015). Figure 8.1 shows the ways in which these trends have evolved over the past 20 years. There is little difference between the two nations in the tendency of the gender differences to reduce, mostly due to a sharp fall in mortality from circulatory disease, which has affected men rather more than women.

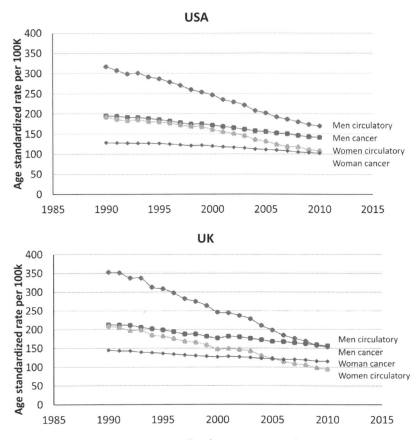

Figure 8.1   Trends in mortality from cancer and circulatory disease in
men and women: United States and United Kingdom
Source: Data from World Health Organization

Gender differences in morbidity (illness) have been widely con-
firmed in representative health surveys in North America and Europe
(Verbrugge 1985; Verbrugge and Wingard 1987; Oksuzyan et al.
2008). In the great majority of these studies, more women than men
suffer from physical complaints such as tiredness, headaches, muscu-
lar aches or pains. These observations have given rise to the idea that
'men die quicker but women are sicker'. However, questions have
also been raised about the validity of studies that show higher illness
rates in women (Macintyre et al. 1996). Health outcome variables
have taken a wide variety of forms, and not all of these show gender

differences of any great importance (Emslie, Hunt and Macintyre 1999; Walters, McDonough and Strohschein 2002). There seems to be more consistency in studies that examine either minor psychological illness, symptoms of anxiety, sickness absence from work (Jenkins 1985a) and functional limitation (Oksuzyan et al. 2008) or depression (Bebbington et al. 1998; Van de Velde et al. 2010).

Some have argued that perhaps when we look solely at morbidity rates in 'men' versus 'women', we are not really making a valid comparison. Men and women occupy such different combinations of social roles that gender itself may have little to do with the health differences that are seen. When an effort is made to compare males and females who are in similar social and economic situations, the gender differences for illness become a great deal smaller or even disappear (Emslie et al. 1999). For example, if one compares a group of male and female full-time low-paid clerical workers in equally routine jobs, all without young families at home or other caring responsibility, the men are, if anything, more likely to report mild psychological illness than the women (Jenkins 1985a, 1985b), although women take more days of sick leave. The gender difference in illness and the need for health care appear to arise as much as anything because many more women work in low-paid routine jobs (Stansfeld et al. 1995) and take major responsibility for caring and domestic work at home (Ladwig et al. 2000). In this study, men in low-paid routine jobs with similar levels of caring work to women suffered similar amounts of illness. To make this even more confusing (or interesting, perhaps), at the time of this research, the more autonomy and responsibility at work a man had, and the higher his pay, the more likely he was to be married with children, whereas the opposite was the case for women. Women in higher-paid professions and managerial positions were in fact more likely than those in low-paid routine work to be unmarried and to have no children (Jenkins and Clare 1985; Emslie et al. 1999; Khlat, Sermet and Le Pape 2000). Changes in the patterns of employment, marriage, childbearing and domestic labour may mean these findings are now out of date, but unfortunately this work has not been followed up.

Explaining gender differences in health

Psycho-social factors

It does not look very likely that a psycho-social approach is going to help us to understand gender differences in health (McDonough and

Walters 2001). The main reason for women's longer lives has been a relatively low risk of heart disease under the age of 60, the most common cause of death in adults in industrialized nations up to this age. This is despite the fact that, in most studies, women are found to have less autonomy and power at work, and to earn less money than men. One might say the same thing for the ERi. If we think about social support, women are found in some studies to have more close relationships than men, although men tend to have a wider circle of less intimate friendships. Whereas this might appear to be protective, it is also reported that women's close relationships are as much a burden as a help to them (Rael et al. 1995; Stansfeld et al. 1995; Fuhrer et al. 1999). But this does not appear to translate into disease in the same way.

Risky behaviour

Does health-related behaviour seem a promising way of explaining health differences between women and men? It is likely to play a major role, not only in the form of smoking and heavy drinking, but in other aspects of behaviour, such as taking physical risks and self-harm (Waldron 2000). Until the 1970s, most risky health behaviours were seen less frequently in women. Smoking in public by women in the United States and Europe was frowned upon, and many bars did not even admit women. Fewer women drove cars. During the 1970s and 1980s, however, gender differences in smoking and in alcohol consumption decreased (Johansson et al. 1999). During the 1980s, a series of papers asked whether, as women became more active in the workforce, they would tend to adopt the same types of risky health behaviours as men (Wingard 1984; Passannante and Nathanson 1987; Pugh et al. 1991)? One example of this from the recent past would be the way in which smoking became more acceptable in women during the 'emancipation' of large-scale employment in wartime industries between 1939 and 1945. When, in the 1960s, new research showing the link between smoking and disease became widely known, it was middle-class men who gave up most swiftly. In some countries at present, smoking is nearly as common in women as it is in men. Figure 8.2 shows the very similar way in which smoking decreased in men and women in the United States and United Kingdom after 1965.

We can see that, although there was a sharp convergence in the smoking rates of men and women between 1965 and the late 1980s,

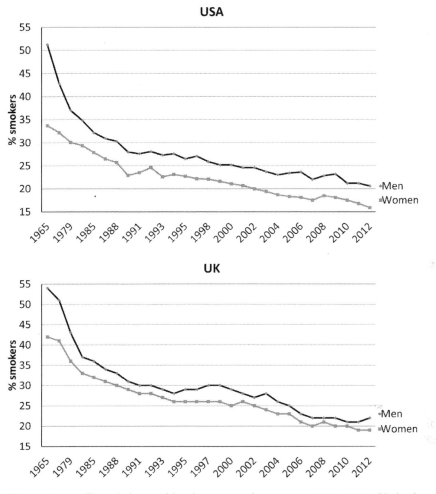

Figure 8.2   Trends in smoking in men and women, 1995–2012, United States and United Kingdom

Source: Health United States, CDC database; Cancer Research UK statistics online

after that, in the United States, the difference remained pretty much the same. In the United Kingdom women's smoking rates did reach a plateau between 1994 and 2001 where they hardly fell at all, but during this time, rates in men actually increased. After around 2005, smoking seems to have decreased at a similar pace in both men and women.

Ideas about changes in behaviour as women's roles change have been described as the 'gender role modernization hypothesis' (Waldron 2000). In order to evaluate this theory, again, we would not expect increasing equalization of risk in all major illnesses at the same time. Gender inequalities in different diseases may show different trends. It is likely that the effect of smoking on lung cancer takes place after a person has been smoking for some considerable time, two to three decades, so that we may continue to see the effects of higher rates of smoking on increasing lung cancer mortality in women for some time to come. However, the timing of the effect of smoking on heart attacks is less clear. Tarry substances in cigarettes stimulate tumour production over a long period. But another effect of tobacco smoke is to reduce the ability of red blood cells to carry oxygen around the body. This is why inhaling tobacco smoke can induce a dizzy feeling. This can force the heart to beat harder in an attempt to keep oxygen flowing to the brain, muscles and other body tissues, which, in someone whose heart is already not working at its best, may set off an attack. If this is one of the ways in which smoking increases the risk of heart attacks in women, we should expect to see heart disease rising more quickly after any increase in smoking among women. In the United States at least, the gender difference in heart disease did not change at all during the period when male and female rates of smoking were becoming more similar. So, overall, gender differences in health behaviours are some help in understanding gender differences in mortality, but the picture is quite complex (Luy and Wegner-Siegmundt 2014).

Materialist factors

Do materialist factors offer any additional help in explaining gender differences in health? In fact, in some ways, gender differences support a materialist theory of health inequality rather strongly. Higher levels of participation in the labour force by men have exposed them to far higher levels of hazard, such as heavy work, extremes of temperature, chemicals, dust and fumes. Although, like everything else to do with gender relationships, this is now changing, it was the norm during most of the history of industrial production for men to work outside the home from the age at which they were legally permitted to work until death or retirement. In contrast, women in most (though not all) regions of most industrial societies participated only intermittently in paid work outside the home.

During the first half of the twentieth century, increasing numbers of regulations were introduced to protect pregnant women because of the concern that there would be insufficient numbers of soldiers for the great wars of that century. These regulations had the effect of excluding women from many of the more hazardous forms of employment. This is not to minimize the hazardous and heavy nature of domestic labour experienced by women as wives, daughters and mothers in working-class households, or as servants in the homes of the rich. However, as contraception became widely understood and available, women effectively gained control of the pace of their own reproductive labour. By the 1970s, women were protected from some of the more hazardous forms of work by legislation and convention, and at the same time they were able to control the amount of energy they expended in reproduction. Women's life expectancy may also have been more influenced than men's by advances in medical technology such as antisepsis and antibiotics, as these resulted in safer confinements and the disappearance of puerperal infection (childbed fever).

Exclusion from work in industries such as mining, ship building and steel making in the mid-twentieth century meant exclusion from the best-paid jobs available to people who had to leave school early to contribute to the budgets of working-class families, and who were thus unable to gain qualifications. An 'advantage' in terms of avoiding certain types of health hazard was combined with a disadvantage in terms of money and living standards. Whereas the majority of women were not dependent solely on their own earning power for their standard of living because they married, the exclusion of working-class women from many higher-paid manual jobs enforced their financial dependency on men. One result of this may have been the higher rates of anxiety and depression seen in women in many surveys. It may be that financial dependency enforced by law, tradition and lack of child care has protected women against material hazards but posed greater psychological risk. In this perspective on gender differences in health, it is suggested that these are the outcome of a complex combination of biology, hazard exposures affected by both tradition and legislation, and changes in medical technology. No studies have systematically examined historical trends in gender differences in health in order to test these ideas.

Is health inequality different in men and women?

We cannot simply move on from looking at gender differences in health to looking at gender differences in health inequality. For one thing, there is no great agreement over whether there really are differences between men and women in the extent of health inequality. In 1988, Moser and colleagues reported that 'accurately to reflect the relation between a woman's life circumstances and mortality it is necessary to utilize other measures than those based solely on occupation' (Moser, Pugh and Goldblatt 1988). In their large longitudinal study, differences between women classified into the Registrar General's social classes (RGSC) according to their own occupations were not very great among the married women, who were in the majority. In the non-married women, differences in mortality risk according to social class based on their occupation were at least as large as those seen in men, but these were the minority. The differences in mortality among married women increased substantially when the researchers included whether the women lived in a household owning one or more cars, and whether the home was owned, rented privately or rented from a local housing authority (low-income housing scheme).

What this means is that whatever it is that produces a higher risk of early death in people in the less advantaged types of occupations, it has less effect by itself on married women than on men. One reason for this could obviously be that married women are less affected by lower levels of control, autonomy and security at work. Or perhaps occupation is not such a good indicator of a married or co-habiting woman's standard of living as it is for a man or a single woman. There are two reasons for this: when a woman is working, her wage may be less than half of the total family income as she will likely be paid less than her male partner; and when she is out of work she will have access to more money than social security benefit alone. Also, we have already seen that legislation in most industrial nations excludes women from several of the most hazardous occupations. So knowing her social class based on her own occupation will not predict hazard exposure as well in a woman as in a man. Then there is the question of status. A woman married to a doctor who works as his secretary has a different 'standing in the community' from one who is simply a secretary and no more than that. So, by all of our criteria of how social position may lead to illness, women's own occupations are poorer measures than men's.

These are rather commonsensical ideas, however, and based on what has been observed in the rather few studies of gender differences in health inequality over the past 30 years or so. As women's social roles change, the ideas need to be constantly checked and revised by new studies, and by looking at different countries. Countries vary enormously in the proportion of women who work, the average amount of their lives that women spend in employment and, to a lesser extent, the sorts of job that women typically do (Hunt and Macintyre 2000). Some of the best international comparisons have been undertaken between Great Britain and Finland by Arber, Lahelma, Rahkonen and colleagues (Arber and Lahelma 1993; Rahkonen et al. 2000). These authors point out that in 1996, doing only domestic work in the home was three times more common in Great Britain (22 per cent of women were 'housewives') than in Finland, where only around 7 per cent had no paid employment. Among those women who were employed, four times as many British women were employed part time (45 per cent versus 10 per cent in Finland; Rahkonen et al. 2000). Do we find, then, that a measure of social class based on occupation is more predictive of health inequality in Finland? Indeed, health differences between social classes defined according to the individual's own job are greater, and more similar to those of men, among Finnish women. We do not get larger inequalities in health in Finnish women by adding housing tenure or marital status to social class (based on occupation) by itself (Arber and Lahelma 1993). This gives support to the idea that, in the United Kingdom in the 1980s and 1990s, measures of social position based on a woman's own occupation were less good predictors of health because they were less strongly linked to living standards and hazard exposures.

Because of this greater effect of the spouse's or partner's social position on women's health seen in British data, it has been argued that we should routinely analyse health inequality in women using only their partners' social class. However, it has been shown, once again in Finland where there are different patterns of employment in women, that this would be a mistake. No differences in the degree of health inequality were found, whether the social position of the woman was defined according to her own or her spouse's occupation (Martikainen 1995; Elo 2009). The same was true for men: the same amount of health inequality was seen whether the man was classified according to his own or to his wife's occupation.

So one reason why health inequality might seem to be less in women than in men is that measures of the individual's own social class or prestige may not accurately reflect the risks and advantages experienced by women. The other reason we might find less inequality in mortality risk in women is a more biological one: the main causes of death during working age in women are not the same as those in men. Whereas for men the most common cause is heart disease, which is quite strongly related to socio-economic position, in women one of the most common causes of death in western nations is breast cancer, which does not have a social gradient. If anything, breast cancer is more common in more privileged women, the complete opposite of the social pattern seen for heart disease and lung cancer. When studies have examined inequality in heart disease mortality in men and women in Finland, where occupational measures of socio-economic position more accurately reflect women's life experiences, the degree of inequality was even greater in women than in men (Pekkanen et al. 1995).

Reasons for gender differences in health inequality

However that may be, in most countries men and women do relate differently to the world of employment, and health inequality is not the same in the two genders. Which of the aetiological pathways might be involved in different ways in men and women? Differences in health behaviours, as we have seen according to the 'gender role modernization hypothesis', may be changing. But are social variations in health behaviours different in men and women? Social class differences in smoking in Britain and the United States at present are similar in both genders, while class differences in unsafe levels of alcohol consumption are different. Women in more advantaged social positions are less likely to smoke, but more likely to be high-level alcohol consumers than their less privileged sisters. If we wanted to test the plausibility of a behavioural explanation for gender differences in health inequality, we would have to go through each of the risky behaviours and compare the degree of inequality in each one. And we would have to see whether that degree of inequality was greater or smaller when we classified women according to their own or their partners' occupations. One example of risky behaviour that does seem to show a large gender difference is that which leads to accidental and violent injury and death. However, increasingly, unsafe driving (for example) results in the deaths of pedestrians (who are in the majority female, and either children or older people), rather than in the death or injury of the (male) driver. There is little evidence as to whether men in more privileged social groups drive more safely, although they are certain to have newer and safer cars which they can afford to maintain. In the case of diet, there is once again little evidence as to whether inequality in diet healthiness is greater in men than women. Traditionally, women were more likely to have the skills to cook fresh food. However, this may be one of the many aspects of gender role differences that is changing rapidly.

What of the psycho-social pathway to health inequality? Could this be operating differently in men and women? Or, indeed, could such differences vary between nations with higher and lower rates of paid employment for women? If work stress of some kind is one of the causes of health inequality, then we would expect inequality to be greater in men, who are tied to paid employment for more of their lives. But if this is so, we should see less difference in nations where women spend more time in paid employment – which does seem to be the case, if we compare just the Finnish and British studies. Women in Britain whose occupations would be classified according to the British NS-SEC as having lower levels of power and autonomy have a smaller health disadvantage compared to those in 'better' jobs than men (Sacker et al. 2000). This is most likely because women spend less of their lives tied to paid employment and thus have less exposure to this kind of risk factor. In Finland, as we have seen, where most women spend most of their working age in paid employment, the differences are far less, and for heart disease in which control at work is likely to be an important risk factor, inequality in women's mortality is greater than it is in men (Pekkanen et al. 1995). This kind of evidence indicates that the effect of psycho-social hazards, such as low control and autonomy at work, are implicated in health inequality in the same way in men and women: it is just that, in some countries, men get a higher 'dose' than women over their lifetimes.

How about the psycho-social effects of low status? This is a rather more difficult argument. If we think there is a simple relationship, such as low status in the community leading to poor health, gender differences in health give us a problem. In most countries, it would be agreed that, if anything, women are in general accorded lower status than men. As women in industrial nations live considerably longer than men, this does not seem a very promising line of argument (although in some developing nations women's status is even lower, and in fact men's life expectancy is higher than that of women). Can we say that there is less status difference between women in more and less advantaged economic or employment circumstances than between men? And we would have to add to this that this 'difference in differences' was itself different for Finland than for Britain, for example. Do we really think that men who are consultant surgeons, or earning £150,000 a year, are 'further away' in status terms from labourers and bus conductors than are their female equivalents? It is rather hard to think about, and there is little evidence to bring to bear.

If we are going to look at differences in health inequality between men and women, we need to be aware of the problems involved in different definitions of inequality. It may be that health is affected by all three types of inequality: social class based on employment relations; status; and material living standards (Bartley 1999; Sacker et al. 2001). For men, a single indicator of social position, such as occupational class, gives a fairly good picture of where they stand on all three of these. But for women this is less the case, at least in societies where a lot of women do not spend most of their lives in full-time paid employment. The problems involved in understanding gender differences in health inequality have only begun to be addressed, and they seem to be most helpfully analysed by international and comparative studies (Arber and Lahelma 1993; Martikainen 1995; Rahkonen et al. 2000). But these problems also have the advantage of forcing us to think more carefully about what inequality is and about the different ways in which it contributes to ill health.

Further reading

This has a lot to say about women's health generally, not just that of women in poverty:

Graham, H., *Hardship and Health in Women's Lives*. London: Harvester Wheatsheaf, 1993.

Good recent papers:

Emslie, C. (2014), Gender and life expectancy, in W. Cockerman et al. (eds), *The Wiley Blackwell Encyclopedia of Health, Illness, Behavior, and Society*. London: John Wiley & Sons, pp. 617−920.

Thoits, P. A. (2010), Stress and health: major findings and policy implications. *Journal of Health and Social Behavior* 51 (1 SUPPL): S41−S53.

Thorslund, M., Wastesson, J. W., Agahi, N., Lagergren, M. and Parker, M. G. (2013), The rise and fall of women's advantage: a comparison of national trends in life expectancy at age 65 years. *European Journal of Ageing* 10(4): 271−7.

9

Ethnic Inequalities in Health

What is meant by 'race' or 'ethnicity'?

Definitions of what is a 'race' or what constitutes 'ethnicity' vary over time and between countries (Jones 2001; Aspinall 2002). The term 'race' has been used to refer to groups of people who are thought to differ from each other in some biological way, whereas 'ethnicity' refers to cultural differences, such as language or religion. During the 1970s and 1980s, the term 'race' became discredited as a useful concept for scientific research on human health (Cooper 1984; Rathwell and Phillips 1986), as it was realized that there was no scientific basis for the idea that groups of people defined as 'races' shared biological features that had significance for health (Senior and Bhopal 1994; Kaufman et al. 2015). 'Race' is now regarded as a socially and politically constructed concept that is used to justify the inferior treatment and greater exploitation of certain groups within a given society (Cooper 1986). 'Ethnicity' is usually defined in terms of the combination of common geographical origin and linguistic and/ or religious differences from the majority or dominant population. So we may think of the Polish communities in England and Scotland as an ethnic group, for example, because they have ancestors from Poland, many still speak Polish and almost all are Catholic.

In many nations, the official statistical organizations have definitions of race and/or ethnicity which are used in censuses and official surveys. These definitions change rapidly and are the subject of so much debate that one could devote an entire book to this topic alone. The US government defines four 'races': white, black, American Indian/Alaskan Native and Asian or Pacific Islander. Hispanic people are described not as a race but as an ethnic group. Ethnic identification in Great Britain has been classified in many different ways, which differ over time, and between England and Wales, Scotland and Northern Ireland (Aspinall 2002). In the 2001 Census of England and Wales, respondents were asked how they would choose to classify themselves and were given the following choices:

White

> British
> Irish
> Any other white background

Mixed

> White and black Caribbean
> White and black African
> White and Asian
> Any other mixed background

Asian or Asian British

> Indian
> Pakistani
> Bangladeshi

Any other Asian background

Black or black British

> Caribbean
> African
> Any other black background

Other ethnic groups

> Chinese
> Any other ethnic groups

Thus the 2001 Census in Great Britain offered quite a large number of possible definitions. Censuses are carried out by separate authorities in England and Wales, in Scotland and in Northern Ireland.
    In the 2001 Census of Northern Ireland, people were asked:

To which of these ethnic groups do you consider you belong?

> White
> Chinese

Irish traveller
Indian
Pakistani
Bangladeshi
Black Caribbean
Black African
Black other

Mixed ethnic group, *please write in*

What religion, religious denomination or body do you belong to?

Roman Catholic
Presbyterian Church in Ireland
Church of Ireland
Methodist Church in Ireland
Other, *please write in*

(If answer is 'no religion')

What religion, religious denomination or body were you brought up in?
Roman Catholic
Presbyterian Church in Ireland
Church of Ireland
Methodist Church in Ireland
Other, *please write in*

The way in which the questions are posed on the census forms show two things. One is the huge differences between the nations (all of which belong to the United Kingdom) in what is considered a relevant ethnic difference. The other is the great importance given to religious background in Northern Ireland. Even if a person there answered that they had no religious affiliation, they were asked to answer further questions in an attempt to discover the religion in which they were brought up. This ethnic categorization derives its significance, of course, from the specific political situation in Ireland. Other ethnic categories will be similarly affected by the political and economic histories of the regions where they are used, and any relationship of ethnicity with health needs to be interpreted in this light.

The problem with the concept of ethnicity is that the notion of ethnic differences in health was at one time used to imply that health problems in groups of people subjected to discrimination and racial harassment were due to their culture (dietary customs, for example).

In many ways this was considered to be just as bad as attributing health differences to biology. It was still an excuse, in the eyes of many, for giving insufficient attention to the position of ethnic or racial minority groups in the social structure, and to the ways in which they have been exploited, often over a long period of history, to the benefit of the majority and more powerful groups. For this reason, most groups who are in any context defined as a racial or ethnic minority support the recording by official surveys of race or ethnicity in one form or another: in order to monitor discrimination and its consequences (Krieger 2000).

In this chapter, I will use the term 'racial or ethnic minority' to refer to any group of people that is likely to be at risk of unfavourable treatment because of its national origins, shared social histories, or religion. In some contexts, the term 'ethnic group' does not seem suitable. On the other hand, the biological-determinist overtones of the term 'race' are both scientifically incorrect and unattractive. It must also be acknowledged that an ethnic or racial group does not by any means have to be of a numerical minority in order to experience forms of discrimination and inequity that might be expected to influence their health. The idea of the 'ethnic majority' is based more importantly on power than on numbers. None of these are fully satisfactory terms. Inequalities between members of different ethnic groups will be situated within a framework of socio-economic inequalities (Nazroo 2001). It will be argued that ethnic inequality in health can best be understood in terms of where members of different groups are situated within social structures, rather than cultural or biological differences between groups (Cooper 1986; Nazroo 1998). However, differences between people that are defined in terms of race or ethnicity, and that give rise to inequalities in life chances, appear in different places for different reasons in history, reasons which are linked to economic and political forces. For this reason, the experiences of these groups can seldom be entirely captured in terms of their income, social class or living conditions at a single point in time alone (Williams 1996; Krieger 1999, 2000; Kuzawa and Sweet 2009).

The largest-scale historical phenomena giving rise to the existence of racial or ethnic minority groups in industrial nations at the present time have been slavery and colonialism. Slavery brought many thousands of people forcibly from Africa to the Americas in the eighteenth and nineteenth centuries. Slavery was enormously important in the development of the economic system we would now call industrial capitalism, the exploitation of African people allowing massive accumulations of wealth that later led to the rise of whole industries in the

United Kingdom and the United States. British colonialism moved many groups of people round the world in various ways. Three of these streams of migration are most relevant to the present discussion. The first of these was the mass recruitment of Irish workers to build canals and railways in Great Britain in the eighteenth and early nineteenth centuries (Abbotts et al. 1997). Then there was the post-war migration of people from the Caribbean Islands and South Asia (India, Pakistan and Bangladesh), recruited to make up for severe shortages of workers in the United Kingdom. In the late 1960s and 1970s, there was also movement of people who had originally migrated from India to Kenya and Uganda when these were all part of the British Empire, who were then expelled from the African nations. In 1974, people migrated from Cyprus at the time of the Turkish invasion of the island. However, the Immigration Act of 1962 brought an end to large-scale migration from the 'New Commonwealth' nations to Britain (the 'Old Commonwealth' nations being Australia, Canada and New Zealand; Smaje 1995).

What are defined as the characteristic differences in appearance between races or ethnic groups are indefinite and bound to their social and historical context (Williams 1997; Dyson 1998; Jones 2001). Both the definition of a group as ethnically or racially distinct and the expression of discriminatory attitudes and practices are outcomes of economic and social forces. In the 1930s, there were 'race riots' in West London (United Kingdom) against Welsh people. They were regarded as unwanted aliens at that time because people from Wales were brought in to work at lower wages in the new industries that were springing up, displacing Londoners. In Switzerland in the 1960s and 1970s, myths abounded about the strange cooking and sexual behaviour of Italians. The status of an 'ethnic minority' was in this case due to the position of Italian guest workers, brought in to do unskilled and hazardous jobs at lower wages than Swiss citizens would have accepted. Korean workers in Japan occupy a somewhat similar position. In the early twenty-first century, hundreds of thousands of people from poorer Eastern European nations migrated to Great Britain and other richer European nations, leading to discriminatory stereotyping and harassment, for example of Polish and Romanian people. These are examples of the ways in which economic forces produce 'ethnic minority' status. If an outsider were to see an Italian and a Swiss person sitting side by side in a café, it would be impossible to tell which was which. Nor would it be possible for the average British, American or Swiss to tell the difference between a Welsh person and an English person. In the United States, England, Wales and Scotland, studies of health inequality pay no attention to religion itself. But in the Netherlands, it is customary automatically to 'adjust' statistically for Catholic and Protestant religion because the health differences between these groups are so consistent, in the same way that one takes account of gender. So we can see that the components of 'race/ethnicity' that are seen as important in terms of defining a group that might be at risk of some kind of health disadvantage depend on time and place.

Ethnicity, biology and health

In this light, it is no surprise that most researchers now consider it a mistake to explain health differences between races or ethnic groups in terms of biology. Many studies in the past were based on the assumption that there are biological similarities among members of the same racial groups (genetic homogeneity) and differences between groups that might give rise to differences in disease risk. This is very rarely true. Certain genes do influence some of the characteristics that are used in some situations to distinguish racial or ethnic groups, such as hair or skin colour. But these genes do not seem to be very important for the ways in which the body works or responds to disease hazards (Cruickshank and Beevers 1989; Cavalli-Sforza, Menozzi and Piazza 1994; Senior and Bhopal 1994; Gravlee 2009).

In most respects, the genetic differences between groups of people defined in terms of their ethnicity are less than the genetic differences between individuals within any of those groups. Knowing an individual's racial or ethnic group, for example, is little help in predicting what their blood group will be (Jones 1981). It is not particularly surprising that the genes that determine hair, eye or skin colour, for example, do not predict ethnic or racial differences in disease vulnerability. After all, it is not hair, eye or skin colour that create an 'ethnic minority' category. Genes may determine (to some extent) who has auburn hair, green eyes and freckly skin, but not the countries in which people with this appearance might or might not be regarded as similar in the sense of constituting a racial or ethnic minority. People of this appearance might be viewed as an ethnic minority in the Spanish Basque country, but not in Italy, for example.

However, in David Williams's words, race or ethnicity can, in many places, act as a 'master status', as sex and age do (Williams 1997). They are one of the first things that people register when they first meet each other. A stream of assumptions follow about what a person is 'like' (Jones 2001). Because of this, when discovering pockets of illness in social groups who are regarded as racially or ethnically 'different', doctors have tended to think first of biological or cultural causes. Nazroo (Nazroo 1997) has described this as the 'traditional epidemiological approach'. It focuses on particular diseases and how biological or cultural variations across ethnic groups may be used to provide clues to aetiology. This can lead to 'blaming' members of minority groups for their greater vulnerability to certain diseases. He contrasts this with the 'race relations approach' which 'raises questions about the motives for, and the methods used in, work on ethnicity and health and the implications that this has for the potentially discriminatory conclusions drawn. It focuses on the health disadvantages faced by ethnic minority groups and how the health services . . . may be failing to find appropriate ways to meet needs' (Nazroo 1997: 2–3).

Understanding of disease causation that is sufficient to help in prevention and treatment is more likely to be gained by paying attention to differences in material and psycho-social hazards across the life course (Onwuachi Saunders and Hawkins 1993; Lillieblanton et al. 1996; Lillieblanton and Laveist 1996). Dressler and colleagues (Dressler, Oths and Gravlee 2005) tested three conventional models of health inequalities affecting African-American people in a US study. They term these the 'racial-genetic model', the 'health behaviour or lifestyle model' and the 'socio-economic status model'. No one model was found to explain the health differences in the study, so they arrived at a fourth, 'social structural model'. Like Williams, Dressler and his team conclude that skin colour is a kind of 'master status', which serves as a criterion of social class in colour-conscious societies such as that of the United States and most European nations. The reason for differences in health between, in particular, white and black Americans is the effect that their racial master status has on access to better education, jobs and careers: in other words, discrimination.

There is, however, a considerable debate on the meaning of this kind of exercise. Many studies take two different ethnic or racial groups and adjust for various measures that are plausible explanations for higher levels of ill health or mortality in one of them. If all these adjustments still leave an excess of ill health, how is this to be viewed (Kaufman 2014)? In the past, studies concluded that this remaining difference was due to 'racial' genetic differences. This kind of explanation, as we have seen, is now largely discredited.

How great are ethnic or racial differences in health?

What do facts and figures on differences in health between racial or ethnic groups actually reveal? Table 9.1 shows the differences in mortality risk between the racial and ethnic groups defined in US official statistics for some of the most common causes of death in the US population. It uses direct standardization, as described in chapter 3, to give a rate per 100,000 of the population after taking account of any possible age differences between the racial/ethnic groups.

In 2013, mortality from all causes in black or African-American men was 22 per cent higher and in women 15 per cent higher than for white men and women. In women, in contrast, the other races/ethnic groups had either an advantage or little difference in mortality rates. All the major causes of death were lower in white than in black men and women: heart disease, lung cancer and even breast cancer (which is often thought to be linked to affluence). Particularly striking is the fact that the risk of death by homicide was over seven times greater for black than for white American men. The result of all these differences was that life expectancy for non-Hispanic black people (men and women together) was 74.8 years, compared to 78.8 years in white people, a difference of four years. This was a reduction since 1990, when the difference was seven years (Miniño 2013).

Figure 9.1 shows that there was considerable improvement in ethnic/racial inequalities in mortality between 2001 and 2011. In particular, mortality in black or African-American men fell more sharply than that in white American men.

The US government keeps much more comprehensive statistics on racial or ethnic differences in health (called 'health disparities') than governments of many other nations. This is in sharp contrast to the lack of data on differences between social classes. The opposite is the case in the United Kingdom. As we have seen, official government reports on class differences in health in England and Wales go back to 1921, and it has been this unique data series that gave rise to the present-day study of health inequality. However, perhaps in part because there are far fewer people classified as coming from racial or ethnic minorities in the United Kingdom than in the United States, data on ethnic differences in health in Great Britain are harder to come by.

Before the census of 1991, British censuses only collected information on country of birth. Table 9.2 shows the standardized mortality ratios (SMRs) for people aged 20 and over, comparing the death rates of people born in various geographical regions. This study used

Table 9.1 Mortality from leading causes by race/ethnicity in men and women, United States 2013

Cause of death	Hispanic		Asian or Pacific Islander		American Indian/Alaskan Native		Black or African American		White	
	Women	Men	Women	Men	Women	Men	Women	Men	Women	Men
Lung cancer	13.2	26.6	18	30.6	22.9	34.4	34.1	65.7	36.7	53.7
Breast cancer	14.6		11.1		10.1		28.3		20.4	
Diabetes	23	30.4	13.1	19.4	30.9	37.9	34.3	44	15.7	23.8
Homicide	1.6	7.3	0.9	2.2	2.4	8.3	4.9	31.6	1.7	4.4
AMI (heart attack)	18.6	33.4	13.4	24.8	17.1	30.2	30.1	46.2	23.8	43.4
Cerebrovascular disease (stroke)	27.6	31.8	27.9	31.2	25.5	22.7	44.7	54.1	34.2	35
All causes	623.5	863.5	343.0	487.8	508.3	689.1	720.6	1052.8	623.5	859.2

Note: Age standardized mortality per 100,000.
Source: Centers for Disease Control and Prevention, National Center for Health Statistics 2012

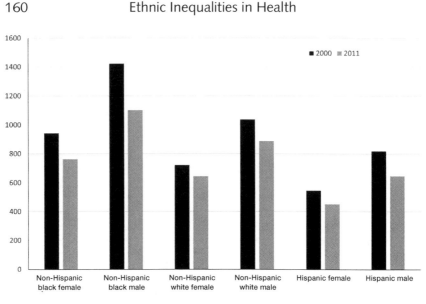

Figure 9.1   Trends in ethnic/racial inequality in mortality, United States, 2000 and 2011

Source: Miniño 2013

the SMR which is seldom used today but can be understood to tell us how far mortality in a certain group is above or below the average for the whole population (see chapter 3 and its Appendix).

From this, we can see that people born in England and Wales had a slightly lower than average risk of death, though not as low as that of people born in China or Hong Kong. In contrast, men born in Ireland had an almost 30% and women more than a 10% greater than average risk of death, and men (but not women) born in Bangladesh a 20% greater risk. Here, we must remember that ethnic group is only being defined in terms of 'country of origin', which is a very inadequate measure. In most countries, ethnic group is determined about when a death is registered, but in England and Wales people were asked where the deceased person had been born. Many people who would regard themselves as belonging to a minority group were born in the United Kingdom. Also, the categories are far too broad. Within India, Pakistan and Bangladesh, there are three major religious groups: Hindu, Sikh and Muslim. Cutting across these religious groups, in turn, are a far larger number of possible regional and social classifications, such as caste groups.

As in the United States, the implications of race or ethnicity for health in Britain are very mixed. Table 9.1 uses direct standardization,

Table 9.2 Mortality from all causes (standardized mortality ratio) by sex, cause and country of birth for people aged 20 years and over, 2001–2003

	SMR					
	Men			Women		
	All causes	IHD	Cerebrovascular disease	All causes	IHD	Cerebrovascular disease
England & Wales	97	96	95	97	97	97
Scotland	113	104	113	109	107	107
Ireland	128	118	127	113	108	111
E. Europe	102	111	112	96	104	100
East Africa	105	141	124	108	130	112
North Africa	100	97	131	107	111	112
West Africa	117	61	234	121	81	131
West Indies	102	73	160	98	96	137
Middle East	98	115	96	97	105	98
Bangladesh	120	175	249	98	167	207
India	96	131	116	104	149	122
Pakistan	99	162	141	106	174	139
China/Hong Kong	83	66	125	82	67	114

Source: Compiled with data from Wild et al. 2007: Tables 1, 4 and 5

whereas Table 9.2 uses indirect standardization and reports relative mortality risk in terms of the SMR, so it is not possible to compare risks between the two nations. The directly standardized rates in the first table can be understood just like a percentage, whereas the SMR is a ratio that compares rates of illness to a 'population average'. In Table 9.2, the risk for everyone regardless of country of origin (separately for men and women) is set to be 100, and the figures for each country compare the risk of mortality relative to this 'average' of 100 for all men and all women. All we can see is the comparison between each ethnic group and the population as a whole. But we can see that both men and women originating in Scotland, Ireland and West Africa have a higher overall relative mortality risk than the rest of the population, while people from China or Hong Kong have a low risk. Both men and women from Bangladesh, the West Indies and West Africa have a very high risk of death from cerebrovascular disease (stroke).

All of these mortality statistics need to be read with great caution (Bhopal 2000; Wild et al. 2007). In the first waves of any migration, migrants tend to be fit and healthy people, able and willing to face the hazards of going far from home in order to make a better life for themselves. Some migrant groups keep close contact with their home countries and return there when they become sick or old. There is, for example, a very great difference between being an African American whose ancestors were brought forcibly to America 200 years ago, and a Hispanic person whose parents migrated more recently from Latin America. There can be no return to Africa for the former, whereas the latter may well have widespread family ties in their parents' home nation, and will probably still share a common language with them. Similarly, the families of most people from South Asia who were resident in the United Kingdom in the 1980s will have arrived relatively recently. In contrast, large-scale migration of people from the Caribbean took place in the 1950s. The great majority of black British people of Caribbean descent were born in the United Kingdom. So the figures in Table 9.2 for people of Caribbean descent only apply to a rather unrepresentative group of more recent migrants. They do not necessarily represent the health of all people of Caribbean descent.

Official statistics for the risk of death (mortality statistics) therefore may not give us a very good picture of health differences between races or ethnic groups. Official government mortality statistics depend on having a good system for recording deaths, recording the ethnic group to which a deceased person belonged, and recording the numbers of persons in the ethnic group in the country as a whole. Only in this way is it possible to get an accurate 'rate' (the number of deaths divided by the population and then multiplied by 100 for a percentage, or by whatever other number is required to get rates per 1,000, 100,000 and so on). There are various ways in which inaccuracies can creep into this kind of procedure, most of which can be envisaged by common sense. If members of some ethnic groups are less likely than others to be accurately classified in a national census, but their origins are accurately recorded when they die, then their apparent death rate will be too high. To calculate the rate, the 'correct' number of deaths in this group will have been divided by a population number that is lower than it should be. If, for some reason, ethnicity or race is not correctly classified when a person's death is officially registered, then the death rate will be too low. The same will happen if a large number of people from a certain group return to the country from which they, or their forebears, originated when they become old or ill. So perhaps we should look outside official records at studies specifically designed to investigate health in different racial or ethnic groups.

Ethnicity and socio-economic conditions

Nazroo has reported on a variety of health problems in various groups in the United Kingdom, using the first large study designed for this purpose. Because this was an important study, I am going to describe the findings here despite the fact that it uses subjective health measures and gives no data on objectively measured disease or mortality. He is sharply critical of lumping groups together in an unconsidered manner and of ignoring the importance of socio-economic position and circumstances. For example, within the category of people with Indian family origins, he distinguishes Hindus, Sikhs, Muslims and Christians, and shows that the difference in self-reported general health between these groups, as well as between each of these and white people, was considerable. While the general health of Hindu and Christian people from ethnic minorities differed little from whites, that of Muslims was considerably worse (Nazroo 1998). Furthermore, within groups classified broadly according to ethnic origins, there were large health differences according to socio-economic circumstances.

When he looked at individual diseases, the importance of socio-economic circumstances was equally striking. In this study, as in others, diabetes was higher in people of Caribbean origins, Indian people who had migrated from both India and Africa, Pakistani and Bangladeshi people than it was in whites. However, within each of these ethnic groupings, the disease was more prevalent among those in workless households and those engaged in manual occupations. When the excess risk of a number of diseases in ethnic minority groups was adjusted for the average standard of living in each group, this excess was greatly reduced and in many cases disappeared altogether (Nazroo 1997: 103–7).

The attention paid in this report to the more precise definition of ethnicity enabled it to show that high rates of ill health relative to the white population were a far greater problem for Pakistani and Bangladeshi people than for other groups, such as Indian and Chinese. A more careful definition of socio-economic position and circumstances was the other important innovation. Rather than using social class alone, Nazroo devised an index of social conditions that included household overcrowding, quality of household amenities and ownership of consumer durables. It was this careful attention to defining both the groups involved and the nature of the disadvantages experienced that allowed many of the 'ethnic' differences to be explained (Nazroo 2001). The logical next step for research would have been to adopt this more careful way of measuring socio-economic circumstances and ethnicity, but use it to investigate differences in objective health measures ('biomarkers' such as blood pressure or lung function) and mortality. Unfortunately, this has not happened.

Social ecology of ethnicity and health

Residential area is another important variable to examine when trying to understand ethnic differences in health (Brulle and Pellow 2006; Crowder and Downey 2010; White and Borrell 2011). People defined as belonging to ethnic or racial minorities do not only tend to find themselves in less advantaged occupations with lower incomes but also in areas that suffer from environmental disadvantage (Acevedo-Garcia et al. 2003; Northridge et al. 2003). In some studies, once account has been taken of income, social class and area of residence, there are no visible 'ethnic effects' at all. In other words, the ethnic 'minority' groups studied were in no poorer health than members of the ethnic 'majority' living in the same conditions in similar areas (Sundquist et al. 1996; Chandola 2001).

The economic system that created migration patterns of African people to and within the United States, and of Irish, Indian, Pakistani and Bangladeshi people to and within England and Wales, has not disappeared. In particular, the need for labour power to carry out large-scale agricultural and industrial projects, combined with the problem of what happens to these workers after economic recessions and changes in patterns of employment, still remains. The areas in towns and cities where immigrants have congregated while they worked in these industries often remain polluted, run down and underdeveloped. When the work is finished, as with the railways, or the industry becomes obsolete, as with the textile, pottery and steel industries, those who worked in them are often forgotten. Hard and hazardous labour is replaced by unemployment. But there is often no good infrastructure of schooling and further education to equip the children of those whose labour has built the old industries to move on and benefit from change.

It is not possible to compare the mortality of first-generation African-American people to that of their descendants born in the United States, as these events took place long before the existence of censuses and health surveys. But we can relate the health disadvantage of African Americans today to the alarming deterioration in the health experience of the children and grandchildren of Irish people who had migrated to England and Wales at the end of the nineteenth century. Whereas first-generation people from the Irish Republic had around 35 per cent higher risk of death between 1971 and 1985, second-generation Irish people had a 54 per cent higher risk (Harding and Balarajan 1996; Harding, Rosato and Teyhan 2008). The reasons for this persistent and worsening health disadvantage among people of Irish descent are not understood, any more than we clearly understand the reasons for the health disadvantage suffered by African-American people. These questions need to be addressed by consideration of political as well as economic factors. Groups that are discriminated against often find it impossible to break into local power structures that determine which areas will have new schools, better transport and improved health services. The social geography of racism and its implications for health are only just beginning to be understood (Krieger 2012). For example, Chandola has reported that a combination of social class, a measure of material standard of living and an area-based measure of local deprivation explains away all of the health differences between British South Asians and the white population (Chandola 2001). Increasing use is now being made of new research methods, combined with measures that take account of social and economic conditions, both contemporary and (where relevant) over historical time. These methods may eventually come to be extended beyond the investigation of ethnic or racial differences in health and improve our understanding of differences between social classes and status groups as well.

Overall, these studies from both the United Kingdom and the United States seem to support the idea that socio-economic position and circumstances are important reasons for such ethnic or racial differences as we do see in the statistics. Health differences between racial or ethnic groups are nothing like as clear or consistent as socio-economic differences. In many groups defined as racial or ethnic minorities, cultural norms mean that smoking, alcohol consumption and diet are more favourable to health than those of the majority population, despite the fact that most of the groups studied are subject to various forms of discrimination. When studies attempt to explain the ethnic health inequalities that do exist, however, social class, education and income do not seem to be the whole answer (Muennig and Murphy 2011; VanderWeele and Robinson 2013). It seems that we should also take account of the environment in which people live (Zaman and Brunner 2008). Areas with very high concentrations of certain ethnic and racial groups seem to experience lower levels of services and worse environmental conditions that add to the disadvantages measured in individual socio-economic terms. This brings us back to the questions concerned with the historical forces that result in any group migrating from their region of origin to a different region (Williams and Ecob 1999). One interesting aspect of the new approach is that it widens out our perspective from concentration on individual nations towards consideration of global forces over long periods of time (Bhopal and Rafnsson 2012). This new way of looking at ethnic differences in health is at an early stage of development. It is likely to have important implications for the ways in which we analyse all forms of health inequality.

Further reading

A very useful book covering a wide range of relevant issues:
Smaje, C. (1995), *Health, 'Race' and Ethnicity*. London: Kings Fund Institute.

Report of a specific study as well as presenting an account of the author's particular approach to ethnic difference in health:
Nazroo, J. (1997), *The Health of Britain's Ethnic Minorities*. London: PSI.

Good recent papers:

Brulle, R. J. and Pellow, D. N. (2006), Environmental justice: human health and environmental inequalities. *Annual Review of Public Health* 27: 103–24.

Crowder, K. and Downey, L. (2010), Inter-neighborhood migration, race, and environmental hazards: modeling micro-level processes of environmental inequality. *American Journal of Sociology* 115(4): 1110–49.

Gravlee, C. C. (2009), How race becomes biology: embodiment of social inequality. *American Journal of Physical Anthropology* 139(1): 47–57.

10

Health Inequality in the Life Course

Our capacity to study heath inequality is beginning to be transformed by an approach that has developed very rapidly in the early twenty-first century, known as the 'life-course approach' (Shuey and Willson 2014). This is not just another one of the aetiological models, although I treated it that way in the first edition of this book. Rather, it is the framework into which all our explanatory models now need to fit. Stressful events and hazardous exposures can no longer be thought of as just happening and having their effect on health at a single time point. They are experienced by people who each have a history, going right back to their gestation. It is a lot easier to see why social and material circumstances have such powerful effects when we think of them as part of a series of 'vicious' and 'virtuous' circles, in which events at one point in time influence future events. In these sequences, health can be both an outcome of previous events and also a cause of future ones.

In demography and sociology these are not new ideas (Kuh and ben Shlomo 2004). Life-course studies in sociology go a long way back and have been given major impetus by the work of Glen Elder and colleagues (Elder and Rockwell 1979). Epidemiologists started to take the life course seriously because of work by David Barker and his research group (Barker 1992, 1995). This group developed an approach that came to be known as developmental origins of health and disease (or DOHaD). It began with the observation that, in some studies, those born with a lower than normal birthweight had a higher probability of various major diseases in mid- to later life and lower life expectancy. The early studies were based on data that were less than ideal in the absence of 'cradle to grave' birth cohorts that later became available. But the results were replicated in a number of other data sets from the Nordic nations which keep fuller records of population health over life (Eriksson et al. 2001). In the following 20 years, the relationship has been studied many times (Risnes et al. 2011). Health problems in adult life seem to occur both in people who were of low birthweight after a normal length of gestation, and in people who were born prematurely (Crump et al. 2011). This work was very much more biological than social but fits in well with the present interest in the 'social-biological interface'. There were specific biological theories that could potentially explain the relationships of low birthweight to different diseases: diabetes was more common because the pancreas had not developed normally during gestation; lung disease was more common because of delayed lung development; and so on.

These very influential studies led some social epidemiologists to begin to investigate the causes of low birthweight itself. Mothers in poorer economic circumstances are more at risk of having low birthweight babies (Marmot Review Team 2010; Räisänen et al. 2013). Linking the medical studies to sociological studies of the life course, some people began to ask: to what extent does the socio-economic disadvantage that increases the risk of low birthweight continue across the life of the child and into adulthood (Bartley et al. 1994)? This raised the question of the ways in which social and biological adversities may combine and interact with each other right across life and ultimately become an important part of the reasons for health inequality (Foverskov and Holm 2016). For example, the biological problems associated with low birthweight might have their own origins in social circumstances during gestation, and then in turn produce poorer childhood health with knock-on effects on education. This could be a reason why children born into poorer circumstances do less well in school and are less likely to get better paid jobs later (Case and Paxson 2010). If such longer-term relationships between social circumstances and health were involved in producing health inequality, it provided a clue to an important puzzle. Studies have repeatedly found, not just a difference in health between very rich and very poor, but rather a 'fine-grained' health gradient. The life-course approach suggested that this 'fine grain' may be a result of complex combinations of circumstances taking place over time (Davey Smith, Ben-Shlomo and Lynch 2002).

Another strength of a life-course approach is that it allows us to combine different aetiological factors that the individual has experienced at different ages. The vast majority of serious diseases have a social gradient. But a life-course approach allows this to happen according to different processes which will be specific to each disease outcome. For example, there are very similar social gradients in mortality from lung cancer and from accidents (Drever et al. 1997: Tables 10.3, 10.13), yet no one would claim that the causal factors are the same.

The influence of the life-course approach on research in health inequality has greatly increased over the past 10 years. It seems strange now that we ever relied so much on cross-sectional data that only gave health and social information at a single point in time. Absorbing the messages of life-course research into policy debates on health inequality may take some time, but the latest report from the Institute of Health Equity recommended 'the life course [is] emerging as the right way to plan action on the social determinants of health' (Marmot 2013: 8).

Critical and sensitive period models of health in the life course

Within the broad category of life-course explanations, there are different models which are widely used in studies. The first of these is the 'critical period' model, according to which a hazard or adverse experience must take place at a certain age in order to have an effect on later health. This idea is taken from biology, for example, there are certain things that have to happen at a certain time in the development of a foetus, and certain hazards (such as exposure of the pregnant mother to German measles) that are only dangerous at a certain time during gestation. The original work on birthweight and later health is regarded as an illustration of this 'critical period' phenomenon. During the gestation of the human embryo, there are times when specific organs must develop. If the organ misses its developmental time-window, it will be far less likely or even impossible for normal development to take place later in gestation

A variation on the critical-period concept is that of a 'sensitive period'. In this model, there are certain times in the life course when an exposure, while not inevitably leading to a disease, is more likely to have such an outcome than at other times. The sensitivity of the period may be a result of social or biological factors. For example, parental divorce or moving to a more overcrowded home may be more harmful to educational attainment if it takes place just at the time of national examinations. In some branches of psychology, there are also sensitive-period theories relating to the development of personality. If something goes wrong, such as depression of the parents, during a certain period of psychological development, the individual is more likely to carry forward problems into later life. A more biological example is the relationship between regular bedtimes for children and the development of the brain. In early childhood, recent research has shown that not having a regular bedtime is clearly harmful in this respect. In later childhood, after starting school, the harm is far less (Kelly, Kelly and Sacker 2013a, 2013b).

A number of studies have shown that the level of social disadvantage during a person's childhood was related to their risk of mortality in middle age (Davey Smith et al. 1998a; Claussen, Davey Smith and Thelle 2003; Galobardes, Lynch and Davey Smith 2004; Power, Hyppönen and Davey Smith 2004).

Figure 10.1 shows the results of one of the early influential studies relating childhood social circumstances to mortality in midlife. Study participants whose fathers were in semiskilled or unskilled manual occupations according to the Registrar General's class schema

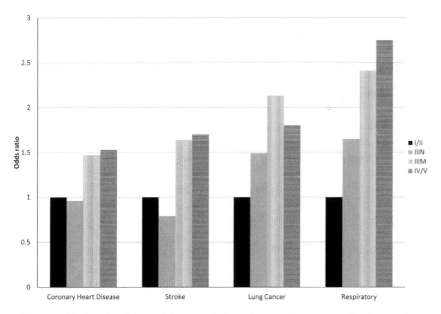

Figure 10.1   Social position at birth and mortality: mortality by major causes in relation to father's social class, men in West of Scotland aged 34–64, 1970–3

Source: Date from Davey Smith et al. 1998a

were 50 per cent more likely to die of heart disease or stroke and more than two and a half times more likely to die of respiratory disease than those whose fathers had been employed in professional or managerial work. Many other studies followed, confirming the findings (Galobardes, Lynch and Davey Smith 2008).

Does this mean that childhood is a 'critical period' for later health? Not necessarily (Hallqvist et al. 2004; Pudrovska and Anikputa 2014). In order for this to be true, we would need to see that socio-economic disadvantage in childhood was related to later poor health, regardless of social conditions in adolescence or early and later adulthood, which is not always found (Kamphuis et al. 2013).

A related model of life-course aetiology looks for interactions between experiences. In some cases, it seems that an experience is only damaging to health in certain groups of people, namely, those who are vulnerable due to previous exposures or experiences. A biomedical example here that may be familiar is exposure to the mumps virus: it can cause serious disease in adults who have not been exposed to the virus in childhood and developed immunity, but it is otherwise harmless. An example that mixes the social and biological is given by a paper using Swedish data that indicate inequality in coronary heart disease between men according to social class or income group might be greater in those of low birthweight (Barker et al. 2001).

Accumulation of advantage and risk across the life course

Studies were also able to show not just that social position in childhood could predict disease in later life, but that those who spent more time in a less advantaged position (in many studies defined in terms of manual work) were also at higher risk of mortality from all major causes (Davey Smith et al. 1997; Hart, Davey Smith and Blane 1998). This became known as the 'accumulation model', that is, finding the effects of the ways in which one hazard or advantage adds to the effects of others (Singh-Manoux et al. 2004; Pollitt, Rose and Kaufman 2005; Chen, Martin and Matthews 2007). In this model of life-course influences on health, it does not matter when a hazard or advantage is experienced, but it does matter whether other hazards or advantages precede it or follow it (Pensola and Martikainen 2003). It is quite a crude model because most studies just add up all the hazards, regardless not only of when they happened but also of what kind of hazard they are. However, hazard 'scores' of this kind have been found to have powerful relationships to many different health outcomes (Bartley and Plewis 2002; Tabassum et al. 2008; Pudrovska and Anikputa 2014).

Figure 10.2 shows how the risk of different major causes of mortality increases with the amount of time a person has spent in the less advantaged manual social classes. The first measurement of social position in this study took place in childhood, the second when the person got their first job and the third in middle age. The numbers in Figure 10.2 are expressed differently to those in Figure 10.1. But we can see that heart disease mortality was just over 40 per 1,000 person-years in those whose fathers' jobs and own jobs at both time points were non-manual, compared to more than 80/1,000 person-years in those whose childhood and adulthood social position had been in a manual social class. This is roughly double the risk, which shows how powerful accumulated social position can be as a predictor of mortality risk.

Table 10.1 illustrates what the rates of illness would look like in four groups of people with different childhood and adulthood socioeconomic circumstances if their health had been affected over time in an accumulative manner.

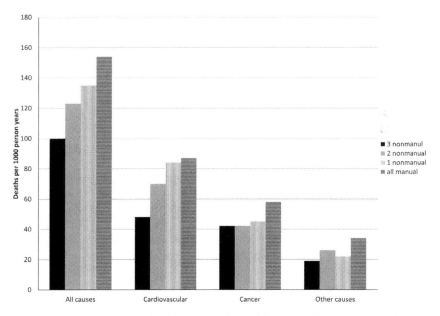

Figure 10.2   Mortality by occupation of father and own occupation
at 2 time points in adulthood

Source: Data from Davey Smith et al. 1997

Table 10.1   Accumulation of health risk over the life course

Parents' social position	Own social position	
	More advantaged	Less advantaged
More advantaged	C	D
% ill	10	8
Less advantaged	A	B
% ill	8	4

What the table shows can be summarized as follows:

1 Group A comes from a disadvantaged background and has ended up in an advantaged social position.
2 Group B comes from a disadvantaged background and has stayed there.
3 Group C comes from an advantaged background and has stayed there.
4 Group D comes from an advantaged background and has ended up in a disadvantaged social position.

We can see that it makes no difference to the percentage of people who are ill whether they moved from a less advantaged to a more advantaged social group (8 per cent are ill), or the other way round (8 per cent are also ill). It is as if time spent in a disadvantaged position gives people a 'risk score': they score more highly on risk the more time they have spent in disadvantage (Hallqvist et al. 2004). There is now evidence from quite a few studies to show that this accumulative pattern lies behind not only the social inequality in disease and mortality, but also several forms of risky behaviours. For example, Hilary Graham found that while 22 per cent of British women were smokers, this rose to 46 per cent of those with no educational qualification, 50 per cent of those with no qualification and a low-skilled job, 67 per cent for women who also lived in social housing and 73 per cent for women who were also having to claim social assistance benefits (Graham 1998; Graham et al. 2006).

The question then arises: what can explain these accumulative patterns? 'Social class' is an abstraction (see chapter 1). Working and housing conditions may damage health directly, but they cannot literally cause people to smoke. We need to know far more about what social conditions in childhood and other stages of life can tell us about things that make sense in terms of causing ill health. In 2014, for example, a paper from a strong research team admitted: 'The relative contribution of early or later life socio-economic position (SEP) to later life health is not fully understood' (Ploubidis et al. 2014).

Selection explanations: 'personal characteristics' in the life course

In many studies, education has been shown to have a powerful relationship to health, and well-educated people in North America, Australia and Northern European countries tend to engage in 'healthier lifestyles'. This is often taken to mean that health inequality may be no more than an expression of 'natural' inequalities in intelligence or other psychological characteristics. Figure 10.3 shows this idea in graphical form.

In the last 10 years, this interpretation of the evidence has gained considerable strength (see Introduction and chapter 1). Some researchers believe that favourable psychological characteristics, perhaps genetic in origin, may help the individual to pass exams, or otherwise to increase her or his 'human capital', which is defined by economists in terms of education, skills and work experience (Caspi et al. 1998; Krapohl and Plomin 2015). These 'human capital' characteristics may include intelligence, conscientiousness, coping skills and similar constructs. Those with these higher levels of human capital then get better jobs and therefore find themselves better placed in terms of income, status, work autonomy and power in the workplace (Bond and Saunders 1999). At the present time,

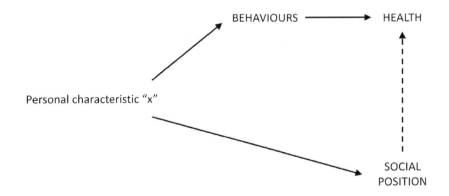

Figure 10.3   Indirect selection as a reason for health inequality

the evidence relating genetic factors to intelligence and thus to edu-cational attainment and adult social position is regarded by genetics experts as rather weak (Rietveld et al. 2013). Even weaker is the evidence that the ability of parents to pass on social advantages to their children (which is very powerful) has anything to do with genes (Conley et al. 2015). On the contrary, a cleverly designed study of adopted children in Sweden showed that the income and wealth of adoptees was more closely related to that of their (genetically unre-lated) adoptive parents than to that of their own biological parents (Black et al. 2015).

What would we need to see in order to know whether character-istics such as intelligence or coping ability that people are born with are a 'cause' of both adult social position (class, status, income) and adult health? That is, how could we carry out some tests of Mackenbach's hypothesis that health inequality is now a 'personal' matter (Chapman et al. 2010; Mackenbach 2010c)? We would need to see that young people with 'favourable' personality traits, such as high conscientiousness perhaps, passed their exams, went on to higher education and gravitated into professional and managerial occupations, engaged in heath-protective practices in terms of their lifestyle and had better health. People with low conscientiousness would need to be found in the alternative life pathways of low educa-tional attainment and less advantaged occupations. And this would have to be regardless of their own family background. This kind of research remains to be done, but it might look a bit like Tables 10.2–10.4.

Forced expiratory volume in 1 second (FEV1) is a measure of how well a person's lungs are working, and of course is strongly influenced by smoking. FEV1 is measured by getting the study participant to blow as hard as they can into a device called a spirometer, which counts how much air per second is blown into it. A high value of FEV1 indicates stronger lungs and so is healthier than a low one. The data in Tables 10.2–10.4 are real, and are taken from the 1958 British Birth Cohort Study. Participants in this study have been fol-lowed from birth to the present day, generating a wide range of meas-ures of health and social circumstances. Between the ages of 45 and 46, around 9,000 participants in this study were visited by a nurse who measured their underlying health such as blood pressure, cho-lesterol and lung function. I have included only men in these tables for simplicity and because men are more likely to be exposed to the kinds of work hazard that can influence the lungs. Table 10.2 shows that a higher proportion of men in manual occupations had low lung

Table 10.2   Social inequality in lung function in men born in 1958

Adult class	Lung function		Odds
	Normal FEV1 %	Low FEV1 %	
Non manual	80	20	0.25
Manual	70	30	0.43
Odds Ratio			1.71

Source: Data from 1958 British Birth Cohort Study

function (in the bottom 20 per cent of the distribution for everyone). The odds ratio comparing the risk of low lung function between manual and non-manual men is 1:71, that is, men in manual occupations were 70 per cent more likely to have low lung function than those in non-manual occupations. If we wanted to see how much of this relationship might be due to the fact that children born to fathers in manual occupations are more likely to become manual workers themselves, we would draw a table like Table 10.3.

Here, we can partly see the 'accumulation' effect, in that the highest risk of poor lung function, 31 per cent, is seen in men who were in the manual class both at birth and in adulthood, and the lowest proportion, 17 per cent, is seen in those who were in the non-manual class at both stages of the life course. The odds ratio here, as discussed in chapter 3, is an average of the two individual ORs

Table 10.3   Influence of childhood social class on the relationship of adult social class to lung function in men born in 1958

Adult class	Childhood class					
	Non manual			Manual		
	Normal FEV	Low FEV	Odds	Normal FEV	Low FEV	Odds
Non- manual	83	17	0.20	78	22	0.28
Manual	71	28	0.39	69	31	0.44
			1.92			1.59
Common (weighted) OR			1.63			

Source: Data from 1958 British Birth Cohort Study

weighted according to how many people were in each group (so if you try to take the average yourself, it will not come out right!). We can look at the proportional reduction in the odds ratio (see chapter 3 again), which will be

$$(1.71-1.63)/(1.73-1)$$

which gives approximately 14 per cent reduction. So we can say that around 14 per cent of the social class differences in lung function at age 45–6 were due to exposures associated with being in a less advantaged social class in childhood.

But what if we also think that more intelligent children, who had healthier behaviours, were more likely to end up in non-manual classes regardless of where they started out? This would happen if the more intelligent children born into manual classes tended to migrate into the non-manual class between adolescence and age 46. If this has happened, then when we adjust for a measure of intelligence, the risk will be the same in both of the adult social groups because it is not social class that affects lung function but intelligence. This is a bit like Table 3.1 in chapter 3, except that (a) these are real data and (b) we have added childhood social class to the analysis. Table 10.4 shows the results.

Here, we can see that men who had high cognitive skills at age 7 also had better lung function at age 45–6, regardless of their childhood or adulthood social class. So there may well be something about cognitive skill that protects the lungs, and this may well be the ability to understand and act upon health education advice. The highest proportion with poor lung function, 33 per cent, was found in the group with lower cognitive skills combined with both childhood and adulthood manual social class. But in the luckier men with higher intelligence and a non-manual family background, manual adult class was still associated with a greater risk of poor lung function. So although cognition is doing something to explain how healthy people's lungs are in midlife, it is by no means the whole story for inequality. The amount of the excess risk of poor lung function that has been explained by adding both childhood class and cognitive function to our model is:

$$(1.73-1.59)/(1.73-1) \text{ which is around } 20\%$$

which also means that around 80 per cent, the great majority of the social class difference in lung function at age 45–6, needs to be explained by the conditions of life in manual social classes. Cognitive function ('intelligence') does play some role in explaining

Table 10.4 Effect of adjustment for childhood social class and cognitive skill at age 7 on social class differences in lung function at age 45–6

High cognitive skill at 7 years

Adult class	Childhood class Non-manual			Childhood class Manual		
	Normal FEV %	Low FEV %	Odds	Normal FEV %	Low FEV %	Odds
Non-manual	85	15	0.17	81	19	0.23
Manual	82	19	0.23	78	22	0.28
OR			1.31			1.20

Low cognitive skill at 7 years

Adult class	Childhood class Non-manual			Childhood class Manual		
	Normal FEV %	Low FEV %	Odds	Normal FEV %	Low FEV %	Odds
Non-manual	82	18	0.22	78	22	0.28
Manual	67	32	0.48	67	33	0.49
OR			2.18			1.75
Common (weighted) OR			1.59			

Source: Data from 1958 British Birth Cohort Study

the relationship of social class to lung function in this case, but less than that of childhood social class. And a clear class difference remains in adulthood. Smoking will play a role in explaining these results but not because of 'intelligence' to any major extent.

However, in a life course perspective, this is too simple. Although the evidence is only growing rather slowly (Evans and Kim 2010), it does look increasingly as if low 'intelligence', bad personality traits and many kinds of ill health in childhood are *themselves* a result of accumulated disadvantages of different kinds, starting from even before birth (Hair et al. 2015). Figure 10.4 shows an example of the ways in which early childhood adversities are related to test performance in both English and mathematics in 7-year-old children in the 2000 British Birth Cohort, the Millennium Cohort Study (MCS).

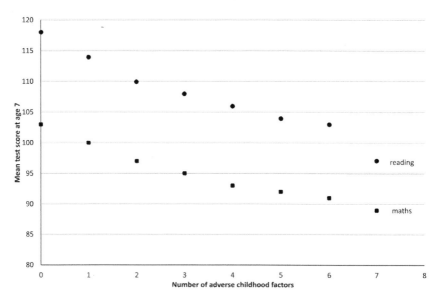

Figure 10.4   Relationship of number of early childhood adversities*
with maths and reading scores at age 7, girls and boys, Millennium
Cohort Study
*Adversities are: low birthweight; not being breastfed; maternal depression; having a lone parent; family income below 60% of the median; parental unemployment; low maternal educational qualifications; damp housing; social housing; area deprivation (lowest quintile of Index of Multiple Deprivation).

Source: Kelly 2012: 5

This is not exactly 'accumulation of risk' because the presence of one adversity (let's say maternal depression) can itself make another adversity (such as not being breastfed) more likely (Lager, Bremberg and Vågerö 2009; Najman et al. 2009; Loucks et al. 2012). Studies are beginning to take into account the fact that adversities of different kinds tend to be closely linked right across the life course. People whose parents were poor tend to grow up in worse housing, live in more polluted areas, go to less excellent schools, and pass fewer school exams. At present, there seems to be little research that looks at what happens to those children who have favourable personal characteristics (intelligence or conscientiousness, for example) but are caught up in material disadvantage as children when they go through the school system and into employment. Nor do we know a great deal about people with lower levels of intelligence, conscientiousness and so on in childhood but who are spared material adversity and go to 'better' schools.

Pathways of life-course aetiology

Perhaps the model that offers the most promise at the present time is a more sophisticated version of that which looks at pathways. Conventionally, life-course researchers talk about a pathway model when a certain hazard (or advantage) may increase (or decrease) the risk of a disease only because it increases the probability of some other aetiological factor. For example, in some studies (Heck and Pamuk 1997; Pudrovska and Anikputa 2012) women who have been highly successful in education have a higher risk of breast cancer. It is unlikely that educational study itself causes cancer, and more likely that these women's subsequent careers have resulted in later childbearing (or none at all) which has been linked to breast cancer for biological (hormonal) reasons.

But just as education cannot literally cause cancer, social position, whether measured in terms of class, status or income and wealth, cannot literally cause any disease. The typical measures of social risk, no matter how many times we measure them, are no more than markers or hints of what is going on in the relationship between the social and physical environment and the body. A typical life-course study using a simple pathway model would look, for example, at whether having parents in a less advantaged social position only resulted in higher mortality among those whose own jobs were more hazardous. In this example, work hazards are a biologically plausible risk factor, and the importance of disadvantaged childhood social class was that it tended to channel people into more dangerous jobs. An important example comes from Lynch and colleagues (Lynch et al. 1994), an American team who took income as their definition of socio-economic position and circumstances in the childhoods and adult lives of around 2,600 Finnish men. Income in adulthood was related to death from heart disease and from all other causes. Having been poor in earlier life only made a difference to those who were also poor as adults. The more affluent adults with poorer childhoods had the same risk of mortality as those who had never experienced low income. Because this early study used income as its measure of adulthood risk exposure, it has not actually pinned down the biologically plausible pathway. But low income tends to be paid to people doing dirtier, more dangerous jobs and in turn pays for less healthy housing and residential conditions.

How social conditions get under the skin over the life course

Unfortunately, most life-course epidemiology still does not focus on the need to understand the ways in which social, economic and cultural environments lead to exposures that are biologically plausible in the sense that they 'directly' set off a disease process in the same way as a virus or bacterium. There is plenty of descriptive research on smoking and diet, which are biologically plausible factors that directly affect the cells and tissues of the body. But we still do not understand why smoking and overweight are so strongly related to social position, or why this is only true in some nations. Effective policies to reduce health inequality are at the very least obliged to understand these pathways.

Recent work is beginning to take a more systematic approach to understanding this kind of complex pathway and how it works over time. Blane and colleagues have set out a simple framework made up of exposures, processes and principles (Blane et al. 2013). Exposures are categorized into structural, behavioural/cultural and interpersonal. Structural exposures are ones that result from the way in which a society is organized. Examples include the degree of income inequality which determines the amount of time a person may spend at or below the minimum income for healthy living (see chapters 6 and 7), the way industry is organized which determines how many jobs are hazardous or stressful, and the availability of good quality housing. Behavioural/cultural exposures are described as '[h]abits and behaviours which affect health and are, at least to some extent, subject to individual autonomy, choice and decision-making', though the authors recognize the importance of cultural norms, for example those around alcohol in Muslim communities and smoking in Hispanic-American people (see chapter 4). Interpersonal exposures include social integration and social support and other '[a]spects of social interaction which affect emotions and feelings' (see chapter 5). Emotional relationships may be particularly important in early life when young children are developing their ability to respond to later stresses (Evans and Kim 2007; Miller, Chen and Parker 2011).

The processes in this framework are all biological, as these are the ways in which any exposure acts upon the body to produce disease. The processes are categorized as material, central nervous system (CNS)-mediated and epigenetic. Material processes include infection by bacteria or viruses, and vitamin deficiencies in pregnant mothers resulting in diseases such as neural tube defects in the baby, as well as the cancer-causing properties of some chemical and dusts such as asbestos. CNS processes are the ones where the biological effect works through a nervous system-to-hormonal pathway. These include the biological consequences of the fight-or-flight response (see chapter 5). Epigenetic processes are relatively newly discovered and not well understood, but could fill an important gap in our understanding. The term 'epigenetic' refers to the way in which genes are 'turned on' or 'turned off' according to what is going on around them. Stress in infancy, for example, is thought to influence later mental health in part because a stressful environment affects the ways in which certain genes function. In this way, stress can have a very long-term effect by changing the way that, for example, a certain part of the nervous system is regulated (Turecki and Meaney 2014).

This framework then adds four principles. The first of these is that 'each type of social exposure can work through any or all of the biological processes'. For example, a person's occupation may determine the amount of fumes, dust or heavy lifting that they experience, as well as the amount of stress. Obesity will work through a direct effect on blood fats and sugars, and on blood pressure, but may also result in social isolation and stigma with consequent CNS-mediated effects. The second principle is that '[b]oth social exposures and biological processes can cumulate and interact'. For example, living in a poor area may result in inhaling higher levels of pollution, less incentive to take outdoor exercise and a greater acceptance of smoking. The third principle warns us not to expect exposures and processes to take the same forms or have the same effects in people of all ages and at all phases of their life course. This acknowledges the possibility of critical periods, for example early childhood. The fourth principle reminds us that exposures and processes can be positive as well as negative.

This framework offers a more organized way to analyse, for example, the body of work on developmental origins of health and disease (DOHaD). Low birthweight is more common in families with lower income and more adverse living conditions (structural exposure). Poverty is associated with higher levels of family conflict, with a risk to the development of an adequate stress response (interpersonal exposure, CNS-mediated and epigenetic processes). Children brought up in poorer families are more at risk of household crowding, damp and noise (material process). This in turn may result in more illnesses leading to missing school, and greater difficulty in studying at home, so that they are more likely to do badly in school. A young person without qualifications has a higher risk of exposure to low income, hazardous working conditions and poor housing as an adult (structural exposure, material process) and is more likely to be a smoker (behavioural exposure). Children of stressed parents are more likely to have a brain architecture that makes it harder for them to cope with adult adversities, and to form their own stable relationships as adults (interpersonal exposure, epigenetic process). This may result in a double jeopardy whereby higher levels of occupational and income-related stresses are combined with lack of social support.

Life-course and health behaviours: individual choice or circumstances?

The framework shown in Table 10.5 is not in itself a model of how health develops over the life course, only of the kinds of exposures and processes that are likely to be involved. For example, it does not relate structural or interpersonal exposures at one point in life to later health behaviours, while we know that these two are in reality closely linked. Although the authors of the framework admit that behavioural exposures are only to some extent a matter of personal choice, they do not go any further into the question of why risky behaviours are so strongly linked to social position (in some nations more than in others). As health behaviours figure so dominantly in the literature on health inequality (see Introduction and chapter 4), it is helpful to look more closely at why health-risk behaviours are, at least in many industrial nations, so closely linked to social position. Some recent literature has tackled this question in interesting ways.

Table 10.5 Framework for understanding social-to-biological transitions

	Exposures								
	Structural			Behavioural/cultural			Interpersonal		
	Material	CNS-mediated	Epigenetic	Material	CNS-mediated	Epigenetic	Material	CNS-mediated	Epigenetic
Processes									
	Principles								

Exposures may work through any biological process
Exposures and processes can cumulate or interact
May take different forms at different life-course stages
May be positive or negative

In the earlier work on life-course influences on health inequality, some researchers examined the extent to which an adverse earlier life experience might be related to riskier behaviours in adulthood. Do children with less privileged backgrounds have poorer health as adults because they smoke more, eat worse diets, binge drink and take less exercise? Van de Mheen and her colleagues found that perhaps around 14 per cent of the difference in health between men with more and less socially advantaged childhoods could be explained by health behaviours (van de Mheen et al. 1998). A Finnish study found that a major cause of higher mortality in young adults from less advantaged social backgrounds was alcohol-related disease and accidents. The daughters and (particularly) sons of manual workers were more at risk of dying from alcohol-related accidents and violence, and from alcoholic liver and pancreatic disease (Pensola and Valkonen 2000).

Another way to look at this is to ask: how far should the riskier health behaviours in people with a less advantaged life course, right back to childhood, be regarded as individual choice and how far the result of early adversity? Research into this question is not that common but is increasing as more relevant data become available (Heraclides, Witte and Brunner 2008; Kamphuis et al. 2013). Perhaps the most important of these studies is that by Giesinger and colleagues. They found that while lifetime smoking (expressed as 'pack-years') explained over half of the inequality in mortality in the 1946 British birth cohort study, half of this effect was itself due to the less socially advantaged backgrounds of the smokers. In this way, Giesinger and colleagues have turned the older question on its head: if early life social circumstances are such a powerful predictor of adult health behaviour, we need to think more carefully about what we mean by 'behavioural' explanations for health inequality (see chapter 4).

New and important advances in this kind of thinking has linked life-course ideas to ideas from philosophy about individual responsibility versus the force of circumstances. In sociology, this kind of approach would use the terms 'agency' and 'structure'. Drawing on the work of philosophers such as Barry and Roemer, a research group in France is developing an approach that combines the 'behavioural' explanation for health inequality discussed in chapter 4 with concepts of social justice. How far should we regard both social advantage and good health as the result of individual 'effort', and how far the result of 'circumstances beyond the control of the individual' (Jusot, Tubeuf and Trannoy 2012; Jusot et al. 2013)? Jusot and her colleagues do not consider personality factors such as conscientiousness or coping ability which have been mentioned in earlier research. But

I suspect that they would regard these, too, as in part outcomes of accumulated advantage and adversity over early life.

The researchers separated individual health behaviour into the proportion that was explained by disadvantages in childhood (parental poor health, unemployment or insecure employment, disadvantaged social class) and the proportion that occurred in people with no evident major childhood disadvantages. They defined the latter as appearing to be 'purely due to choice'. They included in their definition of 'circumstantial causes of poor health in adulthood' both the material measures (parents' social and economic disadvantage) and risky health behaviours in those with a disadvantaged childhood. This is very similar to what was done in the analysis by Giesinger and colleagues. Using these definitions, Jusot and her colleagues concluded that about 45 per cent of adult health inequality in a sample of the French population should be attributed to 'circumstances beyond the control of the individual' and about 6–7 per cent to freely chosen health behaviours (with the rest being accounted for by demographic factors such as sex and age; Jusot et al. 2012). When this research group studied a similar research question in the British 1958 birth cohort (Tubeuf et al. 2012), they found that childhood adversity explained around 20 per cent of inequality in adult self-rated health, while adult health behaviours explained around 32 per cent. However, when they took account of the fact that childhood social adversity predicted adult health behaviours to quite a large extent, the independent effect of chosen behaviour was reduced to 25 per cent. So, in their final analysis, the contributions of life-course disadvantage (structural exposure in Blane and colleagues' terminology) and chosen lifestyle were very similar. This difference between the two nations is consistent with the studies described in chapter 4 which showed that riskier health behaviour has a weaker relationship to adult social position in France than is the case in the United Kingdom.

The work by Giesinger and team is stronger, however, both in their outcome measure, which is mortality rather than self-rated health, and in their measurement of health behaviours. Readers may remember that a far higher estimate of the importance of health behaviours for health inequality was found in some (though not all) studies which measured behaviours several times, rather than just once (see chapter 4). Now that we have so much more life-course data, this method will no doubt become the norm. Unlike the French studies, Giesinger and colleagues used the 'pack-years' of smoking that is available in the 1946 birth cohort which multiplies the average number of cigarettes smoked daily by the number of years for which the survey member has smoked. Using this method, they found that just more than 50 per cent of the social class difference in mortality was explained. However, when they, like Tubeuf and colleagues, subtracted the proportion of smoking that was associated with life-course disadvantages, the effect was reduced by almost half, to 28 per cent (Giesinger et al. 2014).

Taking all this evidence together gives quite a consistent picture of the importance of life course socio-economic circumstances for health directly, and through the influence of circumstances over time on health-damaging behaviour. But researchers are only just beginning to develop conceptual models that are able to take in more of the complexity of life course information that combines social, psychological and biological factors. It is a very exciting prospect for the future which will take us nearer to understanding health inequality.

Further reading

This has become the standard reference text on life-course epidemiology:
Kuh, D. and ben Shlomo, Y. (2004), *A Life Course Approach to Chronic Disease Epidemiology*, 2nd edn. Oxford: Oxford University Press.

A reader-friendly short account of some recent life-course research in health:
Bartley M. (ed.) (2013), *Life Gets Under Your Skin*. London: UCL Department of Epidemiology and Public Health.

A concise history of how life-course studies in health developed:
Blane, D., Netuveli, G. and Stone, J. (2007), The development of life course epidemiology. *Revue d'Epidemiologie et de Santé Publique* 55: 31–8.

A new model for understanding how the social becomes biological:
Blane, D. (2013), Social-biological transitions: how does the social become biological. *Longitudinal and Life Course Studies* 4: 136–46.

Papers beginning to look at effects of early life on brain development:
Evans, G. W. and Kim, P. (2007), Childhood poverty and health cumulative risk exposure and stress dysregulation. *Psychological Science* 18: 953–7.
Hanson, J., Hair, N., Chandra, A., Moss, E., Bhattacharya, J., Pollack, S. D. and Wolfe, B. (2012), Brain development and poverty: a first look, in B. Wolfe, W. Evans and T. E. Seeman (eds), *The Biological Consequences of Socioeconomic Inequalities*. New York: Russell Sage, pp. 187–215.

An example of 'accumulation':
Willson, A. E., Shuey, K. M. and Elder Jr, G. H. (2007), Cumulative advantage processes as mechanisms of inequality in life course health. *American Journal of Sociology* 112: 1886–1924.

11
The Way Forward for Research and Policy Debate

One of the most important reasons why the first edition of this book carefully reviewed alternative explanations for health inequality was the need to increase the relevance of research at a time when reducing health inequality was taken seriously as a policy issue. Researchers in the 1950s and 1960s had been dismayed to find that the inception of the British National Health Service in 1947 had not been followed by a decrease in health inequality. By the 1990s, it was clear that health inequality had in fact steadily increased (see chapter 2). However, the idea that health care free at the time of use would decrease health inequality was based on a mistaken explanatory model. Not unreasonably, in the period before the Second World War, many commentators assumed that the inequalities in health between richer and poorer areas and social groups were due to the fact that medical care had to be paid for and was beyond the means of many people. It was thought that everyone was equally likely to get serious diseases and that the reason for longer life expectancy in richer areas or social groups was that these people could afford treatment.

Although the existence of health inequality had not been an explicit major reason for the setting up of a nationalized health service free at the time of use, it was a shock when it emerged during the 1950s that health inequality had continued to increase (Morris and Heady 1955). In an astonishing echo of the words of Mackenbach on discovering that health inequality is not less marked in the more egalitarian European welfare states, Morris and Heady wrote:

[although] full employment and higher real wages and expanding social services have led to a relatively greater improvement in the situation of the building and dock labourers of social class five and the miners of

class three, . . . than of clerks and professional people. . . . [giving rise
to . . .] the emerging principle of modern public health – that individual
behaviour and personal responsibility are becoming crucial to further
advance (Morris and Heady 1955: 556–7, 559)

Students of social policy will, however, be familiar with Titmuss's
ideas about who were the real beneficiaries of the post-war welfare
state in Britain (Titmuss 1958, 1968; Sinfield 1978). Titmuss coined
the terms 'occupational welfare' and 'fiscal welfare' to take account
of two facts. The first of these was that the new levels of state provision in health, education and social work had created a large number
of new white-collar jobs that greatly expanded the opportunities for
relatively secure, safe and well-paid work in clerical, administrative and semi-professional jobs. The second aspect of occupational
welfare was that there were a large number of privileges that went
along with clerical and administrative work, such as subsidized car
ownership and occupational pensions that were not available to most
manual workers, however much the pay of the latter group might
have improved. A third aspect of middle-class (white collar) privilege
that became increasingly evident was their greater ability to get the
best out of free education and health care by using their inside knowledge and articulacy.

We have seen from the trends shown in chapter 2 that inequality
in mortality between the social classes continued to increase until the
early 2000s, since when it has remained stable. It is now no longer
a matter for debate that having access to health services, important
though it is, happens too late to protect people against the health
consequences of poverty, work hazards, powerlessness or low social
status. The diseases that caused most suffering and early mortality
in the late twentieth century, and that accounted for most of the
inequality in health, were not infections or medical crises that could
be dealt with by drugs or surgery. They were chronic conditions,
such as heart disease and cancer, which have long, complex and often
hidden aetiology. The damp home experienced in childhood, or even
the poorly nourished mother-to-be during a person's gestation, could
have consequences much later on. Other long-term behavioural patterns, such as smoking and diet, are now also known to play a part
in causing the major health problems of modern populations. Health
services can do little or nothing about these kinds of risk factors. Even
worse, it is possible that a concentration of money and attention on
health services perpetuates a mistaken idea of what causes health
inequality, and thereby of how to reduce it.

It is now widely acknowledged, certainly in the United Kingdom, the Nordic nations and the Netherlands (where most research on health inequality has taken place), as well as increasingly in the United States (Adler et al. 1993), that a so-called 'upstream model' of explanation is needed. An upstream model concentrates on things that happen earlier in the development of diseases and on prevention rather than cure. Once this has been opted for, the problem is to decide which upstream model is closest to reality and will therefore prove the most effective guide to policy. The structure of this book has, accordingly, worked through several alternative (though not necessarily contradictory) explanations. The aim has been to clarify each type of explanation as far as possible, and to help the reader to decide for themselves, in any given case for any particular condition, which is the most accurate.

Do we need trials of policy options?

In chapter 3, the question of causality and the need for randomized trials were briefly discussed. To recapitulate, it is often not completely understood exactly why drug X improves the state of someone with disease Y. So in order to prove that it does, drug X is given to a randomly selected group of people, and a 'sugar pill' or placebo, with no drug in it, is given to another similar group. These trials are described as 'randomized' because those who get the real drug and those who do not are selected completely at random (by the equivalent of tossing a coin), so that any differences between the group that gets the medicine and that which does not occur by chance. This would ensure that there could not be any other factor, for example, the motivation of those who take the medicine, which might also make participants more likely to recover from the disease. The trials are also called 'control', or 'controlled', because of the inclusion of a group of people who have not been given the drug, called the 'control group', in order to compare the progress of the disease in the two groups. When the patients do not know whether they are receiving a pill that contains the drug or a placebo, trials are called 'single blind'. They are called 'double blind' when neither the patient nor the doctor knows whether the patient is receiving the treatment or the placebo.

The reason why you need a control group of people who are not getting the drug but think they are (and whose doctors think they are) is the power of the mind over the body. People can show enormous improvement in many health conditions when they think they have good reason to be getting better, even though they may be doing no more than swallowing a sugar pill. Even subtle differences in the behaviour of the doctor who administers the treatment are known to influence the way the patient feels, which is why the doctor as well as the patient must be 'blinded'. This capacity for what we think is happening to us to affect how we feel, and thereby some of the biological processes in the body (see chapter 5), is called the 'placebo effect'. The power of the placebo effect is in fact one reason to believe that psycho-social factors do form part of the explanation for health inequality. But it is also one reason why it is very difficult, if not impossible, to apply the test of the randomized double-blind trial to potential cures for health inequality.

One virtue of the trial is that it can prevent us from deluding ourselves as to the results of treatments or interventions. Take the recent arguments in the United Kingdom and the United States about whether the combined vaccine for measles, mumps and rubella (MMR vaccine) causes autism in children. If a randomized trial could be done, it would be possible to see whether the vaccinated children were more likely to become autistic than the unvaccinated ones. If the selection of those to be vaccinated and those not were truly random, there would be no confounding factors, such as the parents' education level or social class, to influence the results. If, even though they had been chosen purely on the toss of a coin, more of the vaccinated children became autistic, this would be very damning evidence against MMR. But it would be quite impossible to tell a random group of parents that their children had been put into either of the groups. Most would strongly object to being denied vaccination; others would refuse it because they already believed it to be linked to autism.

The absence of this kind of evidence causes all kinds of problems for basing policy on the kind of research we have on health inequality. There are plenty of examples of policies to improve health generally that may have accidentally increased health inequality. In the United States and increasingly in the United Kingdom and other European nations, smoking has been forbidden in more and more workplaces, so that at the present time there are few US or UK offices where it is permitted. One irony of this policy has been the increasing concentration of smoking among people with no paid employment, including mothers of young children (Marsh and McKay 1994). As smoking is more likely to be forbidden in offices, which are full of white-collar workers, than in factories or building sites, another possible effect of this policy change has been to increase the differences in smoking between the social classes (Jarvis 1997). Social inequality in smoking (and in health) is much greater in the United States and the United Kingdom than it is in countries such as Spain and Greece where anti-smoking policies are as yet less widespread. So there is a good case to be made for the assertion that if we want policies that will reduce health inequality, as well as improving health overall, they need to be specially designed for the purpose.

It is not very easy to meet the criteria needed for the popular and plausible idea that policy should be evidence based. Even when we do have evidence from randomized trials, the results often do not agree. In clinical medicine, databases such as the Cochrane Collaboration collect large numbers of studies (for example, of different types of treatment for complications during the birth of a baby) and use systematic methods to decide on the success of which methods (or drugs) is best supported by the evidence. The results of administering different drugs can be collected together and summarized by methods known as 'meta-analysis': sophisticated statistics that show up inconsistencies between trials before deciding what the overall message is for health care. In social policy this type of evidence-based approach has come to be known as a 'what works?' approach. But, as discussed above, it is usually not possible in social policy intervention studies to create a similar situation to the double- (or even single-) blind randomized control trial, because people can hardly be given more money, or better services, without being aware of the fact.

Nor is it usually possible to carry out even non-blinded trials where one group is given a service and another is not. This is because in most cases it is so obvious that the service is beneficial in some way or other (even if it may not actually benefit health in the short term) that the ethics of denying it to some people are not acceptable. A good example of this was the development in the United Kingdom by Jarman of a computerized system for estimating how much social security benefit the patients of a general medical practice were entitled to. A health worker, even one who was not an expert on welfare rights, could sit down with a patient and go through the programme, which would show up any benefits they were not claiming. This could result in the income of some patients rising considerably. How could one carry out a trial of the effects on health of such a service? Even if it had no effect at all on health, there could be no ethical justification for denying a control group of patients the use of the advice service. This would mean they might be denied benefits to which they were entitled by right.

It is for these kinds of reasons that it is very hard to gather much evidence relevant to deciding what might be effective in reducing health inequalities. There have been a few intervention studies dealing with relatively small changes in the social environment. The intervention study is similar to a clinical trial, in that one group of people, or one area, is given a 'dose' of policy (the intervention) and another is not, and results are then compared between the two. Most of these have been based on sensible ideas, which have focused on one particular cause of injury or death. For example, some local authorities in the United Kingdom have funded pubs and bars to provide plastic glasses on Friday and Saturday nights when fights often break out during which glass causes injury. Changes in this kind of hazard are relatively easy to monitor, as reductions in injuries would be expected to take place fairly quickly. Another major study is trying out 'peer-influence' groups in schools, in which some students are recruited and trained to encourage others not to smoke. Smoking levels amongst the children a year or so later are then compared to those in schools where no peer-influence project has been carried out. Because we have no idea whether peer influence will in fact reduce smoking, there is no ethical dilemma (as there would be if we had a strong suspicion that intervention really would achieve lower smoking levels).

However, in general, it is not at all easy to link suggestions for reducing health inequality to 'evidence' in the sense in which it is used in the medical literature. In the report of the Independent Inquiry into Inequality in Health, prepared by Acheson for the British government in 1998, an appendix describes how the evidence gathered was evaluated. The evaluation group included the director of the Cochrane Centre, and the editors of both the *British Medical Journal* and the *Lancet*. In the words of the report, they 'noted that there was a lack of evidence to support many of the suggested policy interventions, and recommended that the Inquiry should make explicit the quality of evidence and argument used to support proposed areas for policy development' (Acheson 1998: 156–7).

International comparative studies

International comparative studies of health inequality have been carried out as one way to produce evidence similar to that of a randomized trial. Differences between nations in social policies, economic policies and cultural variables, such as diet, provide a type of 'natural' experiment. Admittedly, there are many cultural differences between nations, which cause problems about whether answers to questions mean the same thing in different contexts. This is far from the careful design of the clinical trial. But it would be defeatist not to take advantage of what the 'natural experiment' can offer. After all, people do not choose the nation into which they are born – in this sense their social and economic policy environment is randomly allocated. There is no reason to think that there are systematic biological or psychological differences between populations in different countries that would affect the way people reacted to differences in income, working conditions, diet or smoking. This is why the international comparative studies of the team at the Erasmus University in Rotterdam are so important and have been quoted liberally in this book.

In their first study, the Erasmus team came up with some very surprising answers. It seemed that Sweden, with its generous welfare state, high taxes and relatively flat income distribution, had higher levels of health inequality than many other nations (Mackenbach et al. 1997). The nations in the south of Europe around the Mediterranean, such as Spain, France and Italy, had lower levels of health inequality than the Nordic nations (Sweden, Norway, Denmark and Finland; Kunst et al. 1998). At the time, many researchers thought this difference was due to different stages of the 'smoking epidemic', that is, smoking had not yet become associated with lower levels of social and economic advantage (Kunst 1997b). Adopting a behavioural rather than an economic model for the causes of health inequality could to some extent explain these results. Another protective factor in this explanatory model was the Mediterranean diet, which seems to provide some protection to citizens of the Mediterranean nations against social and economic inequalities. In countries where smoking was less concentrated among less privileged social groups, inequality in health between groups defined according to occupational social class also seemed to be lower. The results caused considerable shock. It had been widely thought that health inequality would be greater in countries where the differences in income between social classes, or between those at the top and bottom of the income range, were greater, rather than in nations such as Sweden where taxation and other social policies limit these differences.

Subsequent studies by this research group have continued the bad news about health inequality in different welfare regimes. Between the 1990s and 2000s, the largest increase in inequality in the risk of mortality took place in Norway (see chapter 7). In contrast, the more liberal regimes in England and Wales actually saw the risks of mortality becoming more socially equal. It is true to say that these findings need to be treated with great caution because by the time of this study the Erasmus group had decided to use educational level as their measure of social inequality, and we have seen in chapter 1 that there can be problems in this approach. However, the findings using a measure of social class based on occupation were consistent (Toch-Marquardt et al. 2014).

Implications of recent evidence for policy debate

The introductory chapter of this book has given an account of the Acheson review and subsequent documentation of the evidence on health inequality, and of the policy responses. As we have seen, these policy changes were followed by disappointing results. There have also been changes in the ways in which the official statistics of health inequality in England and Wales have been produced, which has made it more or less impossible to produce findings on trends in health inequality in which one could be really confident. There did seem to be some positive changes. Social class differences in infant mortality seemed to narrow slightly before increasing again after a new government came to power in 2010. Social class differences in mortality also appeared to have stopped increasing, although there are many differences in the methods of measurement. It could also be argued that the policy changes brought in after 1997 did not have enough time to bring about changes in health before the change of government in 2010.

This disappointment with the fruits of policy change in the United Kingdom was accompanied by the ongoing results of the Erasmus programme of international comparisons that continued to show the apparent irrelevance of the generosity of national welfare policies for health inequality. In some of his writing, Mackenbach has interpreted these findings in a pessimistic manner to argue that we should turn back to a previously largely discredited model of health inequality, one based on the selection of individuals with certain types of personal characteristics into different socio-economic positions. In this way, at least some of the current research agenda has increasingly been influenced by Talcott Parsons's structural-functional model of how inequality arises and persists in society. As discussed in chapter 1, this model proposes that it is 'functional' (beneficial) for any society that its most intelligent and socially skilled members are drawn into the most important jobs in industry, the professions and civil administration. To ensure that this happens, these jobs provide high wages, good working conditions and high status. But the good health of their incumbents is not caused by the characteristics of the jobs but by the personal characteristics that qualified them for the jobs in the first place. And in those nations that are more meritocratic, such as the Nordic nations, this process of selection is most efficient and will result in wider inequality between social groups. So no wonder more generous social policies that aim to improve the conditions of those in less advantaged socio-economic circumstances have been futile. The less able members of society were always condemned to poorer health by their riskier health behaviours.

This conclusion is a very long way from the first set of Erasmus studies. These also concluded behavioural differences between people in different socio-economic positions were the most important causes of health inequality. Nevertheless, the Dutch Programme Committee, charged with turning the research information into recommendations for policy, advised the Dutch government that the evidence indicated that community-level policies were also needed to change social differences in health behaviours. Merely to offer yet more health education, or even banning smoking in public places, would be targeted too much at the individual level, a strategy now known, they admitted, to fail. In their final report, the Dutch Programme Committee on Socio-Economic Inequalities in Health concluded that

> current knowledge of effective methods to achieve change in behaviour among lower SES groups remains sketchy. New methodologies, such as the community-based approach, have to date only been subject to minimum assessment . . . [there is a] need for . . . further development of methods, and their monitoring using scientific (effect) assessments. (Programme Committee on Socio-Economic Inequalities in Health 2001: 39)

But as several authors have pointed out, even when policy recommendations have highlighted improvements for the wider society rather than in individual behaviour, real-world policies have suffered from 'lifestyle drift'. Instead of improvements in low-cost housing, there have been yet more campaigns to change health behaviours. The only difference has been these are now targeted at poor areas (labelled 'spearhead areas' at one time in the United Kingdom). There is no reason to think that lectures on healthy behaviour will be more effective when concentrated in poor communities than when they are targeted at the whole population.

Evidence-based policy

What seems to have happened as a result of this complex interplay of research and policy debate is, on the one hand, a tendency towards the capitulation of some of the leading research teams to the politically dominant individualization of health inequality (Katikireddi et al. 2013) and, on the other hand, the disconnection of leading advocates of health equity from research. A full explanation of this trend would need a separate study in the relationship between research and policy (Smith 2013), as well as an understanding of the ways in which the academic world is changing. To give an example, one of the leading health inequality researchers of the 1990s once told me 'Look, if I get an odds ratio of 1:3 for some social factor, I will likely get the paper into a low impact epidemiology journal, but if I get something like that for a gene, I might get it into *Nature*' (a very high impact journal). Academic careers have become far more pressurized, with a great deal more emphasis on 'impact' in two senses. The first of these is 'journal impact', with papers in high-impact journals having an increasing effect on the success of individual academic careers. The second is the demand for 'public impact', which includes the amount of attention a piece of research gets in the media. In fact, in the United Kingdom at present, leading funding bodies demand that 'pathway to impact' is written into the application before any research is even carried out. The trouble is, to cut a long story short, that a series of disconnected single, media-worthy studies does not amount to a coherent body of knowledge that allows the research community to offer responses to perfectly reasonable questions posed as part of policy discussion.

In an intriguing development, some recent studies have indicated that smoking may be about to be overtaken by poor diet and obesity as the major reason for the international differences. It is quite confusing that this takes place at the same time as other studies of individuals (as opposed to whole nations) have boosted the importance of smoking as a cause of health differences between social groups within nations. We have seen that the prevalence of smoking has greatly reduced overall, at least in the United Kingdom and the United States over the past half-century, from around 50 per cent of men and 35–40 per cent of women to around 20 per cent in both genders. And we have remarked that the time trends in smoking do not exactly match trends in the most important cause of smoking-related mortality: lung cancer (see chapter 8). The Erasmus group have taken up these changes and asked 'What would happen to health inequalities if smoking were abolished?', on which Mackenbach comments: 'Smoking is not the fundamental cause of health inequalities, and if underlying inequalities in access to material and immaterial resources remain unchanged, other risk factors may replace smoking as a mediator, so that the effect on health inequalities may in the end be small' (Mackenbach 2011). In this and other examples of research, authors take rather an inconsistent position on the relative importance of material circumstances, stress and behaviour as the major factors in persisting health inequality. In the words of one leading team: 'To translate this evidence into effective public-health interventions, we need more conclusive evidence on the causal components of highly correlated socioeconomic measures and on the major mediators of inequalities.' To which they add: 'Good measurement of SES [*sic*] at individual, family, and community levels remains a major challenge' (Glymour, Clark and Patton 2014). In other words, the research that has accumulated since the Acheson report of 1998, the first edition of the book in 2004 and at the time of writing in 2015 has still not yet enabled us to answer the questions posed by those concerned with social and economic policy who wish to see health inequality reduced.

What would an adequate explanation look like?

There are several characteristics of explanations for health inequality that could serve as a very basic set of requirements for an adequate explanation:

* explanations should be biologically plausible;
* they should show a 'dose–response relationship';
* they should extend to health differences between men and women;
* they should extend to health differences between ethnic groups;
* they should be consistent with trends for whole population over time;
* they should be consistent with international differences.

Biological plausibility has been discussed in some detail in the second section of chapter 10. Nowadays, we would say that what is needed is biological plausibility over the whole of the life course so that, for example, a significant factor may be located in very early life but must be connected to later disease in a way that makes sense in terms of how the body works. For example, a low birthweight baby may have a less well-functioning pancreas, which may then result in diabetes when the larger body in adulthood puts more demands in it.

The 'dose–response relationship' is a well-known criterion for causality in epidemiology. The general idea is that the stronger the hypothetical causal factor, for instance the number of viruses or the amount of asbestos to which the individual has been exposed, the worse the illness will be or the higher the likelihood of contracting the illness. This criterion does not always operate, however, as is the case with blue asbestos and some other similar hazards where the smallest exposure is enough to cause disease. It is this dose–response pattern that gives us some confidence when we see the accumulative patterns over the life course.

The next three criteria for good explanations of health inequality are far less conventional and far less often observed in studies. In fact, it is one of the problems of research over the last 10 years or so that studies are increasingly carried out to relate isolated risk factors to each other at a single point of time or in a single age cohort (Keyes and Galea 2015). Chapter 8 on gender and health inequalities considered this question at some length. It concluded that, for example, a psychosocial model was not particularly consistent with the health differences we observe between men and women, given that women report more stress throughout life but tend to live quite a lot longer than men.

Differences in health between ethnic groups also give us a lot of problems when trying to be consistent in our explanations of health inequality. Some 'minority' ethnic groups have far better health than others, better even than the dominant group. But, on the other hand, it is this kind of puzzle that can lead us away from a racialized perspective on ethnic inequalities in health that depends on whatever the current definitions are of who belongs to an ethnic minority. Rather, it might lead us towards a very innovative set of research questions such as 'Why did members of this group arrive in a given location, what macro-political-economic forces brought them here and what has been their subsequent social history?' In some cases, we would be looking to explain poorer health, such as in Catholic people in the Netherlands and Northern Ireland, or Irish people in England; in other cases, as with the Dutch and British in South Africa or the Mughals in India, we would be trying to explain health advantage. Such an approach needs to be extended to the understanding of health differences between residents in richer and poorer areas, regardless of current definitions of 'ethnicity'.

I have used quite a few examples of time trends in earlier chapters. But these are often neglected. Many of the claims that 'disease X or Y is genetic' make this mistake, for example, by not taking into account how improbable it is that the human genome could change in 30 years enough to account for the decline of heart disease or the rise of obesity. In contrast, research setting time trends in behaviours against trends in health in different nations has begun to provide important insights (Fritzell et al. 2013; Mackenbach et al. 2014). It is worth remembering, also, that the time trends in health inequality produced by the official statistical organizations of England and Wales gave rise to the awareness of health inequality in the first place and of the way in which it increased despite the advent of the welfare state and NHS. This kind of study badly needs to be continued if we are to arrive at better explanations.

It has been international comparative studies that have produced the most important scientific puzzle for health inequality research in the past 10 years. Although the hypothesis that greater welfare generosity and de-commodification of labour power would be associated with smaller health inequalities turned out to be wrong, at least there was a theoretical basis to that idea. Considering welfare regimes forces us to think about macro-level political and economic forces. It also forces us to think about how inequality (as opposed to poverty), even if it is not enormous in material terms, affects ways that individuals feel about their own lives and the value they put on health.

Where would we want health inequality research to be in another 10 years? As someone who occasionally gets asked questions by people who are engaged in policy debate, I would like to be able to answer, with a lot more confidence, from research that is growing organically in a connected way. Because I really don't think that it is possible to point to clear policy implications from the present state of health inequality research. What is needed is a research programme adequate to the purpose of a greater understanding of social factors in health and disease in populations. From this, the policy implications will flow.

Further reading

Glymour, M. M., Clark, C. R. and Patton, K. K. (2014), Socioeconomic determinants of cardiovascular disease: recent findings and future directions. *Current Epidemiology Reports* 1(2): 89–97.

Katikireddi, S. V., Higgins, M., Smith, K. E. and Williams, G. (2013), Health inequalities: the need to move beyond bad behaviours (editorial). *Journal of Epidemiology and Community Health* 67: 715–16.

Smith, K. (2013), *Beyond Evidence-based Policy in Public Health: The Interplay of Ideas*. Basingstoke: Palgrave Macmillan.

References

Abbotts, J., Williams, R., Ford, G., Hunt, K. and West, P. (1997), Morbidity and Irish Catholic descent in Britain: an ethnic and religious minority 150 years on. *Social Science & Medicine* 45: 3–14.

Acevedo-Garcia, D., Lochner, K. A., Osypuk, T. L. and Subramanian, S. V. (2003), Future directions on residential segregation and health research: a multilevel approach. *American Journal of Public Health* 93: 215–21.

Acheson, D. (1998), *Independent Inquiry into Inequalities in Health*. London: The Stationery Office.

Adler, N. E., Boyce, W. T., Chesney, M. A., Folkman, S. and Syme, S. L. (1993), Socioeconomic inequalities in health – no easy solution. *JAMA* 269: 3140–5.

Aittomaki, A., Martikainen, P., Laaksonen, M., Lahelma, E. and Rahkonen, O. (2012), Household economic resources, labour-market advantage and health problems: A study on causal relationships using prospective register data. *Social Science & Medicine* 75: 1303–10.

Anderson, R. T., Sorlie, P., Backlund, E., Johnson, N. and Kaplan, G. A. (1997), Mortality effects of community socioeconomic status. *Epidemiology* 8: 42–7.

Annandale, E. and Hunt, K. (eds) (2000), *Gender Inequalities in Health*. Buckingham: Open University Press.

Arber, S. and Cooper, H. (1999), Gender differences in health in later life: the new paradox? *Social Science & Medicine* 48: 61–76.

Arber, S. and Lahelma, E. (1993), Inequalities in women's and men's ill health: Britain and Finland compared. *Social Science & Medicine* 37: 1055–68.

Aspinall, P. J. (2002), Collective terminology to describe the minority ethnic population. *Sociology* 36: 803–16.

Avendano, M., Glymour, M. M., Banks, J. and Mackenbach, J. P. (2009), Health disadvantage in US adults aged 50 to 74 years: a comparison of the health of rich and poor Americans with that of Europeans. *American Journal of Public Health* 99: 540–8.

Bambra, C. (2007), Going beyond *The Three Worlds of Welfare Capitalism*: regime theory and public health research. *Journal of Epidemiology & Community Health* 61: 1098–1102.

Bambra, C. (2011), Health inequalities and welfare state regimes: theoretical insights on a public health 'puzzle'. *Journal of Epidemiology & Community Health* 65: 740–5.

Bambra, C. (2012), Reducing health inequalities: new data suggest that the English strategy was partially successful (letter). *Journal of Epidemiology & Community Health* 66: 662.

Banks, J., Marmot, M., Oldfield, Z. and Smith, J. P. (2006), Disease and disadvantage in the United States and in England. *JAMA* 295: 2037–45.

Barker, D. J. P. (1992), *Fetal and Infant Origins of Adult Disease*. London: BMJ.

Barker, D. J. (1995), Fetal origins of coronary heart disease. *British Medical Journal* 311: 171–4.

Barker, D. J. P., Forsén, T., Uutela, A., Osmond, C. and Eriksson, J. G. (2001), Size at birth and resilience to effects of poor living conditions in adult life: longitudinal study. *British Medical Journal* 323: 1273–6.

Bartley, M. (1999), Measuring women's social position: the importance of theory. *Journal of Epidemiology and Community Health* 53: 601–3.

Bartley, M. (2012), Explaining health inequality: evidence from the UK. *Social Science & Medicine* 74: 658–60.

Bartley, M., Blane, D. and Montgomery, S. (1997), Health and the life course: why safety nets matter. *British Medical Journal* 314: 1194–6.

Bartley, M. and Plewis, I. (2002), Accumulated labour market disadvantage and limiting long-term illness: data from the 1971–1991 Office for National Statistics' Longitudinal Study. *International Journal of Epidemiology* 31: 336–41.

Bartley, M., Power, C., Blane, D., Smith, G. D. and Shipley, M. (1994), Birth weight and later socioeconomic disadvantage: evidence from the 1958 British cohort study. *British Medical Journal* 309: 1475–8.

Bartley, M., Sacker, A., Firth, D. and Fitzpatrick, R. (1999), Understanding social variation in cardiovascular risk factors in women and men: the advantage of theoretically based measures. *Social Science & Medicine* 49: 831–45.

Batty, G. D., Deary, I. J., Schoon, I. and Gale, C. R. (2007a), Mental ability across childhood in relation to risk factors for premature mortality in adult life: the 1970 British Cohort Study. *Journal of Epidemiology & Community Health* 61: 997–1003.

Batty, G. D., Deary, I. J., Schoon, I. and Gale, C. R. (2007b), Childhood mental ability in relation to cause-specific accidents in adulthood: the 1970 British Cohort Study. *QJM* 100: 405–14.

Beauchamp, A., Peeters, A., Wolfe, R., et al. (2010), Inequalities in cardio-vascular disease mortality: the role of behavioural, physiological and social risk factors. *Journal of Epidemiology & Community Health* 64: 542–8.

Bebbington, P. E., Dunn, G., Jenkins, R., Lewis, G., Brugha, T., Farrell, M. and Meltzer, H. (1998), The influence of age and sex on the prevalence of depressive conditions: report from the National Survey of Psychiatric Morbidity. *Psychological Medicine* 28: 9–19.

Beck, U. (1992), *Risk Society*. London: Sage.

Beckfield, J. and Krieger, N. (2009), Epi + demos + cracy: linking political systems and priorities to the magnitude of health inequities: evidence, gaps, and a research agenda. *Epidemiologic Reviews* 31: 152–77.

Ben Shlomo, Y., White, I. R. and Marmot, M. (1996), Does the variation in the socioeconomic characteristics of an area affect mortality? *British Medical Journal* 312: 1013–14.

Berggvist, K., Yngwe, M. A. and Lundberg, O. (2013), Understanding the role of welfare state characteristics for health and inequalities – an analytical review. *BMC Public Health* 13: doi: 101186/1471.

Berkman, L. F. and Syme, S. L. (1979), Social networks, host resistance, and mortality: a nine-year follow-up study of Alameda County residents. *American Journal of Epidemiology* 109: 186–204.

Berry, J. W., Poortinga, Y. H., Segall, M. H. and Dasen, P. R. (1992), *Cross-Cultural Psychology*. Cambridge: Cambridge University Press.

Beteille, A. (1992), Caste in a South Indian village, in D. Gupta (ed.), *Social Stratification*, Delhi: Oxford University Press, pp. 142–62.

Bhopal, R. (2000), What is the risk of coronary heart disease in South Asians? A review of UK research. *Journal of Public Health Medicine* 22: 375–85.

Bhopal, R. and Rafnsson, S. (2012), Global inequalities in assessment of migrant and ethnic variations in health. *Public Health* 126: 241–4.

Black, D., Morris, J. N. and Townsend, P. (1982), Inequalities in health: the Black Report, in P. Townsend and N. Davidson (eds), *The Black Report and the Health Divide*. Harmondsworth: Penguin, pp. 39–233.

Black, S. E., Devereux, P. J., Lundborg, P. and Majlesi, K. (2015), *Poor Little Rich Kids? The Determinants of the Intergenerational Transmission of Wealth NBER Working Paper 21409*. Cambridge: National Bureau of Economic Research.

Blane, D. (1985), An assessement of the Black Report's explanations of health inequalities. *Sociology of Health & Illness* 7: 231–64.

Blane, D., Bartley, M. and Davey Smith, G. (1997), Disease aetiology and materialist explanations of socioeconomic mortality differentials. *European Journal of Public Health* 7: 385–91.

Blane, D., Berney, L. and Montgomery, S. (2001), Domestic labour, paid employment and women's health: analysis of life course data. *Social Science & Medicine* 52: 959–65.

Blane, D., Kelly-Irving, M., d'Errico, A., Bartley, M. and Montgomery, S.

(2013), Social-biological transitions: how does the social become biological? *Longitudinal & Life Course Studies* 4: 136–46.

Blane, D., Mitchell, R. and Bartley, M. (2000), The 'inverse housing law' and respiratory health. *Journal of Epidemiology & Community Health* 54: 745–9.

Blane, D., Smith, G. D. and Bartley, M. (1993), Social selection – what does it contribute to social-class differences in health? *Sociology of Health & Illness* 15: 2–15.

Blaxter, M. (1990), *Health and Lifestyles*. London: Tavistock.

Boardman H. M. P., Hartley L., Eisinga, A., et al. (2015). Hormone therapy for preventing cardiovascular disease in post-menopausal women Cochrane Database of Systematic Reviews 3. Art. No.: CD002229. DOI: 10.1002/14651858.CD002229.pub4.

Bond, R. and Saunders, P. (1999), Routes to success: influences on occupational attainment of young British males. *British Journal of Sociology* 50: 217–49.

Bosma, H., Marmot, M. G., Hemingway, H., Nicholson, A. C., Brunner, E. and Stansfeld, S. (1997), Low job control and risk of coronary heart disease in Whitehall II (prospective cohort) study. *British Medical Journal* 314: 555–65.

Bosma, H., Peter, R., Siegrist, J. and Marmot, M. (1998), Two alternative job stress models and the risk of coronary heart disease. *American Journal of Public Health* 88: 68–74.

Bosma, H., van de Mheen, H. D. and Mackenbach, J. P. (1999), Social class in childhood and general health in adulthood: questionnaire study of contribution of psychological attributes. *British Medical Journal* 318: 18–22.

Bourdieu, P. (1984a), *Distinction*. London: Routledge.

Bourdieu, P. (1984b), L'Origine et l'évolution des espèces de mélomanes, in P. Bourdieu (ed.), *Questions de Sociologie*. Paris: Editions de Minuit, pp. 155–60.

Bourdieu, P. (1984c), Comment peut-on être sportif? In P. Bourdieu (ed), *Questions de Sociologie*. Paris: Editions de Minuit, pp. 173–95.

Brennenstuhl, S., Quesnel-Vallée, A. and McDonough, P. (2012), Welfare regimes, population health and health inequalities: a research synthesis. *Journal of Epidemiology & Community Health* 66: 397–409.

Brown, G. W. and Harris, T. (1976), *Social Origins of Depression*. London: Tavistock.

Brulle, R. J. and Pellow, D. N. (2006), Environmental justice: human health and environmental inequalities. *Annual Review of Public Health* 27: 103–24.

Brunner, E. (1997), Socioeconomic determinants of health – stress and the biology of inequality. *British Medical Journal* 314: 1472–6.

Brunner, E. (2000), Toward a new social biology, in L. F. Berkman and I. Kawachi (eds), *Social Epidemiology*. Oxford: Oxford University Press, pp. 306–31.

Brunner, E. J., Marmot, M. G., White, I. R., et al. (1993), Gender and employment grade differences in blood cholesterol, apolipoproteins and haemostatic factors in the Whitehall II study. *Atherosclerosis* 102: 195–207.

Buck, D. (2014) Tackling health inequalities: we need a national conversation. Kings Fund blog 25 February. http://www.kingsfund.org.uk/blog/2014/02/tackling-health-inequalities-we-need-national-conversation

Bunton, R. and Burrows, R. (1995), Consumption and health in the 'epidemiological' clinic of late modern medicine, in R. Bunton, S. Nettleton and R. Burrows (eds), *The Sociology of Health Promotion*. London: Routledge, pp. 206–22.

Burgard, S. A. and Lin, K. Y. (2013), Bad jobs, bad health? How work and working conditions contribute to health disparities *American Behavioral Scientist* 57: 1105–27.

Burstrom, B. and Whitehead, M. (2000), Inequality in the social consequences of illness: how well do people with long-term illness fare in the British and Swedish labour markets? *International Journal of Health Services* 30: 435–51.

Cable, N., Bartley, M., Chandola, T. and Sacker, A. (2013), Friends are equally important to men and women, but family matters more for men's well-being. *Journal of Epidemiology & Community Health* 67: 166–71.

Cable, T. A., Meland, E., Soberg, T. and Slagsvold, S. (1999), Lessons from the Oslo Study Diet and Anti-Smoking Trial: a qualitative study of long-term behaviour change. *Scandinavian Journal of Public Health* 27: 206–12.

Cameron, D. and Jones, I. G. (1985), An epidemiological and sociological analysis of the use of alcohol, tobacco and other drugs of solace. *Community Medicine* 7: 18–29.

Carroll, D., Smith, G. D., Sheffield, D., Shipley, M. J. and Marmot, M. G. (1997), The relationship between socioeconomic status, hostility, and blood pressure reactions to mental stress in men: Data from the Whitehall II study. *Health Psychology* 16: 131–6.

Case, A. and Paxson, C. (2010), Causes and consequences of early life health. *Demography* 47 (Suppl.): S65–S85.

Case, A. and Paxson, C. (2011), The long reach of childhood health and circumstance: evidence from the Whitehall II study. *The Economic Journal* 121: F183–F204.

Case, A., Fertig, A. and Paxson, C. (2005), The lasting impact of childhood health and circumstances. *Journal of Health Economics* 24: 365–89.

Caspi, A., Wright, B. R. E., Moffitt, T. E. and Silva, P. A. (1998), Early failure in the labor market: childhood and adolescent predictors of unemployment in the transition to adulthood. *American Sociological Review* 63: 424–51.

Cavalli-Sforza, L. L., Menozzi, P. and Piazza, A. (1994), *The History and Geography of Human Genes*. New Jersey: Princeton University Press.

Centers for Disease Control and Prevention, National Center for Health Statistics (2012), *Health, United States, 2011*. Atlanta: US Department of Health and Human Services.

Chabris, C. S., Lee, J. L., Cesarin, D. and Laibson, D. I. (2015), The Fourth Law of Behaviour Genetics. *Current Directions in Psychological Science* 24(4): 304–12.

Chan, T. W. and Goldthorpe, J. H. (2004), Is there a status order in contemporary British society? Evidence from the occupational structure of friendship. *European Sociological Review* 20: 383–401.

Chan, T. W. and Goldthorpe, J. H. (2007), Class and status: the conceptual distinction and its empirical relevance. *American Sociological Review* 72: 512–32.

Chandola, T. (1998), Social inequality in coronary heart disease: a comparison of occupational classifications. *Social Science & Medicine* 47: 525–33.

Chandola, T. (2001), Ethnic and class differences in health in relation to British South Asians: using the new National Statistics Socio-Economic Classification. *Social Science & Medicine* 52: 1285–96.

Chandola, T., Brunner, E. and Marmot, M. (2006), Chronic stress at work and the metabolic syndrome: prospective study. *British Medical Journal* 332: 521–5.

Chapman, B. P., Fiscella, K., Kawachi, I. and Duberstein, P. R. (2010), Personality, socioeconomic status, and all-cause mortality in the United States. *American Journal of Epidemiology* 171: 83–92.

Chapman, B. P., Roberts, B. and Duberstein, P. (2011), Personality and longevity: knowns, unknowns, and implications for public health and personalized medicine. *Journal of Aging Research* 759170. Epub 201, doi: 104061/2011

Chen, E., Martin, A. D. and Matthews, K. A. (2007), Trajectories of socioeconomic status across children's lifetime predict health (epub). *Pediatrics* 120: e297–e303.

Chen, J. T., Beckfield, J., Waterman, P. D. and Krieger, N. (2013), Can changes in the distributions of and associations between education and income bias temporal comparisons of health disparities? An exploration with causal graphs and simulations. *American Journal of Epidemiology* 177: 870–81.

Choi, B., Dobson, M., Landsbergis, P. A., et al. (2013), Re: 'need for more individual-level meta-analyses in social epidemiology: example of job strain and coronary heart disease'. *American Journal of Epidemiology* 178: 1007–8.

Claussen, B., Davey Smith, G. and Thelle, D. (2003), Impact of childhood and adulthood socioeconomic position on cause specific mortality: the Oslo Mortality Study. *Journal of Epidemiology & Community Health* 57: 40–5.

Coburn, D. (2000), Income inequality, social cohesion and the health status of populations: the role of neo-liberalism. *Social Science & Medicine* 51: 135–46.

Cochrane, A .L. and Moore, F. (1981), Death certification from the epidemiological point of view. *Lancet* 318: 742–3.

Colgrove, J. (2002), The McKeown thesis: a historical controversy and its enduring influence. *American Journal of Public Health* 92: 725–9.

Conley, D., Domingue, B. W., Cesarini, D., Dawes, C., Rietveld, C. A. and Boardman, J. D. (2015), Is the effect of parental education on offspring biased or moderated by genotype? *Sociological Science* 2: 82–105.

Cooper, R. (1984), A note on the biological concept of race and its application in epidemiological research. *American Heart Journal* 108: 715–23.

Cooper, R. (1986), Race, disease and health, in T. Rathwell and D. Phillips (eds), *Health Race and Ethnicity*. London: Croom Helm, pp. 21–79.

Coxon, A. P. M. and Fisher, K. (2002), Criterion validity and occupational classification: the seven economic relations and the NS-SEC, in D. Rose and D. J. Pevalin (eds), *A Researcher's Guide to the National Statistics Socio-Economic Classification*. London: Sage, pp. 107–30.

Crowder, K. and Downey, L. (2010), Inter-neighborhood migration, race, and environmental hazards: modeling micro-level processes of environmental inequality. *American Journal of Sociology* 115: 1110.

Cruickshank, J. and Beevers, D. (1989), *Ethnic Factors in Health and Disease*. Sevenoaks: Wright.

Crump, C., Sundquist, K., Sundquist, J. and Winkleby, M. A. (2011), Gestational age at birth and mortality in young adulthood. *JAMA* 306: 1233–40.

Davey Smith, G. Bartley, M. and Blane, D. (1990), The Black Report on socioeconomic inequalities in health 10 years on. *British Medical Journal* 301: 373–7.

Davey Smith, G., Ben-Shlomo, Y. and Lynch, J. (2002), Life course approaches to inequalities in coronary heart disease risk, in S. Stansfeld and M. Marmot (eds), *Stress and the Heart*. London: BMJ Books, pp. 20–49.

Davey Smith, G., Blane, D. and Bartley, M. (1994), Explanations for socioeconomic differentials in mortality: evidence from Britain and elsewhere. *European Journal of Public Health* 4: 131–44.

Davey Smith, G., Hart, C., Blane, D., Gillis, C. and Hawthorne, V. (1997), Lifetime socioeconomic position and mortality: prospective observational study. *British Medical Journal* 314: 547

Davey Smith, G., Hart, C., Blane, D. and Hole, D. (1998a), Adverse socioeconomic conditions in childhood and cause specific adult mortality: prospective observational study. *British Medical Journal* 316: 1631–5.

Davey Smith, G., Neaton, J. D., Wentworth, D., Stamler, R. and Stamler, J. (1998b), Mortality differences between black and white men in the USA: contribution of income and other risk factors among men screened for the MRFIT. MRFIT Research Group. Multiple Risk Factor Intervention Trial. *Lancet* 351: 934–9.

De Maio, F. (2012), Advancing the income inequality–health hypothesis. *Critical Public Health* 22: 39–46.

Department for Business Innovation and Skills (2014), *Participation Rates in Higher Education Academic Years 2006/7 to 2012/13 (provisional)*. 28 August. London: Department for BIS.

Department of Health (2002), *Tackling Health Inequalities – 2002 Cross-Cutting Review*. London: Department of Health.

Department of Health (2009), *Tackling Health Inequalities: 10 Years On*. London: Department of Health.

Department of Health and Social Security (1980), *Inequalities in Health: Report of a Working Group (The Black Report)*. London: DHSS.

Diderichsen, F. (2002), Impact of income maintenance policies, in J. Mackenbach and M. Bakker (eds), *Reducing Inequalities in Health: A European Perspective*. London: Routledge, pp. 53–66.

Doll, R. and Peto, R. (1981), The causes of cancer: appendix E. *Journal of the National Cancer Institute* 66: 1291–1305.

Dollamore, G. (1999), Examining adult and infant mortality rates using the NS-SEC. *Health Statistics Quarterly* 2: 33–40.

Doniach, I., Swettenham, K. V. and Hathorn, M. K. S. (1975), Prevalence of asbestos bodies in a necropsy series in East London: association with disease, occupation, and domiciliary address. *British Journal of Industrial Medicine* 32: 16–30.

Dowd, J. B. and Goldman, N. (2006), Do biomarkers of stress mediate the relation between socioeconomic status and health? *Journal of Epidemiology & Community Health* 60: 633–9.

Dowd, J. B., Haan, M. N., Blythe, L., Moore, K. and Aiello, A. E. (2008), Socioeconomic gradients in immune response to latent infection. *American Journal of Epidemiology* 167: 112–20.

Dressler, W. W., Oths, K. S. and Gravlee, C. C. (2005), Race and ethnicity in public health research: models to explain health disparities. *Annual Review of Anthropology* 34: 231–52.

Drever, F., Bunting, J. and Harding, D. (1997), Male mortality from major causes of death, in F. Drever and M. Whitehead (eds), *Health Inequality*. London: HMSO, pp. 122–42.

Duncan, G. J., Daly, M. C., McDonough, P. and Williams, D. R. (2002), Optimal indicators of socioeconomic status for health research. *American Journal of Public Health* 92: 1151–7.

Duncan, O. D. (1961), A socioeconomic status for all occupations, in A. J. Reiss Jr (ed.), *Occupations and Social Status*. New York: Free Press, pp. 109–38.

Dunn, J. R. (2010), Health behavior vs the stress of low socioeconomic status and health outcomes. *JAMA* 303: 1199–1200.

Dyson, S. M. (1998), 'Race', ethnicity and haemoglobin disorders. *Social Science & Medicine* 47: 121–31.

Edwards, R., Gillies, V. and Horsley, N. (2014) Policy briefing: the biologisation of poverty. Policy and practice in early years intervention. *Discover Society* 4 (January 14). http://discoversociety.org/2014/01/06/

policy-briefing-the-biologisation-of-poverty-policy-and-practice-in-early-years-intervention/.

Egerton, M. and Halsey, A. H. (1993), Trends by social class and gender in access to higher education in Britain [1]. *Oxford Review of Education* 19: 183–96.

Elder, G. H. and Rockwell, R. C. (1979), The life-course and human development: an ecological perspective. *International Journal of Behavioral Development* 2: 1–21.

Elo, I. T. (2009), Social class differentials in health and mortality: patterns and explanations in comparative perspective. *Annual Review of Sociology* 35: 553–72.

Elstad, J. I. (1998), The psycho-social perspective on inequalities in health, in M. Bartley, D. Blane and G. Davey Smith (eds), *The Sociology of Health Inequalities*. Oxford: Blackwell, pp. 39–58.

Elstad, J. I. (2010), Indirect health-related selection or social causation? Interpreting the educational differences in adolescent health behaviours. *Social Theory & Health* 8: 134–50.

Emslie, C. (2014), Gender and life expectancy, in W. Cockerham et al. (eds), *The Wiley Blackwell Encyclopedia of Health, Illness, Behavior, and Society*. London: John Wiley & Sons, pp. 617–920.

Emslie, C., Hunt, K. and Macintyre, S. (1999), Problematizing gender, work and health: the relationship between gender, occupational grade, working conditions and minor morbidity in full-time bank employees. *Social Science & Medicine* 48: 33–48.

Eng, H. and Mercer, J. B. (1998), Seasonal variations in mortality caused by cardiovascular diseases in Norway and Ireland. *Journal of Cardiovascular Risk* 5: 89–95.

Eng, H. and Mercer, J. B. (2000), The relationship between mortality caused by cardiovascular disease and two climatic factors in densely populated areas in Norway and Ireland. *Journal of Cardiovascular Risk* 7: 369–75.

Erikson, R. and Goldthorpe, J. H. (1992), *The Constant Flux*. Oxford: Clarendon Press.

Eriksson, J. G., Forsén, T., Tuomilehto, J., Osmond, C. and Barker, D. J. P. (2001), Early growth and coronary heart disease in later life: longitudinal study. *British Medical Journal* 322: 949–53.

Esping-Andersen, G. (1990), *The Three Worlds of Welfare Capitalism*. London: Polity Press.

Evandrou, M. and Falkingham, J. (2002), Smoking behaviour and socio-economic status: a cohort analysis, 1974 to 1998. *Health Statistics Quarterly* (Summer): 30–8.

Evans, G. (1992), Testing the validity of the Goldthorpe class schema. *European Sociological Review* 8: 211–32.

Evans, G. W. and Kantrowitz, E. (2002), Socioeconomic status and health: the potential role of environmental risk exposure. *Annual Review of Public Health* 23: 303–31.

Evans, G. W. and Kim, P. (2007), Childhood poverty and health: cumulative risk exposure and stress dysregulation. *Psychological Science* 18: 953–7.

Evans, G. W. and Kim, P. (2010), Multiple risk exposure as a potential explanatory mechanism for the socioeconomic status–health gradient. *Annals of the New York Academy of Sciences* 1186: 174–89.

Evans, G. and Marcynyszyn, L. A. (2004), Environmental justice, cumulative environmental risk, and health among low- and middle-income children in upstate New York. *American Journal of Public Health* 94: 1942–4.

Fassin, D. (2000), Qualifier les inégalités, in A. Leclerc, D. Fassin, H. Grandjean, M. Kaminski and T. Lang (eds), *Les Inégalités Sociales de Santé*. Paris: INSERM/La Decouverte, pp. 124–44.

Featherman, D. L. and Hauser, R. M. (1976), Prestige or socioeconomic scales in the study of occupational achievement? *Sociological Methods & Research* 4: 403–22.

Federico, B., Mackenbach, J. P., Eikemo, T. A., et al. (2013), Educational inequalities in mortality in northern, mid and southern Italy and the contribution of smoking. *Journal of Epidemiology & Community Health* 67: 603–9.

Felice's Log (2014), Social class and the Bennet family in *Pride and Prejudice*, http://felicelog.blogspot.co.uk/2010/09/social-class-and-bennet-family-in-pride.html.

Ferrie, J. E., Shipley, M. J., Marmot, M. G., Stansfeld, S. and Smith, G .D. (1995), Health effects of anticipation of job change and non-employment: longitudinal data from the Whitehall II study. *British Medical Journal* 311: 1264–9.

Fibrinogen Studies Collaboration (2005), Plasma fibrinogen level and the risk of major cardiovascular diseases and nonvascular mortality: an individual participant meta-analysis. *JAMA* 294: 1799–1809.

Foverskov, E. and Holm, A. (2016), Socioeconomic inequality in health in the British household panel: tests of the social causation, health selection and the indirect selection hypothesis using dynamic fixed effects panel models. *Social Science & Medicine* 150: 172–83.

Fox, A. J. and Goldblatt, P. O. (1982), *Longitudinal Study: Socio-Demographic Mortality Differentials*. London: HMSO.

Fox, A. J., Goldblatt, P. O. and Adelstein, A. M. (1982), Selection and mortality differentials. *Journal of Epidemiology & Community Health* 36: 69–79.

Fox, A. J., Goldblatt, P. O. and Jones, D. R. (1985), Social-class mortality differentials – artifact, selection or life circumstances. *Journal of Epidemiology & Community Health* 39: 1–8.

Friedman, M., Rosenman, R. H., Carroll, V. and Tat, R. J. (1958), Changes in the serum cholesterol and blood clotting time in men subjected to cyclic variation of occupational stress. *Circulation* 17: 852–61.

Fritzell, J., Kangas, O., Bacchus Hertzman, J., Blomgren, J. and Hiilamo, H. (2013), Cross-temporal and cross-national poverty and mortality rates among developed countries. *Journal of Environmental & Public Health* 2013, 15 pp.

Fronstin, P., Greenberg, D. H. and Robins, P. K. (2005), The labor market consequences of childhood maladjustment. *Social Science Quarterly* 86: 1170–95.

Fuhrer, R., Stansfeld, S. A., Chemali, J. and Shipley, M. J. (1999), Gender, social relations and mental health: prospective findings from an occupational cohort (Whitehall II study). *Social Science & Medicine* 48: 77–87.

Fukuda, Y. and Hiyoshi, A. (2013), Associations of household expenditure and marital status with cardiovascular risk factors in Japanese adults: analysis of nationally representative surveys. *Journal of Epidemiology* 23: 21–7.

Galea, S., Tracy, M., Hoggatt, K. J., DiMaggio, C. and Karpati, A. (2011), Estimated deaths attributable to social factors in the United States. *American Journal of Public Health* 101: 1456–65.

Gallacher, J. (2008), Commentary: personality and health inequality: inconclusive evidence for an indirect hypothesis. *International Journal of Epidemiology* 37: 602–3.

Gallo, V., Mackenbach, J. P., Ezzati, M., et al. (2012), Social inequalities and mortality in Europe: results from a large multi-national cohort. *PloS One* 7: e39013.

Galobardes, B., Lynch, J. W. and Davey Smith, G. (2004), Childhood socioeconomic circumstances and cause-specific mortality in adulthood: systematic review and interpretation. *Epidemiologic Reviews* 26: 7–21.

Galobardes, B., Lynch, J. W. and Davey Smith, G. (2008), Is the association between childhood socioeconomic circumstances and cause-specific mortality established? Update of a systematic review. *Journal of Epidemiology & Community Health* 62: 387–90.

Gan, Y., Gong, Y., Tong, X., et al. (2014), Depression and the risk of coronary heart disease: a meta-analysis of prospective cohort studies. *BMC Psychiatry* 14(371).

Gardner, M. J., Winter, P. D. and Acheson, E. D. (1982), Variations in cancer mortality among local authority areas in England and Wales: relations with environmental factors and search for causes. *British Medical Journal* 284: 784–7.

Geyer, S., Hemström, Ö., Peter, R. and Vågerö, D. (2006), Education, income, and occupational class cannot be used interchangeably in social epidemiology: empirical evidence against a common practice. *Journal of Epidemiology & Community Health* 60: 804–10.

Giddens, A. (1991), *Modernity and Self-Identity*. Cambridge: Polity Press.

Giesinger, I., Goldblatt, P., Howden-Chapman, P., Marmot, M., Kuh, D. and Brunner, E. (2014), Association of socioeconomic position with smoking and mortality: the contribution of early life circumstances in the 1946 birth cohort. *Journal of Epidemiology & Community Health* 68: 275–9.

Gluckman, P. D., Hanson, M. A., Cooper, C. and Thornburg, K. L. (2008), Effect of in utero and early-life conditions on adult health and disease. *New England Journal of Medicine* 359: 61–73.

Glymour, M. M., Clark, C. R. and Patton, K. K. (2014), Socioeconomic determinants of cardiovascular disease: recent findings and future directions. *Current Epidemiology Reports* 1: 89–97.

Goldberg, D. S. (2012), Social justice, health inequalities and methodological individualism in US health promotion. *Public Health Ethics* 5: 104–15.

Goldblatt, P. (1990), Mortality and alternative social classifications, in P. Goldblatt (ed.), *Longitudinal Study: Mortality and Social Organisation*. London: HMSO, pp. 163–92.

Goldthorpe, J. H., Llewellyn, C. and Payne, C. (1980), *Social Mobility and Class Structure in Modern Britain*. Oxford: Clarendon Press.

Gorey, K. M. and Vena, J. E. (1995), The association of near poverty status with cancer incidence among black-and-white adults. *Journal of Community Health* 20: 359–66.

Gottfredson, L. S. (2004), Intelligence: is it the epidemiologists' elusive 'fundamental cause' of social class inequalities in health? *Journal of Personality & Social Psychology* 86: 174–99.

Graham, H. (1998), Promoting health against inequality. *Health Education Journal* 57: 292–302.

Graham, H., Francis, B., Inskip, H. M. and Harman, J. (2006), Socioeconomic lifecourse influences on women's smoking status in early adulthood. *British Medical Journal* 60: 228–33.

Gravlee, C. C. (2009), How race becomes biology: embodiment of social inequality. *American Journal of Physical Anthropology* 139: 47–57.

Greenwood, D. C., Muir, K. R., Packham, C. J. and Madeley, R. J. (1996), Coronary heart disease: a review of the role of psychosocial stress and social support. *Journal of Public Health Medicine* 18: 221–31.

Grundy, E. (2005), Commentary: the McKeown debate: time for burial. *International Journal of Epidemiology* 34: 529–33.

Gunnbjörnsdóttir, M. I., Franklin, K. A., Norbäck, D., et al. (2006), Prevalence and incidence of respiratory symptoms in relation to indoor dampness: the RHINE study. *Thorax* 61: 221–5.

Hair, N. L., Hanson, J. L., Wolfe, B. L. and Pollak, S. D. (2015), Association of child poverty, brain development, and academic achievement. *JAMA Pediatrics* 169: 822–9.

Halfon, N. and Hochstein, M. (2002), Life course health development: an integrated framework for developing health, policy, and research. *Milbank Quarterly* 80: 433–79.

Hallqvist, J., Lynch, J., Bartley, M., Lang, T. and Blane, D. (2004), Can we disentangle life course processes of accumulation, critical period and social mobility? An analysis of disadvantaged socio-economic positions and myocardial infarction in the Stockholm Heart Epidemiology Program. *Social Science & Medicine* 58: 1555–62.

Hammond, E. C., Selikoff, I. J. and Seidmann, H. (1979), Asbestos exposure, cigarette smoking and death rates. *Annals of the New York Academy of Sciences* 330: 473–90.

Harding, S. and Balarajan, R. (1996), Patterns of mortality in second-generation Irish living in England and Wales: longitudinal study [see comments]. *British Medical Journal* 312: 1389–92.

Harding, S., Rosato, M. and Teyhan, A. (2008), Trends for coronary heart disease and stroke mortality among migrants in England and Wales, 1979–2003: slow declines notable for some groups. *Heart* 94: 463–70.

Hart, C. L., Davey Smith, G. and Blane, D. (1998), Inequalities in mortality by social class measured at three stages of the life course. *American Journal of Public Health* 88: 471–4.

Health and Safety Executive (2014), *Statistics on Fatal Injuries in the Workplace in Great Britain 2014*. www.hse.gov.uk. London: Health and Safety Executive.

Heck, K. E. and Pamuk, E. R. (1997), Explaining the relation between education and postmenopausal breast cancer. *American Journal of Epidemiology* 145: 366–72.

Hemingway, H. and Marmot, M. (1999), Psychosocial factors in the aetiology and prognosis of coronary heart disease: systematic review of prospective cohort studies. *British Medical Journal* 318: 1460–7.

Heraclides, A., Witte, D. and Brunner, E. J. (2008), The association between father's social class and adult obesity is not explained by educational attainment and an unhealthy lifestyle in adulthood. *European Journal of Epidemiology* 23: 573–9.

Hertzman, C., Power, C., Matthews, S. and Manor, O. (2001), Using an interactive framework of society and lifecourse to explain self-rated health in early adulthood. *Social Science & Medicine* 53: 1575–85.

HMSO (1904), *Report of the Inter-Departmental Committee on Physical Deterioration*. London: HMSO.

Hollingshead, A.B. (1971), Commentary on 'the indiscriminate state of social class measurement'. *Social Forces: A Scientific Medium of Social Study & Interpretation* 49: 563–7.

Holt-Lunstad, J., Smith, T. B. and Layton, J. B. (2010), Social relationships and mortality risk: a meta-analytic review. *PLoS Medicine* 7: e1000316.

Holtzman, N. A. (2002), Genetics and social class. *Journal of Epidemiology & Community Health* 56: 529–35.

Howard, J. A. (2000), Social psychology of identities. *Annual Review of Sociology* 26: 367–93.

Howden-Chapman, P. (2010), Evidence-based politics: how successful have government reviews been as policy instruments to reduce health inequalities in England? *Social Science & Medicine* 71: 1240–3.

Huijts, T. and Eikemo, T. (2009), Causality, social selectivity or artefacts? Why socioeconomic inequalities in health are not smallest in the Nordic countries. *European Journal of Public Health* 19: 452–3.

Hunt, K. and Macintyre, S. (2000), Gendre et inégalités de santé, in A. Leclerc, D. Fassin, H. Grandjean, M. Kaminsky and T. Lang (eds), *Les Inégalités Sociales de Santé*. Paris: INSERM/La Decouverte, pp. 264–75.

Investigators, Writing Group for the Women's Health Initiative (2002), Risks and benefits of estrogen plus progestin in healthy postmenopausal women: principal results from the Women's Health Initiative randomized controlled trial. *JAMA* 288: 321–33.

Ioannidis, J. P. A. (2005), Why most published research findings are false. *PLoS Medicine* 2: e124.

Jarvis, M. (1997), Patterns and predictors of smoking cessation in the general population, in C. Bolliger and K. Fagerstrom (eds), *Progress in Respiratory Research: The Tobacco Epidemic*. Basel: S. Karger.

Jenkins, R. (1985a), Minor psychiatric morbidity in employed young men and women and its contribution to sickness absence. *British Journal of Industrial Medicine* 42: 147–54.

Jenkins, R. (1985b), Sex differences in minor psychiatric morbidity: a survey of a homogeneous population. *Social Science & Medicine* (Suppl.) 20: 887–9.

Jenkins, R. and Clare, A. W. (1985), Women and mental illness. *British Medical Journal* 291: 1521–2.

Johansson, L., Thelle, D. S., Solvoll, K., Bjorneboe, G. E. A. and Drevon, C. A. (1999), Healthy dietary habits in relation to social determinants and lifestyle factors. *British Journal of Nutrition* 81: 211–20.

Johnson, J. V., Stewart, W., Hall, E. M., Fredlund, P. and Theorell, T. (1996), Long-term psychosocial work-environment and cardiovascular mortality among Swedish men. *American Journal of Public Health* 86: 324–31.

Jones, C. P. (2001), Invited commentary: 'race', racism and the practice of epidemiology. *American Journal of Epidemiology* 154: 299–304.

Jones, J. (1981), How different are human races? *Nature* 293: 188–90.

Jönsson, D., Rosengren, A., Dotevall, A., Lappas, G. and Wilhelmsen, L. (1999), Job control, job demands and social support at work in relation to cardiovascular risk factors in MONICA 1995, Göteborg. *European Journal of Cardiovascular Risk* 6: 379–85.

Jusot, F., Tubeuf, S. and Trannoy, A. (2012), Differences in health status in France: unequal opportunities or a reflection of risky behaviours? *Economie & Statistique* 455–6.

Jusot, F., Tubeuf, S. and Trannoy, A. (2013), Circumstances and efforts: how important is their correlation for the measurement of inequality of opportunity in health? *Health Economics* 22: 1470–95.

Kamphuis, C. B. M., Turrell, G., Giskes, K., Mackenbach, J. P. and van Lenthe, F. J. (2013), Life course socioeconomic conditions, adulthood risk factors and cardiovascular mortality among men and women: a 17-year follow up of the GLOBE study. *International Journal of Cardiology* 168: 2207–13.

Kaplan, G. A., Pamuk, E. R., Lynch, J. W., Cohen, R. D. and Balfour, J. L. (1996), Inequality in income and mortality in the United States: analysis of mortality and potential pathways. *British Medical Journal* 312: 999–1003.

Karasek, R. (1996), Job strain and the prevalence and outcome of coronary-artery disease. *Circulation* 94: 1140–1.

Karasek, R., Baker, D., Marxer, F., Ahlbom, A. and Theorell, T. (1981), Job decision latitude, job demands, and cardiovascular-disease – a prospective study of Swedish men. *American Journal of Public Health* 71: 694–705.

Katikireddi, S. V., Higgins, M., Smith, K. E. and Williams, G. (2013), Health inequalities: the need to move beyond bad behaviours (editorial). *Journal of Epidemiology & Community Health* 67: 715–16.

Kaufman, J. S. (2014), Race: ritual, regression and reality. *Epidemiology* 25: 485–7.

Kaufman, J. S., Dolman, L., Rushani, D. and Cooper, R. S. (2015), The contribution of genomic research to explaining racial disparities in cardiovascular disease: a systematic review. *American Journal of Epidemiology* 181: 464–72.

Kawachi, I. and Kennedy, B. P. (1997), Socioeconomic determinants of health, 2. Health and social cohesion: Why care about income inequality? *British Medical Journal* 314: 1037–40.

Kawachi, I., Kennedy, B. P., Lochner, K. and Prothrow-Stith, D. (1997), Social capital, income inequality, and mortality. *American Journal of Public Health* 87: 1491–8.

Kelly, Y. (2012), A good start in life, in M. Bartley (ed.), *Life Gets Under Your Skin*. London: UCL Research Department of Epidemiology and Public Health.

Kelly, Y., Kelly, J. and Sacker, A. (2013a), Time for bed: associations with cognitive performance in 7-year-old children: a longitudinal population-based study. *Journal of Epidemiology & Community Health* 67: 926–31.

Kelly, Y., Kelly, J. and Sacker, A. (2013b), Changes in bedtime schedules and behavioural difficulties in 7-year-old children. *Pediatrics* 132: e1184–e1190.

Keyes, K. and Galea, S. (2015), What matters most: quantifying an epidemiology of consequence. *Annals of Epidemiology* 25: 305–11.

Keyes, K. M., Smith, G. D., Koenen, K. C. and Galea, S. (2015), The mathematical limits of genetic prediction for complex chronic disease. *Journal of Epidemiology & Community Health* 69: 574–9.

Khlat, M., Sermet, C. and Le Pape, A. (2000), Women's health in relation with their family and work roles: France in the early 1990s. *Social Science & Medicine* 50: 1807–25.

Kitagawa, E. M. and Hauser, P. M. (1973), *Differential Mortality in the United States: A Study in Socioeconomic Epidemiology*. Cambridge, MA: Harvard University Press.

Kivimäki, M. and Kawachi, I. (2013), Need for more individual-level meta-analyses in social epidemiology: example of job strain and coronary heart disease. *American Journal of Epidemiology* 177: 1–2.

Kivimäki, M., Head, J., Ferrie, J. E., et al. (2007), Hypertension is not the link between job strain and coronary heart disease in the Whitehall II study. *American Journal of Hypertension* 20: 1146–53.

Kivimaki, M., Lawlor, D., Smith, G. D., et al. (2006a), Socioeconomic position, co-occurrence of behaviour-related risk factors, and coronary heart disease: the Finnish public sector study. *American Journal of Public Health* 97: 874–9.

Kivimaki, M., Leino-Arjas, P., Luukkonen, R., Riihimaki, H., Vahtera, J. and Kirjonen, J. (2002), Work stress and risk of cardiovascular mortality: prospective cohort study of industrial employees. *British Medical Journal* 325: 857–62.

Kivimäki, M., Nyberg, S. T., Batty, G. D., et al. (2012), Job strain as a risk factor for coronary heart disease: a collaborative meta-analysis of individual participant data. *Lancet* 380: 1491–7.

Kivimäki, M., Nyberg, S. T., Fransson, E. I., et al. (2013), Associations of job strain and lifestyle risk factors with risk of coronary artery disease: a meta-analysis of individual participant data. *Canadian Medical Association Journal* 185: 763–9.

Kivimaki, M., Virtanen, M., Elovainio, M., Kouvonen, A., Väänänen, A. and Vahtera, J. (2006b), Work stress in the etiology of coronary heart disease – a meta-analysis. *Scandinavian Journal of Work, Environment & Health* 32(6): 431–2.

Kotz, D. and West, R. (2009), Explaining the social gradient in smoking cessation: it's not in the trying, but in the succeeding. *Tobacco Control* 18: 43–6.

Kraaykamp, G., van Eijck, K. and Ultee, W. (2010), Status, class and culture in the Netherlands, in T. W. Chan (ed.), *Social Status and Cultural Consumption*. Cambridge, UK: Cambridge University Press, pp. 169–203.

Krapohl, E. and Plomin, R. (2016), Genetic link between family socio-economic status and children's educational achievement estimated from genome-wide SNPs. *Molecular Psychiatry* 21: 437–43.

Krieger, N. (1999), Embodying inequality: a review of concepts, measures, and methods for studying health consequences of discrimination. *International Journal of Health Services* 29: 295–352.

Krieger, N. (2000), Refiguring 'race': epidemiology, racialized biology, and biological expressions of race relations. *International Journal of Health Services* 30: 211–16.

Krieger, N. (2005), Embodiment: a conceptual glossary for epidemiology. *Journal of Epidemiology & Community Health* 59: 350–5.

Krieger, Nancy (2012), Methods for the scientific study of discrimination and health: an ecosocial approach. *American Journal of Public Health* 102: 936–44.

Krieger, N., Williams, D. R. and Moss, N. E. (1997), Measuring social class in US public health research: concepts, methodologies, and guidelines. *Annual Review of Public Health* 18: 341–78.

Kroeber, A. L. and Kluckhohn, C. (1952), *Culture: A Critical Review of Concepts and Definitions*. Cambridge, MA: Peabody Museum.

Kuh, D. and ben Shlomo, Y. (2004), *A Life Course Approach to Chronic Disease Epidemiology*, 2nd edn. Oxford: Oxford University Press.

Kulhánová, I., Bacigalupe, A., Eikemo, T. A., et al. (2014), Why does Spain have smaller inequalities in mortality? An exploration of potential explanations. *European Journal of Public Health* 24: 370–7.

Kuller, L. H. (2003), Hormone replacement therapy and risk of cardiovascular disease: implications of the results of the women's health initiative. *Arteriosclerosis, Thrombosis, & Vascular Biology* 23: 11–16.

Kunst, A. (1997a), *Cross-National Comparisons of Socio-economic Differences in Mortality*. Den Haag: CIP-Gegevens Koninklijke Bibliotheek.

Kunst, A. (1997b), Cause-specific mortality and occupational class in 11 western countries. *Cross-National Comparisons of Socio-economic Differences in Mortality*. Den Haag: CIP-Gegevens Koninklijke Bibliotheek, pp. 113–24.

Kunst, A. E. and Mackenbach, J. P. (1994a), The size of mortality differences associated with educational level in nine industrialized countries. *American Journal of Public Health* 84: 932–7.

Kunst, A. E. and Mackenbach, J. P. (1994b), International variation in the size of mortality differences associated with occupational status. *International Journal of Epidemiology* 23: 742–50.

Kunst, A. E. and Roskam A.-J. (2009), Using the ESeC to describe socioeconomic inequalities in health in Europe, in D. Rose and E. Harrison (eds), *Social Class in Europe*. London: Routledge, pp. 216–34.

Kunst, A. E., Groenhof, F., Mackenbach, J. P. and Leon, D. A. (1998), Occupational class and cause-specific mortality in middle-aged men in 11 European countries: comparison of population based studies. *British Medical Journal* 316: 1636–42.

Kuzawa, C. W. and Sweet, E. (2009), Epigenetics and the embodiment of race: developmental origins of US racial disparities in cardiovascular health. *American Journal of Human Biology* 21: 2–15.

Laaksonen, M., Talala, K., Martelin, T., et al. (2008), Health behaviours as explanations for educational level differences in cardiovascular and all-cause mortality: a follow-up of 60,000 men and women over 23 years. *European Journal of Public Health* 18: 38–43.

Ladwig, K. H., Marten Mittag, B., Formanek, B. and Dammann, G. (2000), Gender differences of symptom reporting and medical health care utilization in the German population. *European Journal of Epidemiology* 16: 511–18.

Lager, A., Bremberg, S. and Vågerö, D. (2009), The association of early IQ and education with mortality: 65-year longitudinal study in Malmö, Sweden. *British Medical Journal* 339: b5282.

Lahelma, E., Martikainen, P., Rahkonen, O. and Silventoinen, K. (1999), Gender differences in ill health in Finland: patterns, magnitude and change. *Social Science & Medicine* 48: 7–19.

Landsbergis, P. A., Dobson, M., Koutsouras, G. and Schnall, P. (2013), Job strain and ambulatory blood pressure: a meta-analysis and systematic review. *American Journal of Public Health* 103: e61–e71.

Landsbergis, P. A., Dobson, M. and Schnall, P. (2013), Re: 'need for more individual-level meta-analyses in social epidemiology: example of job strain and coronary heart disease'. *American Journal of Epidemiology* 178: 1008–9.

Landsbergis, P. A., Grzywacz, J. G. and LaMontagne, A. D. (2014), Work organization, job insecurity, and occupational health disparities. *American Journal of Industrial Medicine* 57: 495–515.

Landsbergis, P. A., Schnall, P. L., Warren, K., Pickering, T. G. and Schwartz, J. E. (1994), Association between ambulatory blood-pressure and alternative formulations of job strain. *Scandinavian Journal of Work, Environment & Health* 20: 349–63.

Langley Browne, H. W. (1905), A discussion on physical deterioration: its causes and extent. *British Medical Journal*: 929–35.

Langman, L. (1998), Identity, hegemony, and social reproduction. *Current Perspectives on Social Theory* 18: 185–226.

Lantz, P. M., Golberstein, E., House, J. S. and Morenoff, J. (2010), Socio-economic and behavioral risk factors for mortality in a national 19-year prospective study of US adults. *Social Science & Medicine* 70: 1558–66.

Lantz, P. M., House, J. S., Lepkowski, J. M., Williams, D. R., Mero, R. P. and Chen, J. (1998), Socioeconomic factors, health behaviors, and mortality results from a nationally representative prospective study of US adults. *JAMA* 279: 1703–8.

Lantz, P. M., Lynch, J. W., House, J. S., et al. (2001), Socioeconomic disparities in health change in a longitudinal study of US adults: the role of health-risk behaviors. *Social Science & Medicine* 53: 29–40.

Law, C., Parkin, C. and Lewis, H. (2012), Policies to tackle inequalities in child health: why haven't they worked (better)? *Archives of Disease in Childhood* 97: 301–3.

Lillieblanton, M. and Laveist, T. (1996), Race/ethnicity, the social environment, and health. *Social Science & Medicine* 43: 83–91.

Lillieblanton, M., Parsons, P. E., Gayle, H. and Dievler, A. (1996), Racial-differences in health – not just black-and-white, but shades of gray. *Annual Review of Public Health* 17: 411–48.

Link, B. (2002), McKeown and the idea that social conditions are fundamental causes of disease. *American Journal of Public Health* 92: 730–2.

Link, B. G. and Phelan, J. C. (1995), Social conditions as fundamental causes of disease. *Journal of Health & Social Behaviour* 35: 80–94.

Lloyd, E. L. (1991), The role of cold in ischaemic heart disease: a review. *Public Health* 105: 205–15.

Lloyd, O. L. (1978), Respiratory cancer clustering associated with localised industrial air pollution. *Lancet* 311: 318–20.

Loucks, E. B., Buka, S. L., Rogers, M. L., et al. (2012), Education and coronary heart disease risk associations may be affected by early-life common prior causes: a propensity matching analysis. *Annals of Epidemiology* 22: 221–32.

Lundberg, O., Yngwe, M. Å., Stjärne, M. K., et al. (2008), The role of welfare state principles and generosity in social policy programmes for public health: an international comparative study. *Lancet* 372: 1633–40.

Luy, M. and Wegner-Siegmundt, C. (2014), The impact of smoking on gender differences in life expectancy: more heterogeneous than often stated. *European Journal of Public Health* 25: 706–10.

Lynch, J. W., Kaplan, G. A., Cohen, R. D., Kauhanen, J., Wilson, T. W., Smith, N. L. and Salonen, J. T. (1994), Childhood and adult socioeconomic status as predictors of mortality in Finland. *Lancet* 343: 524–7.

Lynch, J. W., Kaplan, G. A., Cohen, R. D., Tuomilehto, J. and Salonen, J. T. (1996), Do cardiovascular risk-factors explain the relation between socio-economic-status, risk of all-cause mortality, cardiovascular mortality, and acute myocardial infarction? *American Journal of Epidemiology* 144: 934–42.

Lynch, J. W., Kaplan, G. A., Pamuk, E. R., et al. (1998), Income inequality and mortality in metropolitan areas of the United States. *American Journal of Public Health* 88: 1074–80.

Lynch, J., Krause, N., Kaplan, G. A., Tuomilehto, J. and Salonen, J. T. (1997), Workplace conditions, socioeconomic status, and the risk of mortality and acute myocardial infarction: the Kuopio Ischemic Heart Disease Risk Factor Study. *American Journal of Public Health* 87: 617–22.

Lynch, J. W., Smith, G. D., Kaplan, G. A. and House, J. S. (2000), Income inequality and mortality: importance to health of individual income, psychosocial environment, or material conditions. *British Medical Journal* 320: 1200–4.

Ma, J., Xu, J., Anderson, R. N. and Jemal, A. (2012), Widening educational disparities in premature death rates in 26 states in the United States, 1993–2007. *PloS One* 7: e41560.

Macintyre, S., Hunt, K. and Sweeting, H. (1996), Gender differences in health: are things really as simple as they seem? *Social Science & Medicine* 42: 617–24.

Mackenbach, J. P. (2010a), Can we reduce health inequalities? An analysis of the English strategy (1997–2010). *Journal of Epidemiology & Community Health* 65: 568–75.

Mackenbach, J. P. (2010b), Has the English strategy to reduce health inequalities failed? *Social Science & Medicine* 71: 1249–53.

Mackenbach, J. P. (2010c), New trends in health inequalities research: now it's personal. *Lancet* 376: 854–5.

Mackenbach, J. P. (2011), What would happen to health inequalities if smoking were eliminated? *British Medical Journal* 342: d3460.

Mackenbach, J. P. (2012), The persistence of health inequalities in modern welfare states: the explanation of a paradox. *Social Science & Medicine* 75: 761–9.

Mackenbach, J. P., Kulhánová, I., Menvielle, G., et al. (2014), Trends in inequalities in premature mortality: a study of 3.2 million deaths in 13 European countries. *Journal of Epidemiology & Community Health* 69: 207–17.

Mackenbach, J. P., Kunst, A. E., Cavelaars, A. E. J. M., Groenhof, F. and Geurts, J. J. M. (1997), Socioeconomic inequalities in morbidity and mortality in western Europe. *Lancet* 349: 1655–9.

Mackenbach, J. P., Looman, C. W. and Kunst, A. E. (1993), Air pollution, lagged effects of temperature, and mortality: the Netherlands 1979–87. *Journal of Epidemiology & Community Health* 47: 121–6.

Mackenbach, J. P., Stirbu, I., and Roskam, A. (2008), Socioeconomic inequalities in health in 22 European countries. *New England Journal of Medicine* 358: 2468–81.

Manson, J. E., Chlebowski, R. T., Stefanick, M. L., et al. (2013), Menopausal hormone therapy and health outcomes during the intervention and extended poststopping phases of the Women's Health Initiative randomized trials. *JAMA* 310: 1353–68.

Marmot, M. (1989), Socioeconomic determinants of CHD mortality. *International Journal of Epidemiology* 18: S196–S202.

Marmot, M. (2010), *Strategic Review of Health Inequalities in England Post-2010: Marmot Review Final Report*. London: University College London.

Marmot, M. (ed.) (2013), *Review of the Social Determinants and the Health Divide in the WHO European Region: Final Report*. Copenhagen: WHO.

Marmot, M. and Brunner, E. (2005), Cohort profile: the Whitehall II study. *International Journal of Epidemiology* 34: 251–6.

Marmot, M., Allen, J. and Goldblatt, P. (2010), A social movement, based on evidence, to reduce inequalities in health. *Social Science & Medicine* 71: 1254–8.

Marmot, M. G., Rose, G., Shipley, M. and Hamilton, P. J. S. (1978), Employment grade and coronary heart disease in British civil servants. *Journal of Epidemiology & Community Health* 32: 244–9.

Marmot, M., Ryff, C. D., Bumpass, L. L., Shipley, M. and Marks, N. F. (1997), Social inequalities in health: next questions and converging evidence. *Social Science & Medicine* 44: 901–10.

Marmot, M. G., Smith, G. D., Stansfeld, S., Patel, C., North, F., Head, J. and White, I. (1991), Health inequalities among British civil servants – the Whitehall II study. *Lancet* 337: 1387–93.

Marmot Review Team (2010), *Fair Society Healthy Lives: Strategic Review of Health Inequalities in England Post-2010*. UCL: Institute of Health Equity.

Marsh, A. and McKay, S. (1994), *Poor Smokers*. London: Policy Studies Institute.

Marshall, G. (1997), *Repositioning Class: Social Inequality in Industrial Societies*. London: Sage.

Marshall, G., Rose, D., Newby, H. and Vogler, C. (1988), *Social Class in Modern Britain*. London: Hutchinson.

Martikainen, P. (1995), Mortality and socioeconomic status among Finnish women. *Population Studies* 49: 71–90.

Martikainen, P., Ishizaki, M., Marmot, M., Nakagawa, H. and Kaganmimori, S. (2001a), Socioeconomic differences in behavioural and biological risk factors: a comparison of a Japanese and an English cohort of employed men. *International Journal of Epidemiology* 30: 833–8.

Martikainen, P., Mäkelä, P., Koskinen, S. and Valkonen, T. (2001b), Income differences in mortality: a register-based follow-up study of three million men and women. *International Journal of Epidemiology* 30: 1397–1405.

Martin, C. J., Platt, S. D. and Hunt, S. (1987), Housing conditions and health. *British Medical Journal* 294: 1125–7.

Matthews, S., Stansfeld, S. and Power, C. (1999), Social support at age 33: the influence of gender, employment status and social class. *Social Science & Medicine* 49: 133–42.

McDonough, P. and Amick III, B. C. (2001), The social context of health selection: a longitudinal study of health and employment. *Social Science & Medicine* 53: 135–45.

McDonough, P. and Walters, V. (2001), Gender and health: reassessing patterns and explanations. *Social Science & Medicine* 52: 547–59.

McEwen, B. S. (1998), Protective and damaging effects of stress mediators. *New England Journal of Medicine* 338: 171–9.

McEwen, B. S. (2013), The brain on stress: toward an integrative approach to brain, body, and behavior. *Perspectives on Psychological Science* 8: 673–5.

McFadden, E., Luben, R., Wareham, N., Bingham, S. and Khaw, K. (2008), Occupational social class, risk factors and cardiovascular disease incidence in men and women: a prospective study in the European Prospective Investigation of Cancer. *European Journal of Epidemiology* 23: 449–58.

Mcisaac, S. J. and Wilkinson, R. G. (1997), Income distribution and cause-specific mortality. *European Journal of Public Health* 7: 45–53.

McKeown, T. (1966), *The Role of Medicine*. Oxford: Blackwell.

Mehta, N. K., House, J. S. and Elliott, M. R. (2015), Dynamics of health behaviours and socioeconomic differences in mortality in the USA. *Journal of Epidemiology & Community Health* 69: 416–22.

Mercer, J. B. (2003), Cold – an underrated risk factor for health. *Environmental Research* 92: 8–13.

Miller, G. E., Chen, E. and Parker, K. J. (2011), Psychological stress in childhood and susceptibility to the chronic diseases of aging: moving toward a model of behavioural and biological mechanisms. *Psychological Bulletin* 137: 959–97.

Miniño, A. M. (2013), *Death in the United States, 2011. NCHS Data Brief No. 115*. March US DHSS, CDC.

Mirowsky, J. and Ross, C. E. (2003), *Education, Social Status and Health.* New York: Aldine de Gruyter.

Mitchell, R., Blane, D. and Bartley, M. (2002), Elevated risk of high blood pressure: climate and the inverse housing law. *International Journal of Epidemiology* 31: 831–8.

Morris, J. N. and Heady, J. A. (1955), Social and biological factors in infant mortality, V: mortality in relation to father's occupation. *Lancet* i: 554–60.

Morris, J. N., Donkin, A. J. M., Wonderling, D., Wilkinson, P. and Dowler, E. A. (2000), A minimum income for healthy living. *Journal of Epidemiology & Community Health* 54: 885–9.

Morris, J. N., Wilkinson, P., Dangour, A. D., Deeming, C. and Fletcher, A. (2007), Defining a minimum income for healthy living (MIHL): older age, England. *International Journal of Epidemiology* 36: 1300–7.

Moser, K., Pugh, H. S. and Goldblatt, P. O. (1988), Inequalities in women's health – looking at mortality differentials using an alternative approach. *British Medical Journal* 296: 1221–4.

Muennig, P. and Murphy, M. (2011), Does racism affect health? Evidence from the United States and the United Kingdom. *Journal of Health Politics, Policy & Law* 36: 187–214.

Muntaner, C., Borrell, C., Ng, E., et al. (2011), Politics, welfare regimes, and population health: controversies and evidence. *Sociology of Health & Illness* 33: 946–64.

Murray, C. J. L., Kulkarni, S. C., Michaud, C., et al. (2006), Eight Americas: investigating mortality disparities across races, counties, and race-counties in the United States. *PLoS Medicine* 3: e260.

Mustard, C. A., Derksen, S., Berthelot, J. M., Wolfson, M. and Roos, L. L. (1997), Age-specific education and income gradients in morbidity and mortality in a Canadian province. *Social Science & Medicine* 45: 383–97.

Myllykangas, M., Pekkanen, J., Rasi, V., Haukkala, A., Vahtera, E. and Salomaa, V. (1995), Hemostatic and other cardiovascular risk-factors, and socioeconomic status among middle-aged Finnish men and women. *International Journal of Epidemiology* 24: 1110–16.

Nabel, E. G. (2013), The Women's Health Initiative – a victory for women and their health. *JAMA* 310: 1349–50.

Nabi, H., Kivimaki, M., Marmot, M. G., et al. (2008), Does personality explain social inequalities in mortality? The French GAZEL cohort study. *International Journal of Epidemiology* 37: 591–602.

Najman, J. M., Hayatbakhsh, M. R., Heron, M. A., Bor, W., O'Callaghan, M. J. and Williams, G. M. (2009), The impact of episodic and chronic poverty on child cognitive development. *Journal of Pediatrics* 154: 284–9.

Nam, C. B. and Terrie, W. E. (1982), Measurement of socioeconomic status from United States census data, in P. H. Rosse and S. L. Nock (eds), *Measuring Social Judgements: The Factorial Survey Approach.* Beverly Hills: Sage, pp. 95–118.

Nandi, A., Glymour, M. M. and Subramanian, S. V. (2014), Association among socioeconomic status, health behaviors, and all-cause mortality in the United States. *Epidemiology* 25: 170–7.

Nathanson, C. (1975), Illness and the feminine role: a theoretical review. *Social Science & Medicine* 9: 57–62.

National Centre for Health Statistics (2012), *Health United States 2011. With special feature on socio-economic status and health*. Hyattsville, MD: National Centre for Health Statistics.

Nazroo, J. Y. (1997), *The Health of Britain's Ethnic Minorities*. London: PSI.

Nazroo, J. (1998), Genetic, cultural or socio-economic vulnerability? Explaining ethnic inequalities in health. *Sociology of Health & Illness* 20: 710–30.

Nazroo, J. Y. (2001), South Asian people and heart disease: an assessment of the importance of socioeconomic position. *Ethnicity & Disease* 11: 401–11.

Nelson, K. and Fritzell, J. (2014), Welfare states and population health: the role of minimum income benefits for mortality. *Social Science & Medicine* 112: 63–71.

Netterstrom, B., Kristensen, T. S., Moller, L., Jensen, G. and Schnohr, P. (1998), Angina pectoris, job strain, and social status: a cross-sectional study of employed urban citizens. *International Journal of Behavioral Medicine* 5: 312–22.

Newhouse, M. L. and Wagner, J. C. (1969), Validation of death certificates in asbestos workers. *British Journal of Industrial Medicine* 26: 302–7.

Northridge, M. E., Stover, G. N., Rosenthal, J. E. and Sgerard, D. (2003), Environmental equity and health: understanding complexity and moving forward. *American Journal of Public Health* 93: 209–14.

Nyberg, S. T., Fransson, E. I., Heikkilä, K., et al. (2014), Job strain as a risk factor for type 2 diabetes: a pooled analysis of 124,808 men and women. *Diabetes Care* 37: 2268–75.

Oakes, J. M. and Rossi, P. H. (2003), The measurement of SES in health research: current practice and steps toward a new approach. *Social Science & Medicine* 56: 769–84.

Office for National Statistics (2012), *Intercensal Mortality Rates by NSSEC, 2001–2010*. London: Office for National Statistics.

Office of Population Censuses and Surveys (1980), *Classification of Occupations*. London: HMSO.

Office of Population Censuses and Surveys (1997), Health Survey for England, 1993 (data collection), 2nd edn. UK Data Service. SN: 3316, http://dx.doi.org/10.5255/UKDA-SN-3316-1.

Oksuzyan, A., Brønnum-Hansen, H. and Jeune, B. (2010), Gender gap in health expectancy. *European Journal of Ageing* 7: 213–18.

Oksuzyan, A., Juel, K., Vaupel, J. W. and Christensen, K. (2008), Men: good health and high mortality: sex differences in health and aging. *Aging Clinical & Experimental Research* 20: 91–102.

O'Neill, M. S., Jerrett, M., Kawachi, I., et al. (2003), Health, wealth, and air pollution: advancing theory and methods. *Environmental Health Perspectives* 111: 1861–70.

Onwuachi Saunders, C. and Hawkins, D. F. (1993), Black–white differences in injury. Race or social class? *Annals of Epidemiology* 3: 150–3.

Osler, M., Godtfredsen, N. S. and Prescott, E. (2008), Childhood social circumstances and health behaviour in midlife: the Metropolit 1953 Danish male birth cohort. *International Journal of Epidemiology* 37: 1367–74.

Osler, M., Prescott, E., Gronbeck, M., Christensen, U., Due, P. and Engholm, G. (2002), Income inequality, individual income, and mortality in Danish adults: analysis of pooled data from two cohort studies. *British Medical Journal* 324: 1–4.

Ostergren, P. O., Lindbladh, E., Isacsson, S. O., Odeberg, H. and Svensson, S. E. (1995), Social network, social support and the concept of control – a qualitative study concerning the validity of certain stressor measures used in quantitative social epidemiology. *Scandinavian Journal of Social Medicine* 23: 95–102.

Parienty, A. (2005), Review of 'La Distinction'. *Alternatives Economiques Poche*: 45–6.

Passannante, M. R. and Nathanson, C. A. (1987), Women in the labour force: are sex mortality differentials changing? *Journal of Occupational Medicine* 29: 21–8.

Pearce, J. R., Richardson, E. A., Mitchell, R. J. and Shortt, N. K. (2010), Environmental justice and health: the implications of the socio-spatial distribution of multiple environmental deprivation for health inequalities in the United Kingdom. *Transactions of the Institute of British Geographers* 35: 522–39.

Pekkanen, J., Tuomilehto, J., Uutela, A., Vartiainen, E. and Nissinen, A. (1995), Social class, health behaviour, and mortality among men and women in eastern Finland. *British Medical Journal* 311: 589–93.

Pensola, T. H. and Martikainen, P. (2003), Cumulative social class and mortality from various causes of adult men. *Journal of Epidemiology & Community Health* 57: 745–51.

Pensola, T. H. and Valkonen, T. (2000), Mortality differences by parental social class from childhood to adulthood. *Journal of Epidemiology & Community Health* 54: 525–9.

Peter, R., Geissler, H. and Siegrist, J. (1998), Associations of effort–reward imbalance at work and reported symptoms in different groups of male and female public transport workers. *Stress Medicine* 14: 175–82.

Pickering, T. G., Devereux, R. B., James, G. D., Gerin, W., Landsbergis, P. and Schnall, P. L. (1996), Environmental influences on blood pressure and the role of job strain. *Journal of Hypertension* 14: S179–S185.

Pickett, K. E. and Pearl, M. (2001), Multilevel analyses of neighbourhood socioeconomic context and health outcomes: a critical review. *Journal of Epidemiology & Community Health* 55: 111–22.

Pierson, C. and Castles, F. G. (2006), *The Welfare State Reader*, 2nd edn. Cambridge: Polity Press.

Platt, S. D., Martin, C. J., Hunt, S. and Lewis, C. W. (1989), Damp housing, mould growth and symptomatic health state. *British Medical Journal* 298: 1673–8.

Ploubidis, G. B., Benova, L., Grundy, E., Laydon, D. and DeStavola, B. (2014), Lifelong socio-economic position and biomarkers of later life health: testing the contribution of competing hypotheses. *Social Science & Medicine* 119: 258–65.

Pluess, M. and Bartley, M. (2015), Childhood conscientiousness predicts the social gradient of smoking in adulthood: a life course analysis. *Journal of Epidemiology & Community Health* 69: 330–8.

Pollitt, R., Rose, K. and Kaufman, J. (2005), Evaluating the evidence for models of life course socioeconomic factors and cardiovascular outcomes: a systematic review. *BMC Public Health* 5: 7.

Popay, J., Whitehead, M. and Hunter, D. J. (2010), Injustice is killing people on a large scale – but what is to be done about it? (Editorial). *Journal of Public Health* 32: 148–9.

Power, C. and Hertzman, C. (1997), Social and biological pathways linking early life and adult disease. *British Medical Bulletin* 53: 210–21.

Power, C. and Matthews, S. (1997), Origins of health inequalities in a national population sample. *Lancet* 350: 1584–9.

Power, C., Hyppönen, E. and Davey Smith, G. (2004), Socioeconomic position in childhood and early adult life and risk of mortality: a prospective study of the mothers of the 1958 British Birth Cohort. *American Journal of Public Health* 95: 1396–1402.

Power, C., Manor, O., Fox, A. J. and Fogelman, K. (1990), Health in childhood and social inequalities in health in young adults. *Journal of the Royal Statistical Society Series A* 153: 17–28.

Prandy, K. (1999), Class, stratification and inequalities in health: a comparison of the Registrar-General's and the Cambridge scale. *Sociology of Health & Illness* 21: 466–84.

Programme Committee on Socio-Economic Inequalities in Health (2001), Reducing socio-economic inequalities in health. Final report and policy recommendations from the Dutch Programme Committee on Socio-Economic Inequalities in Health – second phase. Den Haag: ZON MW.

Pudrovska, T. and Anikputa, B. (2012), The role of early-life socioeconomic status in breast cancer incidence and mortality: unravelling life course mechanisms. *Journal of Aging & Health* 24: 323–44.

Pudrovska, T. and Anikputa, B. (2014), Early-life socioeconomic status and mortality in later life: an integration of four life-course mechanisms. *Journals of Gerontology Series B, Psychological Sciences and Social Sciences* 69: 451–60.

Pugh, H., Power, C., Goldblatt, P. and Arber, S. (1991), Women's lung cancer mortality, socio-economic status and changing smoking patterns. *Social Science & Medicine* 32: 1105–10.

Pulkki, L., Kivimäki, M., Keltikangas-Järvinen, L., Elovainio, M., Leino, M. and Viikari, J. (2003), Contribution of adolescent and early adult personality to the inverse association between education and cardiovascular risk behaviours: prospective population-based cohort study. *International Journal of Epidemiology* 32: 968–75.

Rael, E. G., Stansfeld, S. A., Shipley, M., Head, J., Feeney, A. and Marmot, M. (1995), Sickness absence in the Whitehall II study, London: the role of social support and material problems. *Journal of Epidemiology & Community Health* 49: 474–81.

Rahkonen, O., Arber, S., Lahelma, E., Martikainen, P. and Silentoinen, K. (2000), Understanding income inequalities in health among men and women in Britain and Finland. *International Journal of Health Services* 30: 27–47.

Räisänen, S., Gissler, M., Sankilampi, U., Saari, J., Kramer, M. R. and Heinonen, S. (2013), Contribution of socioeconomic status to the risk of small for gestational age infants: a population-based study of 1,390,165 singleton live births in Finland. *International Journal for Equity in Health* 12: 28–35.

Ramsay, S. E., Morris, R. W., Whincup, P. H., et al. (2009), Socioeconomic inequalities in coronary heart disease risk in older age: contribution of established and novel coronary risk factors. *Journal of Thrombosis & Haemostasis* 7: 1779–86.

Rathwell, T. and Phillips, D. (1986), *Health, Race and Ethnicity*. London: Croom Helm.

Reijneveld, S. A. (1995), Causes of death contributing to urban socio-economic mortality differences in Amsterdam. *International Journal of Epidemiology* 24: 740–9.

Rietveld, C. A., Medland, S. E., Derringer, J., et al. (2013), GWAS of 126,559 individuals identifies genetic variants associated with educational attainment. *Science* 340: 1467–71.

Risnes, K. R., Vatten, L. J., Baker, J. L., et al. (2011), Birthweight and mortality in adulthood: a systematic review and meta-analysis. *International Journal of Epidemiology* 40: 647–61.

Robert, S. and House, J. S. (1996), SES differentials in health by age and alternative indicators of SES. *Journal of Aging & Health* 8: 359–88.

Roberts, I. (1997), Cause specific social class mortality differentials for child injury and poisoning in England and Wales. *Journal of Epidemiology & Community Health* 51: 334–5.

Rogers, R. G., Everett, B. G., Sain Onge, J. M. and Krueger, P. M. (2010), Social, behavioural and biological factors and sex differences in mortality. *Demography* 47: 555–78.

Roos, N. P. and Mustard, C. A. (1997), Variation in health and health care use by socioeconomic status in Winnipeg, Canada: Does the system work well? Yes and no. *Milbank Quarterly* 75: 89–111.

Rose, D. and O'Reilly, K. (1998), *Final Report of the ESRC Review of Government Social Classifications*. Swindon: ESRC/ONS.

Rosengren, A., Orth-Gomer, K., Wedel, H. and Wilhelmsen, L. (1993), Stressful life events, social support, and mortality in men born in 1933. *British Medical Journal* 307: 1102–5.

Ross, N. A., Wolfson, M. C., Dunn, J. R., Berthelot, J. M., Kaplan, G. A. and Lynch, J. W. (2000), Relation between income inequality and mortality in Canada and in the United States: cross-sectional assessment using census data and vital statistics. *British Medical Journal* 320: 898–902.

Rugulies, R. (2002), Depression as a predictor for coronary heart disease. *American Journal of Preventive Medicine* 23: 51–61.

Sacker, A., Bartley, M., Firth, D. and Fitzpatrick, R. (2001), Dimensions of social inequality in the health of women in England: occupational, material and behavioural pathways. *Social Science & Medicine* 52: 763–81.

Sacker, A., Firth, D., Fitzpatrick, R., Lynch, K. and Bartley, M. (2000), Comparing health inequality in men and women: prospective study of mortality 1986–1996. *British Medical Journal* 320: 1303–7.

Savage, M., Devine, F., Cunningham, N., et al. (2013), A new model of social class? Findings from the BBC's Great British Class Survey experiment. *Sociology* 47: 219–50.

Savage, M., Devine, F., Cunningham, N., et al. (2015), On social class, anno 2014. *Sociology* 49: 1011–30.

Scally, G. (2013) "Have we lost the battle to reduce health inequalities?" Kings Fund blog 24 January. http://www.kingsfund.org.uk/time-to-think-differently/blog/have-we-lost-battle-improve-health-inequalities.

Schnall, P. L., Landsbergis, P. A. and Baker, D. (1994), Job strain and cardiovascular-disease. *Annual Review of Public Health* 15: 381–411.

Schnall, P. L., Schwartz, J. E., Landsbergis, P. A., Warren, K. and Pickering, T. G. (1998), A longitudinal study of job strain and ambulatory blood pressure: results from a three-year follow-up. *Psychosomatic Medicine* 60: 697–706.

Schröder, H., Rohlfs, I., Schmelz, E. and Marrugat, J. (2004), Relationship of socioeconomic status with cardiovascular risk factors and lifestyle in a Mediterranean population. *European Journal of Nutrition* 43: 77–85.

Seeman, T. E., Gruenewald, T. L., Cohen, S., Williams, D. R. and Matthews, K. A. (2014), Social relationships and their biological correlates: Coronary Artery Risk Development in Young Adults (CARDIA) study. *Psychoneuroendocrinology* 43: 126–38.

Sen, A. (1992), *Inequality Explained*. Cambridge, MA: Harvard University Press.

Senior, P. A. and Bhopal, R. (1994), Ethnicity as a variable in epidemiological research. *British Medical Journal* 309: 327–30.

Shatenstein, B. and Ghadirian, P. (1998), Influences on diet, health behaviours and their outcome in select ethno-cultural and religious groups. *Nutrition* 14: 223–30.

Shewry, M. C., Smith, W. C. S., Woodward, M. and Tunstallpedoe, H. (1992), Variation in coronary risk-factors by social-status: results from the Scottish Heart Health Study. *British Journal of General Practice* 42: 406–10.

Shively, C. A., Clarkson, T. B. and Kaplan, J. R. (1989), Social deprivation and coronary artery atherosclerosis in the female cynomolgus monkeys. *Atherosclerosis* 77: 69–76.

Shortt, N. K., Richardson, E. A., Mitchell, R. and Pearce, J. (2011), Re-engaging with the physical environment: a health-related environmental classification of the UK. *Area* 43: 76–87.

Shuey, K. M. and Willson, A. E. (2014), Economic hardship in childhood and adult health trajectories: an alternative approach to investigating life-course processes. *Advances in Life Course Research* 22: 49–61.

Siegrist, J. (1995), Emotions and health in occupational life: new scientific findings and policy implications. *Patient Education & Counseling* 25: 227–36.

Siegrist, J. (2000a), Place, social exchange and health: proposed sociological framework. *Social Science & Medicine* 51: 1283–93.

Siegrist, J. (2000b), *Wenner-Gren Foundation International Symposium 2000*. Stockholm: Wenner-Gren Foundation.

Siegrist, J. and Peter, R. (1996), Threat to occupational status control and cardiovascular risk. *Israel Journal of Medical Sciences* 32: 179–84.

Siegrist, J., Klein, D. and Voigt, K. H. (1997), Linking sociological with physiological data: the model of effort–reward imbalance at work. *Acta Physiologica Scandinavica* 161: 112–16.

Siegrist, J., Peter, R., Junge, A., Cremer, P. and Seidel, D. (1990), Low status control, high effort at work and ischemic heart disease: prospective evidence from blue-collar men. *Social Science & Medicine* 31: 1127–34.

Siegrist, J., Peter, R., Motz, W. and Strauer, B. E. (1992), The role of hypertension, left ventricular hypertrophy and psychosocial risks in cardiovascular disease: prospective evidence from blue-collar men. *European Heart Journal* 13 (Suppl D): 89–95.

Silventoinen, K., Tatsuse, T., Martikainen, P., et al. (2013), Occupational class differences in body mass index and weight gain in Japan and Finland. *Journal of Epidemiology* 23: 443–50.

Simon, P. A., Hu, D. J., Diaz, T. and Kerndt, P. R. (1995), Income and AIDS rates in Los Angeles county. *AIDS* 9: 281–84.

Sinfield, A. (1978), Analyses in the social division of welfare. *Journal of Social Policy* 7: 129–56.

Singh-Manoux, A., Ferrie, J. E., Chandola, T. and Marmot, M. (2004), Socioeconomic trajectories across the life course and health outcomes in midlife: evidence for the accumulation hypothesis? *International Journal of Epidemiology* 33: 1072–9.

Skalicka, V., van Lenthe, F., Bambra, C., Krokstad, S. and Mackenbach, J. (2009), Material, psychosocial, behavioural and biomedical factors in the explanation of relative socio-economic inequalities in mortality: evidence from the HUNT study. *International Journal of Epidemiology* 38: 1272–84.

Smaje, C. (1995), *Health, 'Race' and Ethnicity*. London: Kings Fund Institute.

Smith, G. D., Bartley, M. and Blane, D. (1990), The Black Report on socioeconomic inequalities in health 10 years on. *British Medical Journal* 301: 373–7.

Smith, K. (2013), *Beyond Evidence-Based Policy in Public Health: The Interplay of Ideas*. Basingstoke: Palgrave Macmillan.

Srinivas, M. N. (1956), A note on Sanskritization and westernization. *The Far Eastern Quarterly* 15: 481–96.

Stansfeld, S., Feeney, A., Head, J., Canner, R., North, F. and Marmot, M. (1995), Sickness absence for psychiatric illness: the Whitehall II Study. *Social Science & Medicine* 40: 189–97.

Steptoe, A. (2000), Stress, social support and cardiovascular activity over the working day. *International Journal of Psychophysiology* 37: 299–308.

Steptoe, A. and Kivimäki, M. (2013), Stress and cardiovascular disease: an update on current knowledge. *Annual Review of Public Health* 34: 337–54.

Steptoe, A. and Willemsen, G. (2002), Psychophysiological responsivity in coronary heart disease, in S. Stansfeld and M. Marmot (eds), *Stress and the Heart*. London: BMJ Books, pp. 168–80.

Steptoe, A., Roy, M. P., Evans, O. and Snashall, D. (1995), Cardiovascular stress reactivity and job strain as determinants of ambulatory blood pressure at work. *Journal of Hypertension* 13: 201–10.

Stewart, A., Prandy, K. and Blackburn, R. M. (1973), Measuring the class structure. *Nature* 245: 415–17.

Stewart, A., Prandy, K. and Blackburn, R. M. (1980), The measurement of stratification. *Social Stratification and Occupations*. London: Macmillan, pp. 17–70.

Stockwell, E. G., Goza, F. W., Jiang, Y. and Luse, V. O. (1994), Trends in the relationship between socioeconomic-status and infant-mortality in metropolitan Ohio, 1960–1990. *Population Research & Policy Review* 13: 399–410.

Stockwell, E. G., Goza, F. W. and Roach, J. L. (1995), The relationship between socioeconomic status and infant mortality in a metropolitan aggregate, 1989–1991. *Sociological Forum* 10: 297–308.

Stringhini, S., Dugravot, A., Shipley, M., et al. (2011), Health behaviours, socioeconomic status, and mortality: further analyses of the British Whitehall II and the French GAZEL prospective cohorts. *PLoS Medicine* 8: e1000419.

Stringhini, S., Sabia, S., Shipley, M., et al. (2010), Association of socioeconomic position with health behaviors and mortality. *JAMA* 303: 1159–66.

Sundquist, J., Bajekal, M., Jarman, B. and Johansson, S. E. (1996), Underprivileged area score, ethnicity, social-factors and general mortality in district health authorities in England and Wales. *Scandinavian Journal of Primary Health Care* 14: 79–85.

Sweeting, H., Green, M., Benzeval, M. and West, P. (2016), The emergence of health inequalities in early adulthood: evidence on timing and mechanisms from a West of Scotland cohort. *BMC Public Health* 16: 1–15.

Tabassum, F., Kumari, M., Rumley, A., Lowe, G., Power, C. and Strachan, D. P. (2008), Effects of socioeconomic position on inflammatory and hemostatic markers: a life-course analysis in the 1958 British Birth Cohort. *American Journal of Epidemiology* 167: 1332–41.

Theorell, T. (2000), Working conditions and health, in L. F. Berkman and I. Kawachi (eds), *Social Epidemiology*. Oxford: Oxford University Press, pp. 118–36.

Theorell, T. (2014), Commentary triggered by the Individual Participant Data Meta-Analysis Consortium study of job strain and myocardial infarction risk. *Scandinavian Journal of Work, Environment & Health* 4: 89–95.

Theorell, T., Tsutsumi, A., Hallquist, J., et al. (1998), Decision latitude, job strain, and myocardial infarction: a study of working men in Stockholm. The SHEEP Study Group. Stockholm Heart Epidemiology Program. *American Journal of Public Health* 88: 382–88.

Titmuss, R. M. (1958), The social division of welfare: some reflections on the search for equity, in R. M. Titmuss (ed.), *Essays on 'The Welfare State'*. London: George Allen & Unwin.

Titmuss, R. M. (1968), *Commitment to Welfare*. London: Allen & Unwin, pp. 34–55.

Tjepkema, M., Wilkins, R. and Long, A. (2013), Cause-specific mortality by income adequacy in Canada: a 16-year follow-up study. *Health Reports* 24: 14–22.

Toch-Marquardt, M., Menvielle, G., Eikemo, T. A., et al. (2014), Occupational class inequalities in all-cause and cause-specific mortality among middle-aged men in 14 European populations during the early 2000s. *PloS One* 9: e108072.

Torssander, J. and Erikson, R. (2010), Stratification and mortality – a comparison of education, class, status, and income. *European Sociological Review* 26: 465–74.

Townsend, P., Davidson, N. and Whitehead, M. (1986), *The Black Report and the Health Divide*. Harmondsworth: Penguin.

Tubeuf, S., Jusot, F. and Bricard, D. (2012), Mediating role of education and lifestyles in the relationship between early-life conditions and health: evidence from the 1958 British Cohort. *Health Economics* 21: 129–50.

Turecki, G. and Meaney, M. J. (2014), Patterns and predictors of smoking cessation in the general population. *Biological Psychiatry* 79(2): 87–96.

Tylor, E. B. (1871), *Primitive Culture*. London: Murray.

Vahtera, J., Kivimaki, M., Pentti, J. and Theorell, T. (2000), Effect of change in the psychosocial work environment on sickness absence: a seven-year follow-up of initially healthy employees. *Journal of Epidemiology & Community Health* 54: 484–93.

van de Mheen, H., Stronks, K., Looman, C. W. N. and Mackenbach, J. P. (1998), Role of childhood health in the explanation of socioeconomic inequalities in early adult health. *Journal of Epidemiology & Community Health* 52: 15–19.

Van de Velde, S., Bracke, P., Levecque, K. and Meuleman, B. (2010), Gender differences in depression in 25 European countries after eliminating measurement bias in the CES-D 8. *Social Science Research* 39: 396–404.

Van der Kooy, K., van Hout, H., Marwijk, H., Marten, H., Stehouwer, C. and Beekman, A. (2007), Depression and the risk for cardiovascular diseases: systematic review and meta analysis. *International Journal of Geriatric Psychiatry* 22: 613–26.

Van Lenthe, F. J., Gevers, E., Joung, I. M. A., Bosma, H. and Mackenbach, J. P. (2002), Material and behavioral factors in the explanation of educational differences in incidence of acute myocardial infarction: The Globe Study. *Annals of Epidemiology* 12: 535–42.

van Oort, F. V. A., van Lenthe, F. J. and Mackenbach, J. P. (2005), Material, psychosocial, and behavioural factors in the explanation of educational inequalities in mortality in the Netherlands. *Journal of Epidemiology & Community Health* 59 (3): 214–20.

van Rossum, C. T. M., Shipley, M., van de Mheen, H., Grobbee, D. and Marmot, M. G. (2000), Employment grade differences in cause specific mortality. A 25-year follow-up of civil servants from the first Whitehall study. *Journal of Epidemiology & Community Health* 54: 178–84.

VanderWeele, T. J. and Robinson, W. R. (2013), On the causal interpretation of race in regressions adjusting for confounding and mediating variables. *Epidemiology* 25: 473–84.

Vartiainen, E., Pekkanen, J., Koskinen, S., Jousilahti, P., Salomaa, V. and Puska, P. (1998), Do changes in cardiovascular risk factors explain the increasing socioeconomic difference in mortality from ischaemic heart disease in Finland? *Journal of Epidemiology & Community Health* 52: 416–19.

Verbrugge, L. M. (1976), Females and illness: recent trends in sex differences in the United States. *Journal of Health & Social Behavior* 17: 387–403.

Verbrugge, L. M. (1980), Recent trends in sex mortality differentials in the United States. *Women & Health* 5: 17–37.

Verbrugge, L. M. (1985), Gender and health: an update on hypotheses and evidence. *Journal of Health & Social Behavior* 26: 156–82.

Verbrugge, L. M. and Wingard, D. L. (1987), Sex differentials in health and mortality. *Women & Health* 12: 103–45.

Vizard, P. and Obolenskaya, P. (2013), *Labour's Record on Health 1997–2010*. London: LSE Centre for Analysis of Social Exclusion.

von Känel, R., Mills, P. J., Fainman, C. and Dimsdale, J. E. (2001), Effects of psychological stress and psychiatric disorders on blood coagulation and fibrinolysis: a biobehavioural pathway to coronary artery disease? *Psychosomatic Medicine* 63: 531–44.

Vrijkotte, T. G. M., van Doornen, L. J. P. and deGeus, E. J. C. (1999), Work stress and metabolic and hemostatic risk factors. *Psychosomatic Medicine* 61: 796–805.

Wadsworth, M. E. J. (1986), Serious illness in childhood and its association with later life achievements, in R. G. Wilkinson (ed.), *Class and Health*. London: Tavistock, pp. 50–74.

Wadsworth, M. E. J. (1991), *The Imprint of Time*. Oxford: Oxford University Press.

Wadsworth, M. E. J. (1997), Health inequalities in the life course perspective. *Social Science & Medicine* 44: 859–69.

Wahrendorf, M., Sembajwe, G., Zins, M., Berkman, L., Goldberg, M. and Siegrist, J. (2012), Long-term effects of psychosocial work stress in midlife on health functioning after labour market exit – results from the GAZEL Study. *Journals of Gerontology Series B, Psychological Sciences & Social Sciences* 67: 471–80.

Waldron, H. (2013), Mortality differentials by lifetime earnings decile: implications for evaluations of proposed social security law changes. *Social Security Bulletin* 73: 1–37.

Waldron, I. (1976), Why do women live longer than men? *Social Science & Medicine* 10: 349–32.

Waldron, I. (2000), Trends in gender differences in mortality: relationships to changing gender differences in behaviour and other causal factors, in E. Annandale and K. Hunt (eds), *Gender Inequalities in Health*. Buckingham: Open University Press, pp. 150–81.

Walters, V., McDonough, P. and Strohschein, L. (2002), The influence of work, household structure, and social, personal and material resources on gender differences in health: an analysis of the 1994 Canadian National Population Health Survey. *Social Science & Medicine* 54: 677–92.

Wannamethee, S. G. and Shaper, A. G. (1997), Socioeconomic status within social class and mortality: a prospective study in middle-aged British men. *International Journal of Epidemiology* 26: 532–41.

Webb, E., Blane, D. and de Vries, R. (2013), Housing and respiratory health at older ages. *Journal of Epidemiology & Community Health* 67: 280–5.

White, C., Glickman, M., Johnson, B. and Corbin, T. (2007), Social inequalities in adult male mortality by the National Statistics Socio-economic Classification, England and Wales, 2001–03. *Health Statistics Quarterly* 36: 6–23.

White, K. and Borrell, L. N. (2011), Racial/ethnic residential segregation: framing the context of health risk and health disparities. *Health & Place* 17: 438–48.

Whitley, E., Batty, G. D., Hunt, K., Popham, F. and Benzeval, M. (2014), The role of health behaviours across the life course in the socioeconomic patterning of all-cause mortality: the West of Scotland twenty-07 prospective cohort study. *Annals of Behavioural Medicine* 47: 148–57.

Wild, S. H., Fischbacher, C., Brock, A., Griffiths, C. and Bhopal, R. (2007), Mortality from all causes and circulatory disease by country of birth in England and Wales 2001–2003. *Journal of Public Health* 29: 191–8.

Wilkinson, R. G. (1986), Income and mortality, in R. G. Wilkinson (ed.), *Class and Health: Research and Longitudinal Data.* London: Tavistock, pp. 88–114.

Wilkinson, R. G. (1992), National mortality rates – the impact of inequality. *American Journal of Public Health* 82: 1082–4.

Wilkinson, R. G. (1996), *Unhealthy Societies: The Afflictions of Inequality.* London: Routledge.

Wilkinson, R. G. and Pickett, K. E. (2006), Income inequality and population health: a review and explanation of the evidence. *Social Science & Medicine* 62: 1768–84.

Wilkinson, R. G. and Pickett, K. E. (2007), The problems of relative deprivation: why some societies do better than others. *Social Science & Medicine* 65: 1965–78.

Wilkinson, R. and Pickett, K. (2009), *The Spirit Level.* London: Penguin.

Williams, D. R. (1996), Race/ethnicity and socioeconomic-status – measurement and methodological issues. *International Journal of Health Services* 26: 483–505.

Williams, D. R. (1997), Race and health: basic questions, emerging directions. *Annals of Epidemiology* 7: 322–33.

Williams, F. L. and Lloyd, O. (1991), Trends in lung cancer mortality in Scotland and their relation to cigarette smoking and social class. *Scottish Medical Journal* 36: 175–8.

Williams, R. and Ecob, R. (1999), Regional mortality and the Irish in Britain: findings from the ONS Longitudinal Study. *Sociology of Health & Illness* 21: 344–67.

Wingard, D. L. (1984), The sex differential in morbidity, mortality, and lifestyle. *Annual Review of Public Health* 5: 433–58.

Wolfson, M., Kaplan, G., Lynch, J., Ross, N. and Backlund, E. (1999), Relative income inequality and mortality: empirical demonstration. *British Medical Journal* 319: 953–7.

Woodward, M., Tunstall-Pedoe, H., Rumley, A. and Lowe, G. D. O. (2009), Does fibrinogen add to prediction of cardiovascular disease? Results from the Scottish Heart Health Extended Cohort Study. *British Journal of Haematology* 146: 442–6.

Women's Health Initiative (2004) *Questions and Answers about the WHI Postmenopausal Hormone Therapy Trials.* US Department of Health and Human Services. Bethesda: Maryland National Institutes of Health. https://www.nhlbi.nih.gov/whi/whi_faq.htm#q1.

World Health Organization (2015) Mortality database http://apps.who.int/healthinfo/statistics/mortality/whodpms/ (9 March).

Xu, J., Sherry, M. D., Murphy, B. S., Kochanek, K. D. and Bastian, B. A. (2016) Deaths: final data for 2013. *National Vital Statistics Reports* 64: 1–99.

Yang, Y. C., Schorpp, K. and Harris, K. M. (2014), Social support, social strain and inflammation: evidence from a national longitudinal study of US adults. *Social Science & Medicine* 107: 124–35.

Yap, C., Beverland, I. J., Heal, M. R., et al. (2012), Association between long-term exposure to air pollution and specific causes of mortality in Scotland. *Occupational & Environmental Medicine* 69: 916–24.

Zaman, J. and Brunner, E. (2008), Social inequalities and cardiovascular disease in South Asians. *Heart* 94: 406–7.

Index